"He is simply a phenom... occur ever again in theatre history."

"His triumph has been to unite two things ever dissociated in the English mind: hard work and wit." Kenneth Tynan

The plays in this volume demonstrate the extraordinary skill and versatility Coward's writing achieved in the late 1920s.

"Four characters and a maid suffice for *Private Lives* . . . Mr. Coward, as the wayward Elyot, and . . . Miss Gertrude Lawrence, as his Amanda, . . . have been married and divorced and, when they meet on their new honeymoons, each with a dullard attached, they naturally renew old acquaintance and old strife . . . The combination of the characters is perfect . . ." (Ivor Brown, 1930)

Of *Bitter-Sweet* in 1929 James Agate commented that Coward could not quite take credit for "the entire production" though he could fairly be held responsible for "the plot, the dialogue, the lyrics, the melodies as originally executed on a baby grand, the stagecraft, the evening's sparkle, irresponsibility, wit, and fun, the power to conceive its visual delight, and the general notion of what makes a thoroughly good light entertainment."

"Last night," said the Morning Post of 17.2.1927, "an eighteenth-century comedy by Mr. Noël Coward, entitled *The Marquise*, was performed for the first time, and a very amusing and well-constructed piece it proved to be . . . delicious and done with dexterity and delicacy."

In 1930 "I wrote an angry little vilification of war called *Post-Mortem*," explained Coward; "my mind was strongly affected by *Journey's End*, and I had read several current war novels one after the other. I wrote . . . with the utmost sincerity: this, I think, must be fairly obvious to anyone who reads it."

The front cover shows a design from 1975 by Erté, reproduced by courtesy of the Grosvenor Gallery, London.

San Diego Christian College
Library
Santee, CA

in the same series

Coward

Plays: One

(Hay Fever, The Vortex, Fallen Angels, Easy Virtue)

Plays: Three

(Design for Living, Cavalcade, Conversation Piece, *and* Hands Across the Sea, Still Life, Fumed Oak *from* To-night at 8.30)

Plays: Four

(Blithe Spirit, This Happy Breed, Present Laughter, *and* Ways and Means, The Astonished Heart, 'Red Peppers' *from* Tonight at 8.30)

Plays: Five

(Relative Values, Waiting in the Wings, Look After Lulu, Suite in Three Keys)

822
C874co
v.2

NOËL COWARD

Plays: Two

Private Lives

Bitter-Sweet

The Marquise

Post-Mortem

Introduced by Sheridan Morley

Methuen Drama

METHUEN WORLD CLASSICS

This collection first published in Great Britain in 1979 in simultaneous hardback and paperback editions by Eyre Methuen Ltd.
The paperback edition reprinted 1982 by
Methuen London Ltd.
This edition with a new introduction first published in 1986 by
Methuen London Ltd.
Reprinted 1991 by Methuen Drama
an imprint of Reed Consumer Books Ltd
Michelin House, 81 Fulham Road, London SW3 6RB
and Auckland, Melbourne, Singapore and Toronto
and distributed in the United States of America
by Heinemann, a division of Reed Publishing (USA) Inc
361 Hanover Street, Portsmouth, New Hampshire, NH 03801 3959
Reissued with a new cover design 1993

Private Lives was first published in Great Britain in 1930 by Heinemann and republished in 1934 in Play Parade Vol. 1.

Bitter-Sweet was first published in 1929 by Martin Secker. It was republished in 1934 by Heinemann in Play Parade Vo. 1.

The Marquise was first published in 1927 by Ernest Benn as Contemporary British Dramatists Volume 55. It was republished by Heinemann in 1950 in Play Parade Vol. 3.

Post-Mortem was first published in 1931 by Heinemann and republished in 1934 in Play Parade Vol. 1.

Copyright in all the plays is by the Estate of the late Noël Coward.

Introduction copyright © 1986 by Sheridan Morley
Chronology copyright © 1986 by Martin Tickner

ISBN 0 413 46080 0

Printed and bound in Great Britain by
Cox & Wyman Ltd, Reading, Berks.

CAUTION
These plays are fully protected by copyright throughout the world. All applications for performance, etc., should be made *by professionals* to Michael Imison Playwrights Ltd., 28 Almeida Street, London N1 1TD, and *by amateurs* to Samuel French Ltd., 52 Fitzroy Street, London W1P 6JR.

This paperback edition is sold subject to the condition that it shall not, by way of trade or otherwise, be lent, resold, hired out, or otherwise circulated without the publisher's prior consent in any form of binding or cover other than that in which it is published and without a similar condition including this condition being imposed on the subsequent purchaser.

Contents

Introduction

The second of five volumes of plays by Noël Coward in this World Dramatists series opens with the one which more than any other represents his greatest claim to theatrical permanence. Though it is the lightest of light comedies, *Private Lives* has about it a symmetry and durability that have assured it near-constant production in one language or another from the time of its first production in 1930 to the present day. It is in many ways a perfect light comedy, arguably the best to have come out of England in the first half of the twentieth century; and though when it first opened in London many critics reckoned that *Private Lives* could only survive for as long as Gertrude Lawrence and Coward himself played it, the comedy has in fact proved almost consistently successful ever since, a guaranteed copper-bottom audience–puller that has temporarily rescued countless repertory companies from the throes of a bad season. Suitably enough *Private Lives* was also the play which, given a 1963 production by the Hampstead Theatre Club, launched in Noël's own lifetime the sudden revival of interest in his work which he himself gleefully christened 'Dad's Renaissance'.

Yet *Private Lives*, though it has indeed far outlived its original production, is a comedy that, even more than most others by Coward, stands or falls by the way it is played. On paper, one discovers, there is really only a kind of code for actors: brief staccato lines, the very occasional aphorism ('women should be struck regularly, like gongs') and duologues that when spoken take on a sparkling life of their own. The dialogue in this comedy of appalling manners is theatrically effective rather than naturalistic: there is virtually no action beyond a fight at the end of Act Two and another at the end of Act Three; there are no 'cameo' characters to break up the duologues except for the maid, and there is really no plot to sustain the actors if their talents start to fail them. This is in fact a technical exercise of incredible difficulty even for accomplished light comedians.

The roots of *Private Lives* lie in a very different Coward script also published in this volume: originally he had intended the operetta *Bitter-Sweet* to be a vehicle for his old child-actor friend and revue partner Gertrude Lawrence, but when it became clear that her enchanting yet somewhat erratic voice could not possibly sustain so operatic a score, he took it away and promised a play for her instead. Late in 1929 he was setting off on one of his many world tours when, as he recalled in his autobiography *Present Indicative*, 'Gertie had given a farewell party for me and, as a going-away present, a little gold book from Cartier's which when opened and placed on the writing table in my cabin disclosed a clock, calendar and thermometer on one side and an extremely pensive photograph of Gertie herself on the other. This rich gift, although I am sure prompted by the least ulterior of motives, certainly served as a delicate reminder that I had promised to write a play for us both.'

But that might well have been the end of that, had it not been for a sleepless night at the Imperial Hotel in Tokyo a few weeks later: 'the moment I switched out the lights, Gertie appeared in a white Molyneux dress on a terrace in the South of France and refused to go again until four a.m., by which time *Private Lives*, title and all, had constructed itself. In 1923 the play would have been written and typed within a few days of my thinking of it, but in 1929 I had learned the wisdom of not welcoming a new idea too ardently, so I forced it into the back of my mind, trusting to its own integrity to emerge again later on, when it had become sufficiently set and matured.'

A few weeks later, when Coward had reached the Cathay Hotel in Shanghai and was recovering from a sudden bout of influenza, 'the idea by now seemed ripe enough to have a shot at, so I started it, propped up in bed with a writing-block and an Eversharp pencil, and completed it, roughly, in four days. It came easily, and with the exception of a few of the usual "blood and tears" moments, I enjoyed writing it. I thought it a shrewd and witty comedy, well constructed on the whole, but psychologically unstable; however, its entertainment value seemed obvious enough, and its acting opportunities for Gertie and me admirable, so I cabled to her immediately in New York telling her to keep herself free for the autumn, and put the whole thing aside for a few weeks before typing and revising it.'

There followed, as Noël later recalled, 'a tremendous telegraphic bickering' between himself and Gertie: 'She had cabled me in Singapore, rather casually I thought, saying that she had read *Private Lives* and that there was nothing wrong in it that couldn't be fixed. I had wired back curtly that the only thing that was going to be fixed was her performance.

Now cables were arriving at all hours of the day and night, with a typical disregard of expense, saying that she had foolishly committed herself to Charlot for a new revue . . . I finally lost patience and cabled that I intended to do the play with someone else, and I heard nothing further until I arrived back in England.'

By which time Gertrude Lawrence had sorted out her Charlot contracts, and was able to start rehearsing with Noël as author, director and co-star. The other couple in these marital mixed doubles were to be played by Adrianne Allen and a young, moustached Laurence Olivier, and though these roles were considered by their creator 'little better than ninepins, lightly wooden and only there at all in order to be repeatedly knocked down and stood up again by Elyot and Amanda' Coward realised before anyone the importance of having them superbly played. To have given bad parts over to bad actors would have been severely damaging, and on the principle that only a really good actor can play a bore without being boring, Noël told Olivier that the play would do him a great deal of commercial good after his recent and unwise decision to desert *Journey's End* for a disastrous *Beau Geste*. Olivier agreed, and was later to note that much of his comic timing and technique was learnt from Coward during the run of *Private Lives*, as was the discipline not to break into fits of uncontrollable giggles on stage.

With *Private Lives* well into its second week of rehearsal, the then Lord Chamberlain, Lord Cromer, who still had the power of the British stage censor, announced that he was thoroughly unhappy with Act Two in general and the Elyot–Amanda love scene in particular. Considering that they were now supposed to be divorced and married to new and different partners, this affair seemed to him altogether too risqué for public standards of morality in 1930, and his lordship added that unless the act was drastically rewritten, he would regretfully be unable to give permission for *Private Lives* to be publicly performed. Noël repaired instantly to St James's Palace where he read the play, acting out all the parts before Lord Cromer, who was then persuaded that, with some dignified direction, the Elyot–Amanda love scene would after all be acceptable without any cuts.

On 18 August 1930 *Private Lives* therefore had its world première at the King's Theatre in Edinburgh: it was the third time that Noël and Gertie had appeared together on stage (they had started as child-actors in the 1913 *Hannele* and then starred in the 1923 revue *London Calling*) and they were only to work together once more, in *To-night at 8.30* six years later. Yet theirs was to remain one of the most stylish light-comedy partnerships of the century, and nowhere better expressed than in the best comedy of social manners to have come out of England since *The Importance of Being Earnest*, which preceded it by 35 years.

'Gertie and Noël looked so beautiful together,' (wrote Cole Lesley), 'standing in the moonlight that no one who saw them can ever forget; and they played the balcony scene so magically, lightly, tenderly that one was for those fleeting moments brought near to tears by the underlying vulnerability, the evanescence of their love.'

After Edinburgh they toured Liverpool, Birmingham, Manchester and finally Southsea, where *Private Lives* ran into some high moral outrage from the local drama critic: 'This play,' he wrote, 'with the exception of a certain amount of smart backchat, consisted of large buckets of stable manure thrown all over the great audience for more than two hours . . . twenty years ago, such a production would have been unthinkable . . . of course, these four players may in their own private lives be quite moral and even respectable. I know nothing about them, and don't wish to.'

Others were fortunately more enthusiastic: *Private Lives* opened the brand new Phoenix Theatre in the Charing Cross Road with a glittering high-society première on 24 September 1930: 'Don't you just love it,' said Mrs Patrick Campbell, sweeping backstage afterwards, 'when Noël does his little hummings at the piano?'. Reviews next morning were however mixed, more good than bad certainly, but many hallmarked by a kind of grudging, patronising critical tone best captured by Allardyce Nicoll in his *World Drama*: 'an amusing play, no doubt, yet hardly moving farther below the surface than a paper boat in a bathtub and, like the paper boat, ever in imminent danger of becoming a shapeless, sodden mass.'

'Brittle', 'tenuous' and 'thin' were the recurrent adjectives first used to describe *Private Lives* in the press, but there were also references to cocktails, evening dress, repartee and even irreverent allusions to copulation which, noted Noël, 'caused a gratifying number of respectable people to queue up at the box office'. *Private Lives* fast became the most popular play in town, especially when it was announced that Noël and Gertie had only agreed to play it there for three months before moving on to Broadway for the same limited run.

One point about *Private Lives* which went almost entirely unnoticed originally was that, for a light comedy, it was based on just one very serious situation: Amanda and Elyot are unable to live either apart or together and remain only too constantly aware of it. Because of this, there is an underlying sadness about the major love scenes which belies the general impression of a light and flippant comedy. But what the critics first thought of *Private Lives* was on this occasion a matter of supreme irrelevance: the teaming of Coward and Lawrence would have filled the Phoenix to capacity for a three-month season in 1930 if they had chosen merely to read the telephone directory to one another. In that brief London run Coward's partnership with Gertrude Lawrence was generally reckoned to have been the best thing either of them had ever achieved on the stage: together they created a potent theatrical magic, and there was an indefinable chemistry in the public meeting of their two personalities which ensured that each inspired the other to be infinitely better: 'sometimes,' said Noël years later, 'I would look across the stage at Gertie and she would simply take my breath away'.

But the magic of Gertie's performance did not blind Noël to the technical problems of the piece: 'It is a reasonably well-constructed duologue for two experienced performers, with a couple of extra puppets thrown in to assist the plot and to provide contrast. There is a well-written love scene in Act One, and a certain amount of sound sex psychology underlying the quarrel scenes in Act Two. As a complete play it leaves a lot to be desired . . . to begin with, there is no further plot and no further action after Act One, with the exception of the rough-and-tumble at the curtain of Act Two. Before this there is exactly forty minutes of dialogue between the leading protagonists, Amanda and Elyot, which naturally demands from them the maximum of resource and comedy experience, as every night, according to the degree of responsiveness from the audience, the attack and tempo of the performance must inevitably vary. This means a constant ear cocked in the direction of the stalls, listening for the first sinister cough of boredom and, when it comes, a swiftly exchanged glance of warning and an immediate, and, it is to be hoped, imperceptible speeding up of the scene until the next sure-fire laugh breaks and it is permissible to relax and breathe more easily for a moment . . . taken all in all (the second act of *Private Lives*) was more tricky and full of pitfalls than anything I had ever attempted as an actor. But fortunately for me I had the inestimable advantage of playing it with Gertrude Lawrence, and so three quarters of the battle was won before the curtain went up.

'Everything she had been in my mind when I originally conceived the idea in Tokyo came to life on the stage: the witty quick-silver delivery of lines; the romantic quality, tender and alluring; the swift, brittle rages; even the white Molyneux dress . . . Gertie had an astounding sense of the complete reality of the moment, and her moments, dictated by the extreme variability of her moods, changed so swiftly that it was frequently difficult to discover what, apart from eating, sleeping and acting, was true of her at all . . . I have seen many actresses play Amanda in *Private Lives*, some brilliantly, some moderately and one or two abominably. But the part was written for Gertie and, as I conceived it and wrote it, I can say with authority that no actress in the world ever could or ever will come within a mile of her performance of it.'

And for several years after that first definitive performance, no actress ever tried: Noël and Gertie themselves appeared in a brisk charity-matinée parody called *Some Other Private Lives* which moved the whole comedy steeply downmarket to a cockney affair, and the original play rapidly achieved immortality on record (one of the first non-musicals ever to be heard there) with the two stars performing a somewhat impromptu rendering of the main love scenes.

Shortly after *Private Lives* opened at the Phoenix, the publication of the text allowed *The Times* to announce that it was 'unreadable' while their *Literary Supplement* considered with rather more justification that the plot was 'so light as to be almost non-existent'. After years in which Noël had been relentlessly compared to the Parisian boulevardier Sacha Guitry, J. K. Prothero found now a new and more intriguing comparison: 'Mr Coward, brilliant and rootless, emerges more and more as the Aldous Huxley of the theatre. With the same genius for the preposterous, he seizes unerringly on the exuberances and affectations of the moment, but for the purposes of recording only. His satire is not corrective, nor his wit creative. There is the same fundamental lack in his latest as in his earliest plays. He is neither constructive nor combative.' A more enthusiastic critic, Lawrence of Arabia then writing to Noël in private as Aircraftsman Shaw, noted: 'I decided for fun to take some pages of *Private Lives* and strike out all the redundant words: only there were none.'

The first major revival of *Private Lives* on stage came in 1944–5 with John Clements and Kay Hammond (and, later,

Hugh Sinclair and Googie Withers), when it ran at the Apollo in London for 716 performances (Coward and Lawrence had only ever given it a hundred and one) though there had already been an MGM film in 1931 starring Norma Shearer and Robert Montgomery. Major postwar revivals have included the Hampstead production in 1963 ('Can it be,' wondered one critic of this, 'that we have underrated Coward all these years and that *Private Lives*, so far from being a badly dated relic, is in fact the funniest play to have adorned the English theatre in this century?') and then a John Gielgud production in 1972 with Maggie Smith and Robert Stephens, followed by Alan Strachan's Greenwich revival with Maria Aitken and Michael Jayston in 1980 and a somewhat catastrophic Broadway production in which Richard Burton made his last stage appearance (opposite Elizabeth Taylor) in 1982.

Yet the great achievement of *Private Lives* has been survival outside the clenched cigarette-holding hothouse 30s world for which it was first conceived: 'shimmer and spangle and slapstick' was Ivor Brown's original verdict, and he may have got rather closer to the truth of it than the American professor who once spent several thousand words relating the play to Congreve. As the flagship of Coward's theatrical fleet, *Private Lives* still sails at full steam and all its flags bear the same message: 'What shall we do?' asks Elyot in time of crisis. 'Behave exquisitely,' replies Amanda.

Early in the summer of 1928, two years before *Private Lives* went into rehearsal, Noël had begun to think about his first full-scale operetta: 'The idea of *Bitter-Sweet* appeared quite unexpectedly and with no other motivation beyond the fact that I had vaguely discussed with Gladys (Calthrop, his great friend and constant designer) the possibilities of writing a romantic operetta. She and I were staying with Ronald Peake, her family solicitor, in Surrey, and an hour or so before we were due to leave, Mrs Peake happened to play to us on the gramophone a new German orchestral record of *Die Fledermaus*. Immediately a confused picture of uniforms, bustles, chandeliers and gas-lit cafés formed in my mind, and later, when we were driving over Wimbledon Common, we drew the car to a standstill by the roadside and in the shade of a giant horse-chestnut tree mapped out roughly the story of Sari Linden. The uniforms, bustles, chandeliers and gas-lit cafés all fell into place eagerly, as though they had been waiting in the limbo for just this cue to enter. It seemed high time for a little romantic renaissance, and very soon a few of the preliminary melodies began to form in my head. However, the whole idea had to be shelved for a while owing to the urgency of other plans.'

These were for the Broadway production of his revue, *This Year of Grace*, and it was on the way over to star in this that Noël, in mid-Atlantic, wrote the first act; once the revue had been safely launched, he returned to his tale from the Vienna Woods: 'During January and February 1929 I finished *Bitter-Sweet* on which I had been working intermittently for the last few months. The book had been completed long since, but the score had been causing me trouble until one day, when I was in a taxi on my way back to the apartment after a matinée, the "I'll See You Again" waltz dropped into my mind, whole and complete, during a twenty minutes' traffic block. After that everything went smoothly, and I cabled to Cockie in London suggesting that he start making preliminary arrangements regarding theatre, opening dates etc.'

'Cockie' (the impresario C. B. Cochran) did just that, though not without a little local difficulty. Once a title had been found (the suggestion came from Alfred Lunt) the central question was who should play Sari, the character who starts the operetta as a dowager Marchioness in London and then, by flashback to the Vienna of 1880, drops fifty years to become the tragic romantic heroine who loses her lover in a duel. The first idea had of course been Gertrude Lawrence, but when it was realised that her voice could not carry so lengthy or demanding a score, Coward told Cochran in London to approach Evelyn Laye, who in fact created the role on Broadway and took it over at the end of the London run.

She was not however keen to open it in London, and while *Bitter-Sweet* was still without a leading lady, Coward literally ran into Peggy Wood in the lobby of the Algonquin Hotel. Alec Woollcott had already suggested her for Sari, Noël rapidly auditioned her, and within days she was on her way to play the part in London, though Cochran was to express certain doubts about her American accent. Those overcome, *Bitter-Sweet* went into rehearsal at the end of May 1929. It was, wrote Noël afterwards, 'a musical that gave me more complete satisfaction than anything else I had yet written. Not especially on account of its dialogue, or its lyrics, or its music, or its production, but as a whole. In the first place it achieved and sustained the mood of its original conception more satisfactorily than a great deal of my other work. And in the second place, that particular mood of semi-nostalgic sentiment, when well done, invariably affects me very pleasantly. In *Bitter-Sweet* it did seem to me to be well done, and I felt accordingly very happy about it.'

Coward's first venture into the world of operetta was a lavish return to the Viennese past in three acts and six scenes, and its score represents Noël at his closest to Novello (and even Lehar) with lilting, unashamedly sentimental numbers like 'Zigeuner' and 'If Love Were All' as well as the classic 'I'll See You Again' which over the years proved to be one of the greatest song hits he ever had: 'brass bands have blared it, string orchestras have swooned it, Palm Court quartets have murdered it, barrel organs have ground it out in London squares and swing bands have tortured it beyond recognition . . . and I am still very fond of it and very proud of it.'

In the gloom that followed the General Strike, Coward had decided that the time was ripe for a little romantic escapism and *Bitter-Sweet* was just that, a surrender to the charm and the emotion that had filled musical theatre for so many years but laced now with the occasional acidity of 'Green Carnation' and 'Ladies of the Town'. If *Bitter-Sweet* was not one of the original tales from the Vienna Woods, it was a very passable imitation.

The original cast also featured George Metaxa, Ivy St Helier, Robert Newton and Alan Napier, and at stake here was a Cochran budget running to £20,000 as a gesture of considerable faith in Coward's first major work as composer and the first big show for which he alone could be held totally responsible as writer, composer, lyricist and director. 'I would not,' Cochran told the company after seeing their final dress rehearsal, 'part with my rights in this show for a million pounds' and his faith proved wholly justified. A pre-London run in Manchester was a riotous success, and though London reviews were as usual more grudging, James Agate in the *Sunday Times* paid lavish tribute to the sets of Gladys Calthrop and Ernst Stern, and the choreography of Tilly Losch, before adding that 'Mr Coward has done a thundering job'. *The Times* however thought the score 'a naïve medley for a man of Mr Coward's talents' and the fact that Coward had created a one-man English operetta unequalled in its period seemed to go largely unnoticed by critics who conceded not much more than 'thoroughly good light entertainment'. It was left to the fashion editor of *Vogue* to note that 'tiara'd women clapped till the seams of their gloves burst; the older generation could say with more complacency than truth that this was the way they had fallen in love, and the younger generation were wondering if in rejecting romantic love they might not have missed something.'

The journalistic estimate was that *Bitter-Sweet* would run at His Majesty's for about three months: in fact it opened there on July 12 1929 and lasted for eighteen months before transferring to the Palace and ending its run in April 1931 after playing to cut-price audiences at the Lyceum. All in all, nearly a million people saw it during more than 750 London performances, and counting the subsequent Parisian and Broadway productions (where Evelyn Laye did at last get to play a part that might have been written for her) as well as movie rights and song royalties, it would be fair to assume that over the years *Bitter-Sweet* made its author richer by a quarter of a million pounds.

Bitter-Sweet was twice filmed, once with Anna Neagle and Fernand Gravey in a British Films production directed by Herbert Wilcox in 1933, and then in 1941 as an MGM vehicle in Hollywood for Nelson Eddy and Jeanette Macdonald in a production directed by Woody Van Dyke which Noël was to describe in his *Diaries* as 'a nauseating hotchpotch of vulgarity, false values, seedy dialogue, stale sentiment, vile performances and abominable direction'.

It was left to the American author William Bolitho to write the best epitaph for *Bitter-Sweet*: discussing the operetta's quality of lyrical nostalgia he noted 'you find it faintly when you look over old letters the rats have nibbled at, one evening you don't go out; there is a little of it, impure and odorous, in the very sound of barrel organs, in quiet squares in the evenings, puffing out in gusts that intoxicate your heart. It is all right for beasts to have no memories: but we poor humans have to be compensated.'

Recovering from a minor nervous breakdown in America late in 1926, Noël took his manager and friend Jack Wilson for a fortnight's holiday in the Virginia mountains at White Sulphur Springs. But even there, he was unable to rest; by now so keyed up that he could not begin to cope with the meaning of a holiday, he instead began to work on 'an eighteenth-century joke' which was one of the few scripts he ever custom-made for anyone other than Gertrude Lawrence or the Lunts:

'It has long been a habit of wealthy American gentlemen,' Coward wrote later, 'to leave a standing order with their measurements with Savile Row tailors so that, at stated intervals, immaculately cut suits may cross the cold Atlantic and be stepped into without a button having to be altered. The writing of *The Marquise* was a reversal of this process. I left England in the autumn of 1926 with the line and measurements of Marie Tempest clearly in my mind. She had played *Hay Fever* for over a year; her comedy technique was flawless, and I knew from close and happy association with her the consummate grace with which she could handle a scene and the wit with which she could endow a line . . . I wrote *The Marquise* with Marie Tempest speaking every line of it in my mind's ear. It was a swift and pleasant task and when I had finished it I sent it to her. Some months later I arrived in England the day after she had opened in it. I remember sitting in the stage box of the Criterion Theatre just before the rise of the curtain and wondering how much of the actual performance I was about to see would differ from the idealised, imagined performance she had given for me in my room at White Sulphur Springs. It was a curious experience. The curtain rose, the play started and presently in she walked through the French windows, accurate and complete . . . if, with intense concentration, I could detach myself for a moment from Marie Tempest's personality and performance, I might perhaps see what a tenuous, frivolous little piece *The Marquise* is. I might, if only I could forget her in the last act eating an orange and watching Raoul and Esteban fighting a duel, realise how weak and meretricious the plot is. I might, bereft of her memory, read with disdain the whole play; sneer at its flippancy; laugh at its trivial love scenes and shudder at the impertinence of an author who, for no apparent reason except perhaps that pictorially the period is attractive, elects to place a brittle modern comedy in an eighteenth-century setting. But I am not and never shall be bereft of the memory of Marie Tempest, and any reader who shares this privilege will, I am sure, agree that *The Marquise* is gay, brilliant, witty, charming and altogether delightful.'

As usual Coward had proved his own best and most perspicacious critic: with Marie Tempest and some generally good reviews *The Marquise* managed a run of 129 performances at the Criterion in 1927. Without her, it has never in sixty years achieved a West End or Broadway revival, though for a while Coward cherished ambitions of making it over into an operetta for Maggie Teyte.

In April 1930, towards the end of the long voyage which had already produced the script of *Private Lives*, Coward had briefly joined a touring company called The Quaints who were then working in Singapore with a young John Mills and a repertoire including R. C. Sherriff's triumphant First World War play *Journey's End* in which Noël agreed to give a few performances as the intensely tight-lipped Captain Stanhope.

As Coward sailed home through the Suez Canal in an elderly P. & O. steamship, the play stayed very much in his thoughts, not so much because of his own recent and rather too neurotic rendering of the leading role (which he was now rapidly trying to forget) but rather because the general theme of *Journey's End* had moved and impressed him deeply by what it said of the men who had died in the war to end all wars.

Left to himself on board ship, Noël then wrote what could almost have been the sequel to *Journey's End*: a short, sharp look at life in 1930 seen through the eyes of a dying soldier from the trenches who could well have been one of the earlier play's leading characters. *Post-Mortem* is a strange, angry and very uncharacteristic Coward polemic about the betrayed promises and false illusions of the Twenties, unlike any other that Coward ever wrote and one that has still not been professionally produced on any stage. As a vilification of war and some contemporary attitudes towards it, the play offers some of Coward's most powerful writing, but its technique of jumping forwards and backwards in time, together with a tendency for every scene to turn into a tirade, has made it a virtual impossibility for a professional stage director, though there was once the suggestion that Guthrie McClintic would attempt it in America.

Post-Mortem has in fact been occasionally staged, first by captured British soldiers at a prison camp in Germany in 1944, and more recently by a boys' school in Thame in 1966. As a play it would seem to be ideally and almost uncannily suited (in form at least) to the confines and altogether different demands and possibilities of a television production. Realising this, the BBC included a shortened version of it in a series called *The Jazz Age* in the autumn of 1968.

In *Post-Mortem* Coward does not so much write as explode onto paper: the play has a violence that is to be found nowhere else in his work, and he wrote it to release some evidently pent-up furies that could hardly have been allowed to escape into light comedies or period musicals. The result of all the rage in *Post-Mortem* was much the same as the effect created by Noël's performance in *Journey's End*: under-prepared, hastily conceived, hysterical, chaotic, but often very powerful nonetheless. In the fury of his play Coward hits out wildly at the church and state in general and press barons and socialites in particular; one is aware again of the didactic moral preacher of *Poor Little Rich Girl* and *Dance Little Lady*, and as usual Coward was his own best critic:

'There is I believe some of my best writing in *Post-Mortem*, but also some of my worst. I have no deep regrets over it, as I know my intentions to have been of the purest. I passionately believed in the truth of what I was writing: too passionately. The truths I snarled out in that hot, uncomfortable little cabin were all too true and mostly too shallow. Through lack of detachment and lack of real experience of my subject, I muddled the issues of the play. I might have done better had I given more time to it and less vehemence. However, it helped to purge my system of certain accumulated acids . . . Now that the hysteria of its mood has evaporated from my mind, I perceive that it is a slightly more *jejune* gesture than I altogether bargained for. There are certain moments of genuine passion in it which redeem it from bathos, but on the whole I fear that it is sadly confused and unbalanced. All the same, it was an experiment and, far from regretting it, I am exceedingly glad I made it because, as a writer, it undoubtedly did me a power of good. It opened a lot of windows in my brain and allowed me to let off a great deal of steam which might have remained sizzling inside me and combusted later on, to the considerable detriment of *Calvalcade* and *Design For Living*. My emotions while writing it were violent. Much more violent than in any of my previous labours. And I can only say that it was fortunate for my immediate friends that this particular confinement took place on a P. & O. boat returning from the East, where my alternate moans of despair and screams of ecstasy could only disturb two acidulated planters' wives in the adjoining cabin.'

It is tempting to dismiss *Post-Mortem* and its conclusion that 'life is a poor joke' with the thought that the artist and craftsman in Coward have here been defeated by the man with the message, but its theme ('if the men who died in the trenches could only come back now, and see how little we have done to justify their sacrifice') forced those few readers who came across the published text to reconsider him in a more serious political and social light.

Chronology

1899 Born on 16 December in Teddington, Middlesex.
1911 Made first stage appearance in *The Goldfish*, London.
1914 Began writing songs, sketches and short stories (with Esmé Wynne).
1917 His play *Ida Collaborates* (written with Esmé Wynne) produced on a British tour.
1918 Wrote first play as sole author, *The Rat Trap*, produced in Britain in 1926.
1919 Wrote *I'll Leave It To You*, produced in Britain in 1920 and in USA in 1923.
1920 Appeared in London in *I'll Leave It To You.*
1921 Wrote *The Young Idea*, produced in Britain in 1922 and in USA in 1932, and *Sirocco*, produced in Britain in 1927.
1922 Appeared in *The Young Idea.* Wrote songs and sketches for the revue *London Calling!*, produced in 1923, and *The Queen Was in the Parlour*, produced in Britain in 1926 and in USA in 1929. *A Withered Nosegay* published in Britain and (in an expanded version as *Terribly Intimate Portraits*) in USA.
1923 Appeared in London in *London Calling!* Wrote *The Vortex*, produced in Britain in 1924 and in USA in 1925, and *Fallen Angels*, produced in Britain in 1925 and in USA in 1927.
1924 Directed and appeared in *The Vortex* in London. Wrote *Hay Fever*, produced in Britain and USA in 1925, and *Easy Virtue*, produced in USA in 1925 and in Britain in 1926.
1925 Continued appearing in *The Vortex* in London and also in USA. Wrote book, music and lyrics for *On With the Dance*, produced that year in Britain. *Chelsea Buns* published in Britain.
1926 Wrote *This Was A Man*, produced that year in USA, *The Marquise*, produced in Britain and USA in 1927, and *Semi-Monde*, produced in Britain in 1977.
1927 *Easy Virtue*, *The Vortex* and *The Queen Was in the Parlour* filmed. Wrote *Home Chat*, produced in Britain that year and in USA in 1932.

1928 Wrote book, music and lyrics for *This Year of Grace!*, produced in Britain and USA that year – also appeared in American production.

1929 Completed operetta *Bitter-Sweet*, produced in Britain and USA that year. Wrote *Private Lives*, produced in Britain in 1930 and USA in 1931.

1930 Appeared in *Private Lives* in Britain. Wrote *Post-Mortem*, first professional production on British television in 1968, and started *Cavalcade*.

1931 Appeared in *Private Lives* in USA. *Calvalcade* produced in Britain. *Private Lives* filmed. *Collected Sketches and Lyrics* published in Britain (USA 1932).

1932 Wrote book, music and lyrics for *Words and Music*, produced in Britain that year. Also wrote *Design for Living*, produced in USA in 1933 and in Britain in 1939. *The Queen Was in the Parlour* filmed again under the title *Tonight is Ours*. *Cavalcade* filmed. *Spangled Unicorn* published in Britain.

1933 Appeared in USA in *Design for Living*. Wrote *Conversation Piece*, produced in Britain and USA in 1934. *Design for Living* and *Bitter-Sweet* both filmed.

1934 Appeared in *Conversation Piece* in Britain. Wrote *Point Valaine*, produced in USA that year and in Britain in 1944.

1935 Wrote *To-night at 8.30*, produced in Britain that year and in USA in 1936. He appeared in both productions.

1937 Wrote *Operette*, produced in Britain in 1938. First volume of autobiography, *Present Indicative*, published in Britain and USA.

1938 Adapted *Words and Music* for its American production, entitled *Set to Music*.

1939 Wrote *Present Laughter* and *This Happy Breed*. Rehearsals for both interrupted by the war and not produced in Britain until 1942. *Present Laughter* produced in USA in 1946 and *This Happy Breed* in 1949. *To Step Aside* (short stories) published in Britain and USA.

1940 Toured Australia and also wrote *Time Remembered (Salute to the Brave)*, unproduced to date.

1941 Wrote and directed *Blithe Spirit*, produced in Britain and USA that year. Wrote screenplay for *In Which We Serve*.

1942 Appeared in and co-directed (with David Lean) *In Which We Serve*. Toured Britain in *Blithe Spirit*,

Present Laughter and *This Happy Breed. We Were Dancing* (from *To-night at 8.30*) filmed.

1943 Appeared in London in *Present Laughter* and *This Happy Breed* and co-produced film version of the latter.

1944 Toured extensively in South Africa, Far East and Europe. Co-produced film of *Blithe Spirit.* Wrote screenplay for *Brief Encounter* (based on *Still Life* from *To-night at 8.30*). *Middle East Diary* published in Britain and USA.

1945 Wrote *Sigh No More*, produced in Britain that year, and started writing *Pacific 1860*, produced in Britain in 1946.

1946 Started writing *Peace in Our Time*, produced in Britain in 1947.

1947 Appeared in *Present Laughter* in Britain. Wrote *Long Island Sound*, unproduced to date.

1948 Appeared in French production of *Present Laughter* (*Joyeux Chagrins*). Wrote screenplay for *The Astonished Heart* (from *To-night at 8.30*).

1949 Appeared in *The Astonished Heart*. Wrote *Ace of Clubs*, produced in Britain in 1950, and *Home and Colonial*: as *Island Fling* it was produced in USA in 1951 and revised as *South Sea Bubble* in Britain in 1956.

1951 Wrote *Relative Values*, produced in Britain that year, and *Quadrille*, produced in Britain in 1952 and in USA in 1954. Made first cabaret appearance at Café de Paris, London. *Star Quality* (short stories) published in Britain and USA.

1952 Three plays from *To-night at 8.30* filmed as *Meet Me To-night*.

1953 Wrote *After the Ball*, produced in Britain in 1954 and in USA in 1955.

1954 Wrote *Nude with Violin* produced in Britain in 1956 and in USA in 1957. *Future Indefinite* published in Britain and USA.

1955 Cabaret season in Las Vegas, USA. Wrote and appeared in *Together with Music* for US television.

1956 Appeared in *Blithe Spirit* and *This Happy Breed* on US television. Wrote *Volcano*, unproduced to date.

1957 Appeared in USA in *Nude with Violin*.

1958 Appeared in USA in *Present Laughter* and *Nude with Violin*. Adapted Feydeau's *Occupe-toi d'Amélie* as *Look After Lulu*, produced in USA and Britain in 1959. Composed score for the ballet *London Morning*, produced in Britain in 1959.

1959 Wrote *Waiting in the Wings*, produced in Britain in 1960.

1960 His novel *Pomp and Circumstance* published in Britain and USA.

1961 Completed *Sail Away*, produced in USA that year and in Britain in 1962.

1962 Wrote music and lyrics for *The Girl Who Came to Supper*, produced in USA in 1963. *The Collected Short Stories* published in Britain.

1964 Directed *High Spirits* (musical of *Blithe Spirit*) in USA and *Hay Fever* in Britain. *Pretty Polly Barlow* (short stories) published in Britain.

1965 Wrote *Suite in Three Keys*, produced in Britain in 1966 and (as *Noël Coward in Two Keys*) in USA in 1974. *The Lyrics of Noël Coward* published in Britain (USA 1967).

1966 Appeared in Britain in *Suite in Three Keys*. Started writing stage version of *Star Quality*, produced in Britain in 1982.

1967 *Bon Voyage* (short stories) and *Not Yet The Dodo* (verses) published in Britain (USA 1968).

1970 Received knighthood in the British New Year Honours List.

1972 *Cowardly Custard* produced in Britain and *Oh! Coward* in USA.

1973 Died on 26 March in Jamaica.

PRIVATE LIVES

First produced at the Phoenix Theatre, London, (after a preliminary tour), on 24 September 1930 with the following cast:

AMANDA PRYNNE	Gertrude Lawrence
VICTOR PRYNNE, *her husband*	Laurence Olivier
LOUISE, *a maid*	Everly Gregg
SIBYL CHASE	Adrianne Allen
ELYOT CHASE, *her husband*	Noël Coward

Directed by Noël Coward
Designed by G. E. Calthrop

ACT I

The Terrace of a Hotel in France. Summer evening.

ACT II

Amanda's flat in Paris. A few days later. Evening.

ACT III

The same. The next morning.

Time: The Present.

ACT I

The Scene is the terrace of a hotel in France. There are two French windows at the back opening on to two separate suites. The terrace space is divided by a line of small trees in tubs, and, down-stage, running parallel with the footlights, there is a low stone balustrade. Upon each side of the line of tree tubs is a set of suitable terrace furniture, a swinging seat, two or three chairs, and a table. There are orange and white awnings shading the windows, as it is summer.

When the curtain rises it is about eight o'clock in the evening. There is an orchestra playing not very far off. SIBYL CHASE *opens the windows on the Right, and steps out on to the terrace. She is very pretty and blonde, and smartly dressed in travelling clothes. She comes down stage, stretches her arms wide with a little sigh of satisfaction, and regards the view with an ecstatic expression.*

SIBYL (*calling*): Elli, Elli dear, do come out. It's so lovely.

ELYOT (*inside*): Just a minute.

After a pause ELYOT *comes out. He is about thirty, quite slim and pleasant looking, and also in travelling clothes. He walks right down to the balustrade and looks thoughtfully at the view.* SIBIL *stands beside him, and slips her arm through his.*

ELYOT: Not so bad.

SIBYL: It's heavenly. Look at the lights of that yacht reflected in the water. Oh dear, I'm so happy

ELYOT (*smiling*): Are you?

SIBYL: Aren't you?

ELYOT: Of course I am. Tremendously happy.

SIBYL: Just to think, here we are, you and I, married!

ELYOT: Yes, things have come to a pretty pass.

SIBYL: Don't laugh at me, you mustn't be *blasé* about honeymoons just because this is your second.

ELYOT (*frowning*): That's silly.

SIBYL: Have I annoyed you by saying that?

ELYOT: Just a little.

SIBYL: Oh, darling, I'm so sorry. (*She holds her face up to his.*) Kiss me.

ELYOT (*doing so*): There.

SIBYL: Ummm, not so very enthusiastic.

ELYOT (*kissing her again*): That better?

SIBYL: Three times, please, I'm superstitious.

ELYOT (*kissing her*): You really are very sweet.

SIBYL: Are you glad you married me?

ELYOT: Of course I am.

SIBYL: How glad?

ELYOT: Incredibly, magnificently glad.

SIBYL: How lovely.

ELYOT: We ought to go in and dress.

SIBYL: Gladder than before?

ELYOT: Why do you keep harping on that?

SIBYL: It's in my mind, and yours too, I expect.

ELYOT: It isn't anything of the sort.

SIBYL: She was pretty, wasn't she? Amanda?

ELYOT: Very pretty.

SIBYL: Prettier than I am?

ELYOT: Much.

SIBYL: Elyot!

ELYOT: She was pretty and sleek, and her hands were long and slim, and her legs were long and slim, and she danced like an angel. You dance very poorly, by the way.

SIBYL: Could she play the piano as well as I can?

ELYOT: She couldn't play the piano at all.

SIBYL (*triumphantly*): Aha! Had she my talent for organisation?

ELYOT: No, but she hadn't your mother either.

SIBYL: I don't believe you like mother.

ELYOT: Like her! I can't bear her.

SIBYL: Elyot! She's a darling, underneath.

ELYOT: I never got underneath.

SIBYL: It makes me unhappy to think you don't like mother.

ELYOT: Nonsense. I believe the only reason you married me was to get away from her.

SIBYL: I married you because I loved you.

ELYOT: Oh dear, oh dear, oh dear, oh dear!

SIBYL: I love you far more than Amanda loved you. I'd never make you miserable like she did.

ELYOT: We made each other miserable.

SIBYL: It was all her fault, you know it was.

ELYOT (*with vehemence*): Yes, it was. Entirely her fault.

SIBYL: She was a fool to lose you.

ELYOT: We lost each other.

SIBYL: She lost you, with her violent tempers and carryings on.

ELYOT: Will you stop talking about Amanda?

SIBYL: But I'm very glad, because if she hadn't

been uncontrolled, and wicked, and unfaithful, we shouldn't be here now.

ELYOT: She wasn't unfaithful.

SIBYL: How do you know? I bet she was. I bet she was unfaithful every five minutes.

ELYOT: It would take a far more concentrated woman than Amanda to be unfaithful every five minutes.

SIBYL (*anxiously*): You do hate her, don't you?

ELYOT: No, I don't hate her. I think I despise her.

SIBYL (*with satisfaction*): That's much worse.

ELYOT: And yet I'm sorry for her.

SIBYL: Why?

ELYOT: Because she's marked for tragedy; she's bound to make a mess of everything.

SIBYL: If it's all her fault, I don't see that it matters much.

ELYOT: She has some very good qualities.

SIBYL: Considering what a hell she made of your life, I think you are very nice about her. Most men would be vindictive.

ELYOT: What's the use of that? It's all over now, such a long time ago.

SIBYL: Five years isn't very long.

ELYOT (*seriously*): Yes it is.

SIBYL: Do you think you could ever love her again?

ELYOT: Now then, Sibyl.

SIBYL: But could you?

ELYOT: Of course not, I love you.

SIBYL: Yes, but you love me differently; I know that.

ELYOT: More wisely perhaps.

SIBYL: I'm glad. I'd rather have that sort of love.

ELYOT: You're right. Love is no use unless it's wise, and kind, and undramatic. Something steady and sweet, to smooth out your nerves when you're tired. Something tremendously cosy; and unflurried by scenes and jealousies. That's what I want, what I've always wanted really. Oh my dear, I do hope it's not going to be dull for you.

SIBYL: Sweetheart, as tho' you could ever be dull.

ELYOT: I'm much older than you.

SIBYL: Not so very much.

ELYOT: Seven years.

SIBYL (*snuggling up to him*): The music has stopped now and you can hear the sea.

ELYOT: We'll bathe to-morrow morning.

SIBYL: I mustn't get sunburnt.

ELYOT: Why not?

SIBYL: I hate it on women.

ELYOT: Very well, you shan't then. I hope you don't hate it on men.

SIBYL: Of course I don't. It's suitable to men.

ELYOT: You're a completely feminine little creature aren't you?

SIBYL: Why do you say that?

ELYOT: Everything in its place.

SIBYL: What do you mean?

ELYOT: If you feel you'd like me to smoke a pipe, I'll try and master it.

SIBYL: I like a man to be a man, if that's what you mean.

ELYOT: Are you going to understand me, and manage me?

SIBYL: I'm going to try to understand you.

ELYOT: Run me without my knowing it?

SIBYL (*withdrawing slightly*): I think you're being a little unkind.

ELYOT: No, I don't mean to be. I was only wondering.

SIBYL: Well?

ELYOT: I was wondering what was going on inside your mind, what your plans are really?

SIBYL: Plans; Oh, Elli!

ELYOT: Apart from loving me and all that, you must have plans.

SIBYL: I haven't the faintest idea what you're talking about.

ELYOT: Perhaps it's subconscious then, age old instincts working away deep down, mincing up little bits of experience for future use, watching me carefully like a little sharp-eyed, blonde kitten.

SIBYL: How can you be so horrid.

ELYOT: I said Kitten, not Cat.

SIBYL: Kittens grow into cats.

ELYOT: Let that be a warning to you.

SIBYL (*slipping her arm through his again*): What's the matter, darling; are you hungry?

ELYOT: Not a bit.

SIBYL: You're very strange all of a sudden, and rather cruel. Just because I'm feminine. It doesn't mean that I'm crafty and calculating.

ELYOT: I didn't say you were either of those things.

SIBYL: I hate these half masculine women who go banging about.

ELYOT: I hate anybody who goes banging about.

SIBYL: I should think you needed a little quiet womanliness after Amanda.

ELYOT: Why will you keep on talking about her?

SIBYL: It's natural enough, isn't it?

ELYOT: What do you want to find out?

SIBYL: Why did you really let her divorce you?

ELYOT: She divorced me for cruelty, and flagrant infidelity. I spent a whole week-end at Brighton with a lady called Vera Williams. She had the nastiest looking hair brush I have ever seen.

SIBYL: Misplaced chivalry, I call it. Why didn't you divorce her?

ELYOT: It would not have been the action of a gentleman, whatever that may mean.

SIBYL: I think she got off very lightly.

ELYOT: Once and for all will you stop talking about her.

SIBYL: Yes, Elli dear.

ELYOT: I don't wish to see her again or hear her name mentioned.

SIBYL: Very well, darling.

ELYOT: Is that understood?

SIBYL: Yes, darling. Where did you spend your honeymoon?

ELYOT: St. Moritz. Be quiet.

SIBYL: I hate St. Moritz.

ELYOT: So do I, bitterly.

SIBYL: Was she good on skis?

ELYOT: Do you want to dine downstairs here, or at the Casino?

SIBYL: I love you, I love you, I love you.

ELYOT: Good, let's go in and dress.

SIBYL: Kiss me first.

ELYOT (*kissing her*): Casino?

SIBYL: Yes. Are you a gambler? You never told me.

ELYOT: Every now and then.

SIBYL: I shall come and sit just behind your chair and bring you luck.

ELYOT: That will be fatal.

They go off into their suite. There is a slight pause and then VICTOR PRYNNE *enters from the Left suite. He is quite nice looking, about thirty or thirty-five. He is dressed in a light travelling suit. He sniffs the air, looks at the view, and then turns back to the window.*

VICTOR (*calling*): Mandy.

AMANDA (*inside*): What?

VICTOR: Come outside, the view is wonderful.

AMANDA: I'm still damp from the bath. Wait a minute——

VICTOR *lights a cigarette. Presently* AMANDA *comes out on to the terrace. She is quite exquisite with a gay face and a perfect figure. At the moment she is wearing a negligee.*

I shall catch pneumonia, that's what I shall catch.

VICTOR (*looking at her*): God!

AMANDA: I beg your pardon?

VICTOR: You look wonderful.

AMANDA: Thank you, darling.

VICTOR: Like a beautiful advertisement for something.

AMANDA: Nothing peculiar, I hope.

VICTOR: I can hardly believe it's true. You and I, nere alone together, married!

AMANDA (*rubbing her face on his shoulder*): That stuff's very rough.

VICTOR: Don't you like it?

AMANDA: A bit hearty, isn't it?

VICTOR: Do you love me?

AMANDA: Of course, that's why I'm here.

VICTOR: More than——

AMANDA: Now then, none of that.

VICTOR: No, but do you love me more than you loved Elyot?

AMANDA: I don't remember, it's such a long time ago.

VICTOR: Not so very long.

AMANDA (*flinging out her arms*): All my life ago.

VICTOR: I'd like to break his damned neck.

AMANDA (*laughing*): Why?

VICTOR: For making you unhappy.

AMANDA: It was mutual.

VICTOR: Rubbish! It was all his fault, you know it was.

AMANDA: Yes, it was, now I come to think about it.

VICTOR: Swine!

AMANDA: Don't be so vehement, darling.

VICTOR: I'll never treat you like that.

AMANDA: That's right.

VICTOR: I love you too much.

AMANDA: So did he.

VICTOR: Fine sort of love that is. He struck you once, didn't he?

AMANDA: More than once.

VICTOR: Where?

AMANDA: Several places.

VICTOR: What a cad.

AMANDA: I struck him too. Once I broke four

gramophone records over his head. It was very satisfying.

VICTOR: You must have been driven to distraction.

AMANDA: Yes, I was, but don't let's talk about it, please. After all, it's a dreary subject for our honeymoon night.

VICTOR: He didn't know when he was well off.

AMANDA: Look at the lights of that yacht reflected in the water. I wonder whose it is.

VICTOR: We must bathe to-morrow.

AMANDA: Yes. I want to get a nice sunburn.

VICTOR (*reproachfully*): Mandy!

AMANDA: Why, what's the matter?

VICTOR: I hate sunburnt women.

AMANDA: Why?

VICTOR: It's somehow, well, unsuitable.

AMANDA: It's awfully suitable to me, darling.

VICTOR: Of course if you really want to.

AMANDA: I'm absolutely determined. I've got masses of lovely oil to rub all over myself.

VICTOR: Your skin is so beautiful as it is.

AMANDA: Wait and see. When I'm done a nice crisp brown, you'll fall in love with me all over again.

VICTOR: I couldn't love you more than I do now.

AMANDA: Oh, dear. I did so hope our honeymoon was going to be progressive.

VICTOR: Where did you spend the last one?

AMANDA (*warningly*): Victor.

VICTOR: I want to know.

AMANDA: St. Moritz. It was very attractive.

VICTOR: I hate St. Moritz.

AMANDA: So do I.

VICTOR: Did he start quarrelling with you right away?

AMANDA: Within the first few days. I put it down to the high altitudes.

VICTOR: And you loved him?

AMANDA: Yes, Victor.

VICTOR: You poor child.

AMANDA: You must try not to be pompous, dear. (*She turns away.*)

VICTOR (*hurt*): Mandy!

AMANDA: I don't believe I'm a bit like what you think I am.

VICTOR: How do you mean?

AMANDA: I was never a poor child.

VICTOR: Figure of speech, dear, that's all.

AMANDA: I suffered a good deal, and had my heart broken. But it wasn't an innocent girlish heart. It was jagged with sophistication. I've always been sophisticated, far too knowing. That caused many of my rows with Elyot. I irritated him because he knew I could see through him.

VICTOR: I don't mind how much you see through me.

AMANDA: Sweet. (*She kisses him.*)

VICTOR: I'm going to make you happy.

AMANDA: Are you?

VICTOR: Just by looking after you, and seeing that you're all right, you know.

AMANDA (*a trifle wistfully*): No, I don't know.

VICTOR: I think you love me quite differently from the way you loved Elyot.

AMANDA: Do stop harping on Elyot.

VICTOR: It's true, though, isn't it?

AMANDA: I love you much more calmly, if that's what you mean.

VICTOR: More lastingly?

AMANDA: I expect so.

VICTOR: Do you remember when I first met you?

AMANDA: Yes. Distinctly.

VICTOR: At Marion Vale's party.

AMANDA: Yes.

VICTOR: Wasn't it wonderful?

AMANDA: Not really, dear. It was only redeemed from the completely commonplace by the fact of my having hiccoughs.

VICTOR: I never noticed them.

AMANDA: Love at first sight.

VICTOR: Where did you first meet Elyot?

AMANDA: To hell with Elyot.

VICTOR: Mandy!

AMANDA: I forbid you to mention his name again. I'm sick of the sound of it. You must be raving mad. Here we are on the first night of our honeymoon, with the moon coming up, and the music playing, and all you can do is to talk about my first husband. It's downright sacrilegious.

VICTOR: Don't be angry.

AMANDA: Well, it's very annoying.

VICTOR: Will you forgive me?

AMANDA: Yes; only don't do it again.

VICTOR: I promise.

AMANDA: You'd better go and dress now, you haven't bathed yet.

VICTOR: Where shall we dine, downstairs here, or at the Casino?

AMANDA: The Casino is more fun, I think.

VICTOR: We can play Boule afterwards.

AMANDA: No, we can't, dear.

VICTOR: Don't you like dear old Boule?

AMANDA: No, I hate dear old Boule. We'll play a nice game of Chemin de fer.

VICTOR (*apprehensively*): Not at the big table?

AMANDA: Maybe at the biggest table.

VICTOR: You're not a terrible gambler, are you?

AMANDA: Inveterate. Chance rules my life.

VICTOR: What nonsense.

AMANDA: How can you say it's nonsense. It was chance meeting you. It was chancing falling in love; it's chance that we're here, particularly after your driving. Everything that happens is chance.

VICTOR: You know I feel rather scared of you at close quarters.

AMANDA: That promises to be very embarrassing.

VICTOR: You're somehow different now, wilder than I thought you were, more strained.

AMANDA: Wilder! Oh Victor, I've never felt less wild in my life. A little strained, I grant you, but that's the newly married atmosphere; you can't expect anything else. Honeymooning is a very overrated amusement.

VICTOR: You say that because you had a ghastly experience before.

AMANDA: There you go again.

VICTOR: It couldn't fail to embitter you a little.

AMANDA: The honeymoon wasn't such a ghastly experience really; it was afterwards that was so awful.

VICTOR: I intend to make you forget it all entirely.

AMANDA: You won't succeed by making constant references to it.

VICTOR: I wish I knew you better.

AMANDA: It's just as well you don't. The "woman"—in italics—should always retain a certain amount of alluring feminine mystery for the " man "—also in italics.

VICTOR: What about the man? Isn't he allowed to have any mystery?

AMANDA: Absolutely none. Transparent as glass.

VICTOR: Oh, I see.

AMANDA: Never mind, darling; it doesn't necessarily work out like that; it's only supposed to.

VICTOR: I'm glad I'm normal.

AMANDA: What an odd thing to be glad about. Why?

VICTOR: Well, aren't you?

AMANDA: I'm not so sure I'm normal.

VICTOR: Oh, Mandy, of course you are, sweetly, divinely normal.

AMANDA: I haven't any peculiar cravings for Chinamen or old boots, if that's what you mean.

VICTOR (*scandalised*): Mandy!

AMANDA: I think very few people are completely normal really, deep down in their private lives. It all depends on a combination of circumstances. If all the various cosmic thingummys fuse at the same moment, and the right spark is struck, there's no knowing what one mightn't do. That was the trouble with Elyot and me, we were like two violent acids bubbling about in a nasty little matrimonial bottle.

VICTOR: I don't believe you're nearly as complex as you think you are.

AMANDA: I don't think I'm particularly complex, but I know I'm unreliable.

VICTOR: You're frightening me horribly. In what way unreliable?

AMANDA: I'm so apt to see things the wrong way round.

VICTOR: What sort of things?

AMANDA: Morals. What one should do and what one shouldn't.

VICTOR (*fondly*): Darling, you're so sweet.

AMANDA: Thank you, Victor, that's most encouraging. You really must have your bath now. Come along.

VICTOR: Kiss me.

AMANDA (*doing so*): There, dear, hurry now; I've only got to slip my dress on and then I shall be ready.

VICTOR: Give me ten minutes.

AMANDA: I'll bring the cocktails out here when they come.

VICTOR: All right.

AMANDA: Go along now, hurry.

They both disappear into their suite. After a moment's pause ELYOT *steps carefully on to the terrace carrying a tray upon which are two champagne cocktails. He puts the tray down on the table.*

ELYOT (*calling*): Sibyl.

SIBYL (*inside*): Yes.

ELYOT: I've brought the cocktails out here, hurry up.

SIBYL: I can't find my lipstick.

ELYOT: Never mind, send down to the kitchen for some cochineal.

SIBYL: Don't be so silly.

ELYOT: Hurry.

Elyot saunters down to the balustrade. He looks casually over on to the next terrace, and then out at the view. He looks up at the moon and sighs, then he sits down in a chair with his back towards the line of tubs, and lights a cigarette. AMANDA *steps gingerly on to her terrace carrying a tray with two champagne cocktails on it. She is wearing a charmingly simple evening gown, her cloak is flung over her right shoulder. She places the tray carefully on the table, puts her cloak over the back of a chair, and sits down with her back towards* ELYOT. *She takes a small mirror from her handbag, and scrutinizes her face in it The orchestra downstairs strikes up a new melody. Both* ELYOT *and* AMANDA *give a little start. After a moment,* ELYOT *pensively begins to hum the tune the band is playing. It is a sentimental, romantic little tune.* AMANDA *hears him, and clutches at her throat suddenly as though she were suffocating. Then she iumps up noiselessly, and peers over the line of tubs.* ELYOT, *with his back to her, continues to sing obliviously. She sits down again, relaxing with a gesture almost of despair. Then she looks anxiously over her shoulder at the window in case* VICTOR *should be listening, and then, with a little smile, she takes up the melody herself, clearly.* ELYOT *stops dead and gives a gasp, then he jumps up, and stands looking at her. She continues to sing, pretending not to know that he is there. At the end of the song, she turns slowly, and faces him.*

AMANDA: Thoughtful of them to play that, wasn't it?

ELYOT (*in a stifled voice*): What are you doing here?

AMANDA: I'm on honeymoon.

ELYOT: How interesting, so am I.

AMANDA: I hope you're enjoying it.

ELYOT: It hasn't started yet.

AMANDA: Neither has mine.

ELYOT: Oh, my God!

AMANDA: I can't help feeling that this is a little unfortunate.

ELYOT: Are you happy?

AMANDA: Perfectly.

ELYOT: Good. That's all right, then, isn't it?

AMANDA: Are you?

ELYOT: Ecstatically.

AMANDA: I'm delighted to hear it. We shall probably meet again sometime. Au revoir! (*She turns.*)

ELYOT (*firmly*): Good-bye.

She goes indoors without looking back. He stands gazing after her with an expression of horror on his face. SIBYL *comes brightly on to the terrace in a very pretty evening frock.*

SIBYL: Cocktail, please. (ELYOT *doesn't answer.*) Elli, what's the matter?

ELYOT: I feel very odd.

SIBYL: Odd, what do you mean, Ill?

ELYOT: Yes, ill.

SIBYL (*alarmed*): What sort of

ELYOT: We must leave at once.

SIBYL: Leave!

ELYOT: Yes, dear. Leave immediately.

SIBYL: Elli!

ELYOT: I have a strange foreboding.

SIBYL: You must be mad.

ELYOT: Listen, darling. I want you to be very

sweet, and patient, and understanding, and not be upset, or ask any questions, or anything. I have an absolute conviction that our whole future happiness depends upon our leaving here instantly.

SIBYL: Why?

ELYOT: I can't tell you why.

SIBYL: But we've only just come.

ELYOT: I know that, but it can't be helped.

SIBYL: What's happened, what has happened?

ELYOT: Nothing has happened.

SIBYL: You've gone out of your mind.

ELYOT: I haven't gone out of my mind, but I shall if we stay here another hour.

SIBYL: You're not drunk, are you?

ELYOT: Of course I'm not drunk. What time have I had to get drunk?

SIBYL: Come down and have some dinner, darling, and then you'll feel ever so much better.

ELYOT: It's no use trying to humour me. I'm serious.

SIBYL: But darling, please be reasonable. We've only just arrived; everything's unpacked. It's our first night together. We can't go away now.

ELYOT: We can have our first night together in Paris.

SIBYL: We shouldn't get there until the small hours.

ELYOT (*with a great effort at calmness*): Now please, Sibyl, I know it sounds crazy to you, and utterly lacking in reason and sense, but I've got second sight over certain things. I'm almost psychic. I've got the most extraordinary sensation of impending disaster. If we stay here something appalling will happen. I know it.

SIBYL (*firmly*): Hysterical nonsense.

ELYOT: It isn't hysterical nonsense. Presentiments are far from being nonsense. Look at the woman who cancelled her passage on the *Titanic*. All because of a presentiment.

SIBYL: I don't see what that has to do with it.

ELYOT: It has everything to do with it. She obeyed her instincts, that's what she did, and saved her life. All I ask is to be allowed to obey my instincts.

SIBYL: Do you mean that there's going to be an earthquake or something?

ELYOT: Very possibly, very possibly indeed, or perhaps a violent explosion.

SIBYL: They don't have earthquakes in France.

ELYOT: On the contrary, only the other day they felt a distinct shock at Toulon.

SIBYL: Yes, but that's in the South where it's hot.

ELYOT: Don't quibble, Sibyl.

SIBYL: And as for explosions, there's nothing here that can explode.

ELYOT: Oho, isn't there.

SIBYL: Yes, but Elli——

ELYOT: Darling, be sweet. Bear with me. I beseech you to bear with me.

SIBYL: I don't understand. It's horrid of you to do this.

ELYOT: I'm not doing anything. I'm only asking you, imploring you to come away from this place.

SIBYL: But I love it here.

ELYOT: There are thousands of other places far nicer.

SIBYL: It's a pity we didn't go to one of them.

ELYOT: Now, listen, Sibyl——

SIBYL: Yes, but why are you behaving like this, why, why, why?

ELYOT: Don't ask why. Just give in to me. I swear I'll never ask you to give into me over anything again.

SIBYL (*with complete decision*): I won't think of going to-night. It's utterly ridiculous. I've done quite enough travelling for one day, and I'm tired.

ELYOT: You're as obstinate as a mule.

SIBYL: I like that, I must say.

ELYOT (*hotly*): You've got your nasty little feet dug into the ground, and you don't intend to budge an inch, do you?

SIBYL (*with spirit*): No, I do not.

ELYOT: If there's one thing in the world that infuriates me, it's sheer wanton stubbornness. I should like to cut off your head with a meat axe.

SYBIL: How dare you talk to me like that, on our honeymoon night.

ELYOT: Damn our honeymoon night. Damn it, damn it, damn it!

SIBYL (*bursting into tears*): Oh, Elli, Elli——

ELYOT: Stop crying. Will you or will you not come away with me to Paris?

SIBYL: I've never been so miserable in my life. You're hateful and beastly. Mother was perfectly right. She said you had shifty eyes.

ELYOT: Well, she can't talk. Her's are so close together, you couldn't put a needle between them.

SIBYL: You don't love me a little bit. I wish I were dead.

ELYOT: Will you or will you not come to Paris?

SIBYL: No, no I won't.

ELYOT: Oh, my God! (*He stamps indoors.*)

SIBYL (*following him, wailing*): Oh, Elli, Elli, Elli——

VICTOR *comes stamping out of the French windows on the left, followed by* AMANDA.

VICTOR: You were certainly right when you said you weren't normal. You're behaving like a lunatic.

AMANDA: Not at all. All I have done is to ask you a little favour.

VICTOR: Little favour indeed.

AMANDA: If we left now we could be in Paris in a few hours.

VICTOR: If we crossed Siberia by train we could be in China in a fortnight, but I don't see any reason to do it.

AMANDA: Oh, Victor darling—please, please—be sensible, just for my sake.

VICTOR: Sensible!

AMANDA: Yes, sensible. I shall be absolutely miserable if we stay here. You don't want me to be absolutely miserable all through my honeymoon, do you?

VICTOR: But why on earth didn't you think of your sister's tragedy before?

AMANDA: I forgot.

VICTOR: You couldn't forget a thing like that.

AMANDA: I got the places muddled. Then when I saw the Casino there in the moonlight, it all came back to me.

VICTOR: When did all this happen?

AMANDA: Years ago, but it might just as well have been yesterday. I can see her now lying dead, with that dreadful expression on her face. Then all that awful business of taking the body home to England.

It was perfectly horrible.

VICTOR: I never knew you had a sister.

AMANDA: I haven't any more.

VICTOR: There's something behind all this.

AMANDA: Don't be silly. What could there be behind it?

VICTOR: Well, for one thing, I know you're lying.

AMANDA: Victor!

VICTOR: Be honest. Aren't you?

AMANDA: I can't think how you can be so mean and suspicious.

VICTOR (*patiently*): You're lying, Amanda. Aren't you?

AMANDA: Yes, Victor.

VICTOR: You never had a sister, dead or alive?

AMANDA: I believe there was a stillborn one in 1902.

VICTOR: What is your reason for all this?

AMANDA: I told you I was unreliable.

VICTOR: Why do you want to leave so badly?

AMANDA: You'll be angry if I tell you the truth.

VICTOR: What is it?

AMANDA: I warn you.

VICTOR: Tell me. Please teli me.

AMANDA: Elyot's here.

VICTOR: What!

AMANDA: I saw him.

VICTOR: When?

AMANDA: Just now, when you were in the bath.

VICTOR: Where was he?

AMANDA (*hesitatingly*): Down there, in a white suit. (*She points over the balustrade.*)

VICTOR (*sceptically*): White suit?

AMANDA: Why not? It's summer, isn't it?

VICTOR: You're lying again.

AMANDA: I'm not. He's here. I swear he is.

VICTOR: Well, what of it?

AMANDA: I can't enjoy a honeymoon with you, with Elyot liable to bounce in at any moment.

VICTOR: Really, Mandy.

AMANDA: Can't you see how awful it is? It's the most embarrassing thing that ever happened to me in my whole life.

VICTOR: Did he see you?

AMANDA: No, he was running.

VICTOR: What was he running for?

AMANDA: How on earth do I know. Don't be so annoying.

VICTOR: Well, as long as he didn't see you it's all right, isn't it?

AMANDA: It isn't all right at all. We must leave immediately.

VICTOR: But why?

AMANDA: How can you be so appallingly obstinate.

VICTOR: I'm not afraid of him.

AMANDA: Neither am I. It isn't a question of being afraid. It's just a horrible awkward situation.

VICTOR: I'm damned if I can see why our whole honeymoon should be upset by Elyot.

AMANDA: My last one was.

VICTOR: I don't believe he's here at all.

AMANDA: He is I tell you. I saw him.

VICTOR: It was probably an optical illusion. This half light is very deceptive.

AMANDA: It was no such thing.

VICTOR: I absolutely refuse to change all our

plans at the last moment, just because you think you've seen Elyot. It's unreasonable and ridiculous of you to demand it. Even if he is here I can't see that it matters. He'll probably feel much more embarrassed than you, and a damned good job too; and if he annoys you in any way I'll knock him down.

AMANDA: That would be charming.

VICTOR: Now don't let's talk about it any more.

AMANDA: Do you mean to stand there seriously and imagine that the whole thing can be glossed over as easily as that?

VICTOR: I'm not going to leave, Mandy. If I start giving into you as early as this, our lives will be unbearable.

AMANDA (*outraged*): Victor!

VICTOR (*calmly*): You've worked yourself up into a state over a situation which really only exists in your mind.

AMANDA (*controlling herself with an effort*): Please, Victor, please, for this last time I implore you. Let's go to Paris now, to-night. I mean it with all my heart—please——

VICTOR (*with gentle firmness*): No, Mandy!

AMANDA: I see quite clearly that I have been foolish enough to marry a fat old gentleman in a club armchair.

VICTOR: It's no use being cross.

AMANDA: You're a pompous ass.

ICTOR (*horrified*): Mandy!

AMANDA (*enraged*): Pompous ass, that's what I said, and that's what I meant. Blown out with your own importance.

VICTOR: Mandy, control yourself.

AMANDA: Get away from me. I can't bear to think

I'm married to such rugged grandeur.

VICTOR (*with great dignity*): I shall be in the bar. When you are ready to come down and dine, let me know.

AMANDA (*flinging herself into a chair*): Go away, go away.

VICTOR *stalks off, at the same moment that* ELYOT *stamps on, on the other side, followed by* SIBYL *in tears.*

ELYOT: If you don't stop screaming, I'll murder you.

SIBYL: I wish to heaven I'd never seen you in my life, let alone married you. I don't wonder Amanda left you, if you behaved to her as you've behaved to me. I'm going down to have dinner by myself and you can just do what you like about it.

ELYOT: Do, and I hope it chokes you.

SIBYL: Oh Elli, Elli——

She goes wailing indoors. Elyot stamps down to the balustrade and lights a cigarette, obviously trying to control his nerves. Amanda sees him, and comes down too.

AMANDA: Give me one for God's sake.

ELYOT (*hands her his case laconically*): Here.

AMANDA (*taking a cigarette*): I'm in such a rage.

ELYOT (*lighting up*): So am I.

AMANDA: What are we to do?

ELYOT: I don't know.

AMANDA: Whose yacht is that?

ELYOT: The Duke of Westminster's I expect. It always is.

AMANDA: I wish I were on it.

ELYOT: I wish you were too.

AMANDA: There's no need to be nasty.

ELYOT: Yes there is, every need. I've never in my

life felt a greater urge to be nasty.

AMANDA: And you've had some urges in your time, haven't you?

ELYOT: If you start bickering with me, Amanda, I swear I'll throw you over the edge.

AMANDA: Try it, that's all, just try it.

ELYOT: You've upset everything, as usual.

AMANDA: I've upset everything! What about you?

ELYOT: Ever since the first moment I was unlucky enough to set eyes on you, my life has been insupportable.

AMANDA: Oh do shut up, there's no sense in going on like that.

ELYOT: Nothing's any use. There's no escape, ever.

AMANDA: Don't be melodramatic.

ELYOT: Do you want a cocktail? There are two here.

AMANDA: There are two over here as well.

ELYOT: We'll have my two first. (AMANDA *crosses over into* ELYOT's *part of the terrace. He gives her one, and keeps one himself.*)

AMANDA: Shall we get roaring screaming drunk?

ELYOT: I don't think that would help, we did it once before and it was a dismal failure.

AMANDA: It was lovely at the beginning.

ELYOT: You have an immoral memory Amanda. Here's to you. (*They raise their glasses solemnly and drink.*)

AMANDA: I tried to get away the moment after I'd seen you, but he wouldn't budge.

ELYOT: What's his name.

AMANDA: Victor, Victor Prynne.

ELYOT (*toasting*): Mr. and Mrs. Victor Prynne. (*He drinks.*) Mine wouldn't budge either.

AMANDA: What's her name?

ELYOT: Sibyl.

AMANDA (*toasting*): Mr. and Mrs. Elyot Chase. (*She drinks.*) God pity the poor girl.

ELYOT: Are you in love with him?

AMANDA: Of course.

ELYOT: How funny.

AMANDA: I don't see anything particularly funny about it, you're in love with yours aren't you?

ELYOT: Certainly.

AMANDA: There you are then.

ELYOT: There we both are then.

AMANDA: What's she like?

ELYOT: Fair, very pretty, plays the piano beautifully.

AMANDA: Very comforting.

ELYOT: How's yours?

AMANDA: I don't want to discuss him.

ELYOT: Well, it doesn't matter, he'll probably come popping out in a minute and I shall see for myself. Does he know I'm here?

AMANDA: Yes, I told him.

ELYOT (*with sarcasm*): That's going to make things a whole lot easier.

AMANDA: You needn't be frightened, he won't hurt you.

ELYOT: If he comes near me I'll scream the place down.

AMANDA: Does Sibyl know I'm here?

ELYOT: No, I pretended I'd had a presentiment. I tried terribly hard to persuade her to leave for Paris.

AMANDA: I tried too, it's lucky we didn't both succeed, isn't it? Otherwise we should probably all have joined up in Rouen or somewhere.

ELYOT (*laughing*): In some frowsy little hotel.

AMANDA (*laughing too*): Oh dear, it would have been much, much worse.

ELYOT: I can see us all sailing down in the morning for an early start.

AMANDA (*weakly*): Lovely, oh lovely.

ELYOT: Glorious! (*They both laugh helplessly.*)

AMANDA: What's happened to yours?

ELYOT: Didn't you hear her screaming? She's downstairs in the dining-room I think.

AMANDA: Mine is being grand, in the bar.

ELYOT: It really is awfully difficult.

AMANDA: Have you known her long?

ELYOT: About four months, we met in a house party in Norfolk.

AMANDA: Very flat, Norfolk.

ELYOT: How old is dear Victor?

AMANDA: Thirty-four, or five; and Sibyl?

ELYOT: I blush to tell you, only twenty-three.

AMANDA: You've gone a mucker alright.

ELYOT: I shall reserve my opinion of your choice until I've met dear Victor.

AMANDA: I wish you wouldn't go on calling him "Dear Victor." It's extremely irritating.

ELYOT: That's how I see him. Dumpy, and fair, and very considerate, with glasses. Dear Victor.

AMANDA: As I said before I would rather not discuss him. At least I have good taste enough to refrain from making cheap gibes at Sibyl.

ELYOT: You said Norfolk was flat.

AMANDA: That was no reflection on her, unless she made it flatter.

ELYOT: Your voice takes on an acid quality whenever you mention her name.

AMANDA: I'll never mention it again.

ELYOT: Good, and I'll keep off Victor.

AMANDA (*with dignity*): Thank you.

There is silence for a moment. The orchestra starts playing the same tune that they were singing previously.

ELYOT: That orchestra has a remarkable small repertoire.

AMANDA: They don't seem to know anything but this, do they?

She sits down on the balustrade, and sings it, softly, Her eyes are looking out to sea, and her mind is far away. ELYOT *watches her while she sings. When she turns to him at the end, there are tears in her eyes. He looks away awkwardly and lights another cigarette.*

ELYOT: You always had a sweet voice, Amanda.

AMANDA (*a little huskily*): Thank you.

ELYOT: I'm awfully sorry about all this, really I am. I wouldn't have had it happen for the world.

AMANDA: I know. I'm sorry too. It's just rotten luck.

ELYOT: I'll go away to-morrow whatever happens, so don't you worry.

AMANDA: That's nice of you.

ELYOT: I hope everything turns out splendidly for you, and that you'll be very happy.

AMANDA: I hope the same for you, too.

The music, which has been playing continually through this little scene, returns persistently to the refrain. They both look at one another and laugh.

ELYOT: Nasty insistent little tune.

AMANDA: Extraordinary how potent cheap music is.*

ELYOT: What exactly were you remembering at that moment?

AMANDA: The Palace Hotel Skating Rink in the morning, bright strong sunlight, and everybody whirling round in vivid colours, and you kneeling down to put on my skates for me.

ELYOT: You'd fallen on your fanny a few moments before.

AMANDA: It was beastly of you to laugh like that, I felt so humiliated.

ELYOT: Poor darling.

AMANDA: Do you remember waking up in the morning, and standing on the balcony, looking out across the valley?

ELYOT: Blue shadows on white snow, cleanness beyond belief, high above everything in the world. How beautiful it was.

AMANDA: It's nice to think we had a few marvellous moments.

ELYOT: A few: We had heaps really, only they slip away into the background, and one only remembers the bad ones.

AMANDA: Yes. What fools we were to ruin it all. What utter, utter fools.

ELYOT: You feel like that too, do you?

AMANDA (*wearily*): Of course.

ELYOT: Why did we?

AMANDA: The whole business was too much for us.

ELYOT: We were so ridiculously over in love.

AMANDA: Funny wasn't it?

ELYOT (*sadly*): Horribly funny.

* This line was subsequently altered to "Strange how potent cheap music is." See introduction.

AMANDA: Selfishness, cruelty, hatred, possessiveness, petty jealousy. All those qualities came out in us just because we loved each other.

ELYOT: Perhaps they were there anyhow.

AMANDA: No, it's love that does it. To hell with love.

ELYOT: To hell with love.

AMANDA: And yet here we are starting afresh with two quite different people. In love all over again, aren't we? (ELYOT *doesn't answer.*) Aren't we?

ELYOT: No.

AMANDA: Elyot.

ELYOT: We're not in love all over again, and you know it. Good night, Amanda. (*He turns abruptly, and goes towards the French windows.*)

AMANDA: Elyot—don't be silly—come back.

ELYOT: I must go and find Sibyl.

AMANDA: I must go and find Victor.

ELYOT (*savagely*): Well, why don't you?

AMANDA: I don't want to.

ELYOT: It's shameful, shameful of us.

AMANDA: Don't: I feel terrible. Don't leave me for a minute, I shall go mad if you do. We won't talk about ourselves any more, we'll talk about outside things, anything you like, only just don't leave me until I've pulled myself together.

ELYOT: Very well. (*There is a dead silence.*)

AMANDA: What have you been doing lately? During these last years?

ELYOT: Travelling about. I went round the world you know after——

AMANDA (*hurriedly*): Yes, yes, I know. How was it?

ELYOT: The world?

AMANDA: Yes.

ELYOT: Oh, highly enjoyable.

AMANDA: China must be very interesting.

ELYOT: Very big, China.

AMANDA: And Japan——

ELYOT: Very small.

AMANDA: Did you eat sharks' fins, and take your shoes off, and use chopsticks and everything?

ELYOT: Practically everything.

AMANDA: And India, the burning Ghars, or Ghats, or whatever they are, and the Taj Mahal. How was the Taj Mahal?

ELYOT (*looking at her*): Unbelievable, a sort of dream.

AMANDA: That was the moonlight I expect, you must have seen it in the moonlight.

ELYOT (*never taking his eyes off her face*): Yes, moonlight is cruelly deceptive.

AMANDA: And it didn't look like a biscuit box did it? I've always felt that it might.

ELYOT (*quietly*): Darling, darling, I love you so.

AMANDA: And I do hope you met a sacred Elephant. They're lint white I believe, and very, very sweet.

ELYOT: I've never loved anyone else for an instant.

AMANDA (*raising her hand feebly in protest*): No, no, you mustn't—Elyot—stop.

ELYOT: You love me, too, don't you? There's no doubt about it anywhere, is there?

AMANDA: No, no doubt anywhere.

ELYOT: You're looking very lovely you know, in this damned moonlight. Your skin is clear and cool, and your eyes are shining, and you're growing lovelier and lovelier every second as I look at you. You don't hold any mystery for me, darling, do you mind? There isn't a particle of you that I don't know, remember, and want.

AMANDA (*softly*): I'm glad, my sweet.

ELYOT: More than any desire anywhere, deep down in my deepest heart I want you back again—please——

AMANDA (*putting her hand over his mouth*): Don't say any more, you're making me cry so dreadfully.

He pulls her gently into his arms and they stand silently, completely oblivious to everything but the moment, and each other. When finally, they separate, they sit down, rather breathlessly, on the balustrade.

AMANDA: What now? Oh darling, what now?

ELYOT: I don't know, I'm lost, utterly.

AMANDA: We must think quickly, oh quickly——

ELYOT: Escape?

AMANDA: Together?

ELYOT: Yes, of course, now, now.

AMANDA: We can't, we can't, you know we can't.

ELYOT: We must.

AMANDA: It would break Victor's heart.

ELYOT: And Sibyl's too probably, but they 'r bound to suffer anyhow. Think of the hell we'd lead them into if we stayed. Infinitely worse than any cruelty in the world, pretending to love them, and loving each other, so desperately.

AMANDA: We must tell them.

ELYOT: What?

AMANDA: Call them, and tell them.

ELYOT: Oh no, no, that's impossible.

AMANDA: It's honest.

ELYOT: I can't help how honest it is, it's too horrible

to think of. How should we start? What should we say?

AMANDA: We should have to trust to the inspiration of the moment.

ELYOT: It would be a moment completely devoid of inspiration. The most appalling moment imaginable. No, no, we can't, you must see that, we simply can't.

AMANDA: What do you propose to do then? As it is they might appear at any moment.

ELYOT: We've got to decide instantly one way or another. Go away together now, or stay with them, and never see one another again, ever.

AMANDA: Don't be silly, what choice is there?

ELYOT: No choice at all, come—— (*He takes her hand.*)

AMANDA: No, wait, This is sheer raving madness, something's happened to us, we're not sane.

ELYOT: We never were.

AMANDA: Where can we go?

ELYOT: Paris first, my car's in the garage, all ready.

AMANDA: They'll follow us.

ELYOT: That doesn't matter, once the thing's done.

AMANDA: I've got a flat in Paris.

ELYOT: Good.

AMANDA: It's in the Avenue Montaigne. I let it to Freda Lawson, but she's in Biarritz, so it's empty.

ELYOT: Does Victor know?

AMANDA: No, he knows I have one but he hasn't the faintest idea where.

ELYOT: Better and better.

AMANDA: We're being so bad, so terribly bad, we'll suffer for this, I know we shall.

ELYOT: Can't be helped.

AMANDA: Starting all those awful rows all over again.

ELYOT: No, no, we're older and wiser now.

AMANDA: What difference does that make? The first moment either of us gets a bit nervy, off we'll go again.

ELYOT: Stop shilly-shallying, Amanda.

AMANDA: I'm trying to be sensible.

ELYOT: You're only succeeding in being completely idiotic.

AMANDA: Idiotic indeed! What about you?

ELYOT: Now look here Amanda——

AMANDA (*stricken*): Oh my God!

ELYOT (*rushing to her and kissing her*): Darling, darling, I didn't mean it——

AMANDA: I won't move from here unless we have a compact, a sacred, sacred compact never to quarrel again.

ELYOT: Easy to make but difficult to keep.

AMANDA: No, no, it's the bickering that always starts it. The moment we notice we're bickering, either of us, we must promise on our honour to stop dead. We'll invent some phrase or catchword. which when either of us says it, automatically cuts off all conversation for at least five minutes.

ELYOT: Two minutes dear, with an option of renewal.

AMANDA: Very well, what shall it be?

ELYOT (*hurriedly*): Solomon Isaacs.

AMANDA: All right, that'll do.

ELYOT: Come on, come on.

AMANDA: What shall we do if we meet either of them on the way downstairs?

ELYOT: Run like stags.

AMANDA: What about clothes?

ELYOT: I've got a couple of bags I haven't unpacked yet.

AMANDA: I've got a small trunk.

ELYOT: Send the porter up for it.

AMANDA: Oh this is terrible—terrible——

ELYOT: Come on, come on, don't waste time.

AMANDA: Oughtn't we to leave notes or something?

ELYOT: No, no, no, we'll telegraph from somewhere on the road.

AMANDA: Darling, I daren't, it's too wicked of us, I simply daren't:

ELYOT (*seizing her in his arms and kissing her violently*): Now will you behave?

AMANDA: Yes, but Elyot darling——

ELYOT: Solomon Isaacs!

They rush off together through ELYOT'S *suite. After a moment or so,* VICTOR *steps out on to the terrace and looks round anxiously. Then he goes back indoors again, and can be heard calling* "MANDY." *Finally he again comes out on to the terrace and comes despondently down to the balustrade. He hears* SIBYL'S *voice calling* "ELLI" *and looks round as she comes out of the French windows. She jumps slightly upon seeing him.*

VICTOR: Good evening.

SIBYL (*rather flustered*): Good-evening—I was——er—looking for my husband.

VICTOR: Really, that's funny. I was looking for my wife.

SIBYL: Quite a coincidence. (*She laughs nervously.*)

VICTOR (*after a pause*): It's very nice here isn't it?

SIBYL: Lovely.

VICTOR: Have you been here long?

SIBYL: No, we only arrived to-day.

VICTOR: Another coincidence. So did we.

SIBYL: How awfully funny.

VICTOR: Would you care for a cocktail?

SIBYL: Oh no thank you—really——

VICTOR: There are two here on the table.

SIBYL *glances at the two empty glasses on the balustrade, and tosses her head defiantly.*

SIBYL: Thanks very much, I'd love one.

VICTOR: Good, here you are. (SIBYL *comes over to* VICTOR'S *side of the terrace. He hands her one and takes one himself*)

SIBYL: Thank you.

VICTOR (*with rather forced gaiety*): To absent friends. (*He raises his glass.*)

SIBYL (*raising hers*): To absent friends. (*They both laugh rather mirthlessly and then sit down on the balustrade, pensively sipping their cocktails and looking at the view.*) It's awfully pretty isn't it? The moonlight, and the lights of that yacht reflected in the water——

VICTOR: I wonder who it belongs to.

THE CURTAIN SLOWLY FALLS

ACT II

The Scene is AMANDA'S *flat in Paris. A few days have elapsed since Act I. The flat is charmingly furnished, its principal features being a Steinway Grand on the Left, facing slightly up stage. Down stage centre, a very large comfortable sofa, behind which is a small table. There is also another sofa somewhere about, and one or two small tables, and a gramophone. The rest can be left to the discretion and taste of the decorator.*

When the Curtain Rises it is about ten o'clock in the evening. The windows are wide open, and the various street sounds of Paris can be heard but not very loudly as the apartment is high up.

AMANDA *and* ELYOT *are seated opposite one another at the table. They have finished dinner and are dallying over coffee and liqueurs.* AMANDA *is wearing pajamas, and* ELYOT *a comfortable dressing-gown.*

AMANDA: I'm glad we let Louise go. I am afraid she is going to have a cold.

ELYOT: Going to have a cold; she's been grunting and snorting all the evening like a whole herd of Bison.

AMANDA (*thoughtfully*): Bison never sounds right to me somehow. I have a feeling it ought to be Bisons, a flock of Bisons.

ELYOT: You might say a covey of Bisons, or even a school of Bisons.

AMANDA: Yes, lovely. The Royal London School of Bisons. Do you think Louise is happy at home?

ELYOT: No, profoundly miserable.

AMANDA: Family beastly to her?

ELYOT (*with conviction*): Absolutely vile. Knock her about dreadfully I expect, make her eat the most disgusting food, and pull her fringe.

AMANDA (*laughing*): Oh, poor Louise.

ELYOT: Well, you know what the French are.

AMANDA: Oh yes, indeed. I know what the Hungarians are too.

ELYOT: What are they?

AMANDA: Very wistful. It's all those Pretzles I shouldn't wonder.

ELYOT: And the Poostza; I always felt the Poostza was far too big, Danube or no Danube.

AMANDA: Have you ever crossed the Sahara on a Camel?

ELYOT: Frequently. When I was a boy we used to do it all the time. My Grandmother had a lovely seat on a camel.

AMANDA: There's no doubt about it, foreign travel's the thing.

ELYOT: Would you like some brandy?

AMANDA: Just a little. (*He pours some into her glass and some into his own.*)

ELYOT: I'm glad we didn't go out to-night.

AMANDA: Or last night.

ELYOT: Or the night before.

AMANDA: There's no reason to, really, when we're cosy here.

ELYOT: Exactly.

AMANDA: It's nice, isn't it?

ELYOT: Strangely peaceful. It's an awfully bad reflection on our characters. We ought to be absolutely tortured with conscience.

AMANDA: We are, every now and then.

ELYOT: Not nearly enough.

AMANDA: We sent Victor and Sibyl a nice note from wherever it was, what more can they want?

ELYOT: You're even more ruthless than I am.

AMANDA: I don't believe in crying over my bridge before I've eaten it.

ELYOT: Very sensible.

AMANDA: Personally I feel grateful for a miraculous escape. I know now that I should never have been happy with Victor. I was a fool ever to consider it.

ELYOT: You did a little more than consider it.

AMANDA: Well, you can't talk.

ELYOT: I wonder whether they met each other, or whether they've been suffering alone.

AMANDA: Oh dear, don't let's go on about it, it really does make one feel rather awful.

ELYOT: I suppose one or other or both of them will turn up here eventually.

AMANDA: Bound to; it won't be very nice, will it?

ELYOT (*cheerfully*): Perfectly horrible.

AMANDA: Do you realise that we're living in sin?

ELYOT: Not according to the Catholics, Catholics don't recognise divorce. We're married as much as ever we were.

AMANDA: Yes, dear, but we're not Catholics.

ELYOT: Never mind, it's nice to think they'd sort of back us up. We were married in the eyes of heaven, and we still are.

AMANDA: We may be alright in the eyes of Heaven,

but we look like being in the hell of a mess socially.

ELYOT: Who cares?

AMANDA: Are we going to marry again, after Victor and Sibyl divorce us?

ELYOT: I suppose so. What do you think?

AMANDA: I feel rather scared of marriage really.

ELYOT: It is a frowsy business.

AMANDA: I believe it was just the fact of our being married, and clamped together publicly, that wrecked us before.

ELYOT: That, and not knowing how to manage each other.

AMANDA: Do you think we know how to manage each other now?

ELYOT: This week's been very successful. We've hardly used Solomon Isaacs at all.

AMANDA: Solomon Isaacs is so long, let's shorten it to sollocks.

ELYOT: All right.

AMANDA: Darling, you do look awfully sweet in your little dressing-gown.

ELYOT: Yes, it's pretty ravishing, isn't it?

AMANDA: Do you mind if I come round and kiss you?

ELYOT: A pleasure, Lady Agatha.

AMANDA *comes round the table, kisses him, picks up the coffee pot, and returns to her chair.*

AMANDA: What fools we were to subject ourselves to five years' unnecessary suffering.

ELYOT: Perhaps it wasn't unnecessary, perhaps it mellowed and perfected us like beautiful ripe fruit.

AMANDA: When we were together, did you really think I was unfaithful to you?

ELYOT: Yes, practically every day.

AMANDA: I thought you were too; often I used to torture myself with visions of your bouncing about on divans with awful widows.

ELYOT: Why widows?

AMANDA: I was thinking of Claire Lavenham really.

ELYOT: Oh Claire.

AMANDA (*sharply*): What did you say "Oh Claire" like that for? It sounded far too careless to me.

ELYOT (*wistfully*): What a lovely creature she was.

AMANDA: Lovely, lovely, lovely!

ELYOT (*blowing her a kiss*): Darling!

AMANDA: Did you ever have an affair with her? Afterwards I mean?

ELYOT: Why do you want to know?

AMANDA: Curiosity, I suppose.

ELYOT: Dangerous.

AMANDA: Oh not now, not dangerous now. I wouldn't expect you to have been celibate during those five years, any more than I was.

ELYOT (*jumping*): What?

AMANDA: After all, Claire was undeniably attractive. A trifle over vivacious I always thought, but that was probably because she was fundamentally stupid.

ELYOT: What do you mean about not being celibate during those five years?

AMANDA: What do you think I mean?

ELYOT: Oh God! (*He looks down miserably.*)

AMANDA: What's the matter?

ELYOT: You know perfectly well what's the matter.

AMANDA (*gently*): You mustn't be unreasonable, I was only trying to stamp out the memory of you. I expect your affairs well outnumbered mine anyhow.

ELYOT: That is a little different. I'm a man.

AMANDA: Excuse me a moment while I get a caraway biscuit and change my crinoline.

ELYOT: It doesn't suit women to be promiscuous.

AMANDA: It doesn't suit men for women to be promiscuous.

ELYOT (*with sarcasm*): Very modern dear; really your advanced views quite startle me.

AMANDA: Don't be cross, Elyot, I haven't been so dreadfully loose actually. Five years is a long time, and even if I did nip off with someone every now and again, they were none of them very serious.

ELYOT (*rising from the table and walking away*): Oh, do stop it please——

AMANDA: Well, what about you?

ELYOT: Do you want me to tell you?

AMANDA: No, no, I don't—I take everything back—I don't.

ELYOT (*viciously*): I was madly in love with a woman in South Africa.

AMANDA: Did she have a ring through her nose?

ELYOT: Don't be revolting.

AMANDA: We're tormenting one another. Sit down, sweet, I'm scared.

ELYOT (*slowly*): Very well. (*He sits down thoughtfully.*)

AMANDA: We should have said Sollocks ages ago.

ELYOT: We're in love alright.

AMANDA: Don't say it so bitterly. Let's try to get the best out of it this time, instead of the worst.

ELYOT (*stretching his hand across the table*): Hand please.

AMANDA (*clasping it*): Here.

ELYOT: More comfortable?

AMANDA: Much more.

ELYOT (*after a slight pause*): Are you engaged for this dance?

AMANDA: Funnily enough I was, but my partner was suddenly taken ill.

ELYOT (*rising and going to the gramophone*): It's this damned smallpox epidemic.

AMANDA: No, as a matter of fact it was kidney trouble.

ELYOT: You'll dance it with me I hope?

AMANDA (*rising*): I shall be charmed.

ELYOT (*as they dance*): Quite a good floor, isn't it?

AMANDA: Yes, I think it needs a little Borax.

ELYOT: I love Borax.

AMANDA: Is that the Grand Duchess Olga lying under the piano?

ELYOT: Yes, her husband died a few weeks ago, you know, on his way back from Pulborough. So sad.

AMANDA: What on earth was he doing in Pulborough?

ELYOT: Nobody knows exactly, but there have been the usual stories.

AMANDA: I see.

ELYOT: Delightful parties Lady Bundle always gives, doesn't she?

AMANDA: Entrancing. Such a dear old lady.

ELYOT: And so gay: Did you notice her at supper blowing all those shrimps through her ear trumpet?

The tune comes to an end. AMANDA *sits on the edge of the sofa, pensively.*

ELYOT: What are you thinking about?

AMANDA: Nothing in particular.

ELYOT: Come on, I know that face.

AMANDA: Poor Sibyl.

ELYOT: Sibyl?

AMANDA: Yes, I suppose she loves you terribly.

ELYOT: Not as much as all that, she didn't have a chance to get really under way.

AMANDA: I expect she's dreadfully unhappy.

ELYOT: Oh, do shut up, Amanda, we've had all that out before.

AMANDA: We've certainly been pretty busy trying to justify ourselves.

ELYOT: It isn't a question of justifying ourselves, it's the true values of the situation that are really important. The moment we saw one another again we knew it was no use going on. We knew it instantly really, although we tried to pretend to ourselves that we didn't. What we've got to be thankful for is that we made the break straight away, and not later.

AMANDA: You think we should have done it anyhow?

ELYOT: Of course, and things would have been in a worse mess than they are now.

AMANDA: And what if we'd never happened to meet again. Would you have been quite happy with Sibyl?

ELYOT: I expect so.

AMANDA: Oh, Elyot!

ELYOT: You needn't look so stricken. It would havebeen the same with you and Victor. Life would have been smooth, and amicable, and quite charming, wouldn't it?

AMANDA: Poor dear Victor. He certainly did love me.

ELYOT: Splendid.

AMANDA: When I met him I was so lonely and

depressed, I felt that I was getting old, and crumbling away unwanted.

ELYOT: It certainly is horrid when one begins to crumble.

AMANDA (*wistfully*): He used to look at me hopelessly like a lovely spaniel, and I sort of melted like snow in the sunlight.

ELYOT: That must have been an edifying spectacle.

AMANDA: Victor really had a great charm.

ELYOT: You must tell me all about it.

AMANDA: He had a positive mania for looking after me, and protecting me.

ELYOT: That would have died down in time, dear.

AMANDA: You mustn't be rude, there's no necessity to be rude.

ELYOT: I wasn't in the least rude, I merely made a perfectly rational statement.

AMANDA: Your voice was decidedly bitter.

ELYOT: Victor had glorious legs, hadn't he? And fascinating ears.

AMANDA: Don't be silly.

ELYOT: He probably looked radiant in the morning, all flushed and tumbled on the pillow.

AMANDA: I never saw him on the pillow.

ELYOT: I'm surprised to hear it.

AMANDA (*angrily*): Elyot!

ELYOT. There's no need to be cross.

AMANDA: What did you mean by that?

ELYOT: I'm sick of listening to you yap, yap, yap, yap, yap, yapping about Victor.

AMANDA: Now listen Elyot, once and for all——

ELYOT: Oh my dear, Sollocks! Sollocks!—two minutes—Sollocks.

AMANDA: But——

ELYOT (*firmly*): Sollocks!

They sit in dead silence, looking at each other. AMANDA *makes a sign that she wants a cigarette.* ELYOT *gets up, hands her the box, and lights one for her and himself.* AMANDA *rises and walks over to the window, and stands there, looking out for a moment. Presently* ELYOT *joins her. She slips her arm through his, and they kiss lightly. They draw the curtains and then come down and sit side by side on the sofa.* ELYOT *looks at his watch.* AMANDA *raises her eyebrows at him and he nods, then they both sigh, audibly.*

That was a near thing.

AMANDA: It was my fault. I'm terribly sorry, darling.

ELYOT: I was very irritating, I know I was. I'm sure Victor was awfully nice, and you're perfectly right to be sweet about him.

AMANDA: That's downright handsome of you. Sweetheart! (*She kisses him.*)

ELYOT (*leaning back with her on the sofa*): I think I love you more than ever before. Isn't it ridiculous? Put your feet up.

She puts her legs across his, and they snuggle back together in the corner of the sofa, his head resting on her shoulder.

AMANDA: Comfortable?

ELYOT: Almost, wait a minute.

He struggles a bit and then settles down with a sigh.

AMANDA: How long, Oh Lord, how long?

ELYOT (*drowsily*): What do you mean, "how long, Oh Lord, how long?"

AMANDA: This is far too perfect to last.

ELYOT: You have no faith, that's what's wrong with you.

AMANDA: Absolutely none.

ELYOT: Don't you believe in——? (*He nods upwards.*)

AMANDA: No, do you?

ELYOT (*shaking his head*): No. What about——? (*He points downwards.*)

AMANDA: Oh dear no.

ELYOT: Don't you believe in anything?

AMANDA: Oh yes, I believe in being kind to everyone, and giving money to old beggar women, and being as gay as possible.

ELYOT: What about after we're dead?

AMANDA: I think a rather gloomy merging into everything, don't you?

ELYOT: I hope not, I'm a bad merger.

AMANDA: You won't know a thing about it.

ELYOT: I hope for a glorious oblivion, like being under gas.

AMANDA: I always dream the most peculiar things under gas.

ELYOT: Would you be young always? If you could choose?

AMANDA: No, I don't think so, not if it meant having awful bull's glands popped into me.

ELYOT: Cows for you dear. Bulls for me.

AMANDA: We certainly live in a marvellous age.

ELYOT: Too marvellous. It's alright if you happen to be a specialist at something, then you're too concentrated to pay attention to all the other things going on. But, for the ordinary observer, it's too much.

AMANDA (*snuggling closer*): Far, far too much.

ELYOT: Take the radio for instance.

AMANDA: Oh darling, don't let's take the radio.

ELYOT: Well, aeroplanes then, and Cosmic Atoms, and Television, and those gland injections we were talking about just now.

AMANDA: It must be so nasty for the poor animals, being experimented on.

ELYOT: Not when the experiments are successful. Why in Vienna I believe you can see whole lines of decrepit old rats carrying on like Tiller Girls.

AMANDA (*laughing*): Oh, how very, very sweet.

ELYOT (*burying his face in her shoulder*): I do love you so.

AMANDA: Don't blow, dear heart, it gives me the shivers.

ELYOT (*trying to kiss her*): Swivel your face round a bit more.

AMANDA (*obliging*): That better?

ELYOT (*kissing her lingeringly*): Very nice, thank you kindly.

AMANDA (*twining her arms round his neck*): Darling, you're so terribly, terribly dear, and sweet, and attractive. (*She pulls his head down to her again and they kiss lovingly.*)

ELYOT (*softly*): We were raving mad, ever to part, even for an instant.

AMANDA: Utter imbeciles.

ELYOT: I realised it almost immediately, didn't you?

AMANDA: Long before we got our decree.

ELYOT: My heart broke on that damned trip round the world. I saw such beautiful things, darling. Moonlight shining on old Temples, strange barbaric dances in jungle villages, scarlet flamingoes flying over deep, deep blue water. Breathlessly lovely, and completely unexciting because you weren't there to see them with me.

AMANDA (*kissing him again*): Take me please, take me at once, let's make up for lost time.

ELYOT: Next week?

AMANDA: To-morrow.

ELYOT: Done.

AMANDA: I must see those dear Flamingoes. (*There is a pause.*) Eight years all told, we've loved each other. Three married and five divorced.

ELYOT: Angel. Angel. Angel. (*He kisses her passionately.*)

AMANDA (*struggling slightly*): No, Elyot, stop now, stop——

ELYOT: Why should I stop? You know you adore being made love to.

AMANDA (*through his kisses*): It's so soon after dinner.

ELYOT (*jumping up rather angrily*): You really do say most awful things.

AMANDA (*tidying her hair*): I don't see anything particularly awful about that.

ELYOT: No sense of glamour, no sense of glamour at all.

AMANDA: It's difficult to feel really glamorous with a crick in the neck.

ELYOT: Why didn't you say you had a crick in your neck?

AMANDA (*sweetly*): It's gone now.

ELYOT: How convenient. (*He lights a cigarette.*)

AMANDA (*holding out her hand*): I want one please.

ELYOT (*throwing her one*): Here.

AMANDA: Match?

ELYOT (*impatiently*): Wait a minute, can't you?

AMANDA: Chivalrous little love.

ELYOT (*throwing the matches at her*): Here.

AMANDA (*coldly*): Thank you very much indeed. (*There is a silence for a moment.*)

ELYOT: You really can be more irritating than anyone in the world.

AMANDA: I fail to see what I've done that's so terribly irritating.

ELYOT: You have no tact.

AMANDA: Tact. You have no consideration.

ELYOT (*walking up and down*): Too soon after dinner indeed.

AMANDA: Yes, much too soon.

ELYOT: That sort of remark shows rather a common sort of mind I'm afraid.

AMANDA: Oh it does, does it?

ELYOT: Very unpleasant, makes me shudder.

AMANDA: Making all this fuss just because your silly vanity is a little upset.

ELYOT: Vanity: What do you mean, vanity?

AMANDA: You can't bear the thought that there are certain moments when our chemical, what d'you call 'ems, don't fuse properly.

ELYOT (*derisively*): Chemical what d'you call 'ems: Please try to be more explicit.

AMANDA: You know perfectly well what I mean, and don't you try to patronise me.

ELYOT (*loudly*): Now look here, Amanda——

AMANDA (*suddenly*): Darling Sollocks! Oh, for God's sake, Sollocks!

ELYOT: But listen——

AMANDA: Sollocks, Sollocks, Oh dear—triple Sollocks!

They stand looking at one another in silence for a moment, then AMANDA *flings herself down on the sofa and buries her face in the cushions.* ELYOT *looks at her, then goes over to the piano. He sits down and begins to play idly.* AMANDA *raises her head, screws herself round on the sofa, and lies there listening.* ELYOT *blows a kiss to her and goes on playing. He starts to sing softly to her, never taking his eyes off her. When he has finished the little refrain, whatever it was, he still continues to play it looking at her.*

AMANDA: Big romantic stuff, darling.

ELYOT (*smiling*): Yes, big romantic stuff.

He wanders off into another tune. AMANDA *sits up crossed legged on the sofa, and begins to sing it, then, still singing, she comes over and perches on the piano. They sing several old refrains from dead and gone musical comedies finishing with the song that brought them together again in the first Act. Finally* AMANDA *comes down and sits next to him on the piano stool, they both therefore have their backs half turned to the audience. She rests her head on his shoulder, until finally his fingers drop off the keys, and they melt into one another's arms.*

ELYOT (*after a moment*): You're the most thrilling, exciting woman that was ever born.

AMANDA (*standing up, and brushing her hand lightly over his mouth*): Dearest, dearest heart——

He catches at her hand and kisses it, and then her arm, until he is standing up, embracing her ardently. She struggles a little, half laughing, and breaks away, but he catches her, and they finish up on the sofa again, clasped in each other's arms, both completely given up to the passion of the moment, until the telephone bell rings violently, and they both spring apart.

ELYOT: Good God!

AMANDA: Do you think it's them?

ELYOT: I wonder.

AMANDA: Nobody knows we're here except Freda, and she wouldn't ring up.

ELYOT: It must be them then.

AMANDA: What are we to do?

ELYOT (*suddenly*): We're alright darling, aren't we—whatever happens?

AMANDA: Now and always, Sweet.

ELYOT: I don't care then.

He gets up and goes defiantly over to the telephone, which has been ringing incessantly during the little preceding scene.

AMANDA: It was bound to come sooner or later.

ELYOT (*at telephone*): Hallo—hallo—what—comment? Madame, qui? 'allo—'allo—oui c'est ca. Oh, Madame Duvallon—Oui, oui, oui. (*He puts his hand over the mouthpiece.*) It's only somebody wanting to talk to the dear Madame Duvallon.

AMANDA: Who's she?

ELYOT: I haven't the faintest idea. (*At telephone.*) Je regrette beaucoup Monsieur, mais Madame Duvallon viens de partir—cette apres midi, pour Madagascar. (*He hangs up the telephone.*) Whew; that gave me a fright.

AMANDA: It sent shivers up my spine.

ELYOT: What shall we do if they suddenly walk in on us?

AMANDA: Behave exquisitely.

ELYOT: With the most perfect poise?

AMANDA: Certainly, I shall probably do a Court Curtsey.

ELYOT (*sitting on the edge of the sofa*): Things that ought to matter dreadfully, don't matter at all when one's happy, do they?

AMANDA. What is so horrible is that one can't stay happy.

ELYOT: Darling, don't say that.

AMANDA: It's true. The whole business is a very poor joke.

ELYOT: Meaning that sacred and beautiful thing, Love?

AMANDA: Yes, meaning just that.

ELYOT (*striding up and down the room dramatically*): What does it all mean, that's what I ask myself in my ceaseless quest for ultimate truth. Dear God, what does it all mean?

AMANDA: Don't laugh at me, I'm serious.

ELYOT (*seriously*): You mustn't be serious, my dear one, it's just what they want.

AMANDA: Who's they?

ELYOT: All the futile moralists who try to make life unbearable. Laugh at them. Be flippant. Laugh at everything, all their sacred shibboleths. Flippancy brings out the acid in their damned sweetness and light.

AMANDA: If I laugh at everything, I must laugh at us too.

ELYOT: Certainly you must. We're figures of fun alright.

AMANDA: How long will it last, this ludicrous, overbearing love of ours?

ELYOT: Who knows?

AMANDA: Shall we always want to bicker and fight?

ELYOT: No, that desire will fade, along with our passion.

AMANDA: Oh dear, shall we like that?

ELYOT: It all depends on how well we've played.

AMANDA: What happens if one of us dies? Does the one that's left still laugh?

ELYOT: Yes, yes, with all his might.

AMANDA (*wistfully clutching his hand*): That's serious enough, isn't it?

ELYOT: No, no, it isn't. Death's very laughable, such a cunning little mystery. All done with mirrors.

AMANDA: Darling, I believe you're talking nonsense.

ELYOT: So is everyone else in the long run. Let's be superficial and pity the poor Philosophers. Let's blow trumpets and squeakers, and enjoy the party as much as we can, like very small, quite idiotic school-children. Let's savour the delight of the moment. Come and kiss me darling, before your body rots, and worms pop in and out of your eye sockets.

AMANDA: Elyot, worms don't pop.

ELYOT (*kissing her*): I don't mind what you do see? You can paint yourself bright green all over, and dance naked in the Place Vendome, and rush off madly with all the men in the world, and I shan't say a word, as long as you love me best.

AMANDA: Thank you, dear. The same applies to you, except that if I catch you so much as looking at another woman, I'll kill you.

ELYOT: Do you remember that awful scene we had in Venice?

AMANDA: Which particular one?

ELYOT: The one when you bought that little painted wooden snake on the Piazza, and put it on my bed.

AMANDA: Oh Charles. That was his name, Charles. He did wriggle so beautifully.

ELYOT: Horrible thing, I hated it.

AMANDA: Yes, I know you did. You threw it out of the window into the Grand Canal. I don't think I'll ever forgive you for that.

ELYOT: How long did the row last?

AMANDA: It went on intermittently for days.

ELYOT: The worst one was in Cannes when your curling irons burnt a hole in my new dressing-gown. (*He laughs.*)

AMANDA: It burnt my comb too, and all the towels in the bathroom.

ELYOT: That was a rouser, wasn't it?

AMANDA: That was the first time you ever hit me.

ELYOT: I didn't hit you very hard.

AMANDA: The manager came in and found us rolling on the floor, biting and scratching like panthers. Oh dear, oh dear—— (*She laughs helplessly.*)

ELYOT: I shall never forget his face. (*They both collapse with laughter.*)

AMANDA: How ridiculous, how utterly, utterly ridiculous.

ELYOT: We were very much younger then.

AMANDA: And very much sillier.

ELYOT: As a matter of fact the real cause of that row was Peter Burden.

AMANDA: You knew there was nothing in that.

ELYOT: I didn't know anything of the sort, you took presents from him.

AMANDA: Presents: only a trivial little brooch.

ELYOT: I remember it well, bristling with diamonds. In the worst possible taste.

AMANDA: Not at all, it was very pretty. I still have it, and I wear it often.

ELYOT: You went out of your way to torture me over Peter Burden.

AMANDA: No, I didn't, you worked the whole thing up in your jealous imagination.

ELYOT: You must admit that he was in love with you, wasn't he?

AMANDA: Just a little perhaps. Nothing serious.

ELYOT: You let him kiss you. You said you did.

AMANDA: Well, what of it?

ELYOT: What of it!

AMANDA: It gave him a lot of pleasure, and it didn't hurt me.

ELYOT: What about me?

AMANDA: If you hadn't been so suspicious and nosey you'd never have known a thing about it.

ELYOT: That's a nice point of view I must say.

AMANDA: Oh dear, I'm bored with this conversation.

ELYOT: So am I, bored stiff. (*He goes over to the table.*) Want some brandy?

AMANDA: No thanks.

ELYOT: I'll have a little, I think.

AMANDA: I don't see why you want it, you've already had two glasses.

ELYOT: No particular reason, anyhow they were very small ones.

AMANDA: It seems so silly to go on, and on, and on with a thing.

ELYOT (*pouring himself out a glassful*): You can hardly call three liqueur glasses in a whole evening going on, and on, and on.

AMANDA: It's become a habit with you.

ELYOT: You needn't be so grand, just because you don't happen to want any yourself at the moment.

AMANDA: Don't be so stupid.

ELYOT (*irritably*): Really Amanda——

AMANDA: What?

ELYOT: Nothing. (AMANDA *sits down on the sofa, and, taking a small mirror from her bag, gazes at her face critically, and then uses some lipstick and powder. A trifle nastily.*) Going out somewhere dear?

AMANDA: No, just making myself fascinating for you.

ELYOT: That reply has broken my heart.

AMANDA: The woman's job is to allure the man. Watch me a minute will you?

ELYOT: As a matter of fact that's perfectly true.

AMANDA: Oh, no, it isn't.

ELYOT: Yes it is.

AMANDA (*snappily*): Oh be quiet.

ELYOT: It's a pity you didn't have any more brandy; it might have made you a little less disagreeable.

AMANDA: It doesn't seem to have worked such wonders with you.

ELYOT: Snap, snap, snap; like a little adder.

AMANDA: Adders don't snap, they sting.

ELYOT: Nonsense, they have a little bag of venom behind their fangs and they snap.

AMANDA: They sting.

ELYOT: They snap.

AMANDA (*with exasperation*): I don't care, do you understand? I don't care. I don't mind if they bark, and roll about like hoops.

ELYOT (*after a slight pause*): Did you see much of

Peter Burden after our divorce?

AMANDA: Yes, I did, quite a lot.

ELYOT: I suppose you let him kiss you a good deal more then.

AMANDA: Mind your own business.

ELYOT: You must have had a riotous time. (AMANDA *doesn't answer, so he stalks about the room.*) No restraint at all—very enjoyable—you never had much anyhow.

AMANDA: You're quite insufferable; I expect it's because you're drunk.

ELYOT: I'm not in the least drunk.

AMANDA: You always had a weak head.

ELYOT: I think I mentioned once before that I have only had three minute liqueur glasses of brandy the whole evening long. A child of two couldn't get drunk on that.

AMANDA: On the contrary, a child of two could get violently drunk on only one glass of brandy.

ELYOT: Very interesting. How about a child of four, and a child of six, and a child of nine?

AMANDA (*turning her head away*): Oh do shut up.

ELYOT (*witheringly*): We might get up a splendid little debate about that, you know, Intemperate Tots.

AMANDA: Not very funny, dear; you'd better have some more brandy.

ELYOT: Very good idea, I will. (*He pours out another glass and gulps it down defiantly.*)

AMANDA: Ridiculous ass.

ELYOT: I beg your pardon?

AMANDA: I said ridiculous ass!

ELYOT (*with great dignity*): Thank you. (*There is a silence.* AMANDA *gets up, and turns the gramophone on.*)

You'd better turn that off, I think.

AMANDA (*coldly*): Why?

ELYOT: It's very late and it will annoy the people upstairs.

AMANDA: There aren't any people upstairs. It's a photographer's studio.

ELYOT: There are people downstairs, I suppose?

AMANDA: They're away in Tunis.

ELYOT: This is no time of the year for Tunis. (*He turns the gramophone off.*)

AMANDA (*icily*): Turn it on again, please.

ELYOT: I'll do no such thing.

AMANDA: Very well, if you insist on being boorish and idiotic. (*She gets up and turns it on again.*)

ELYOT: Turn it off. It's driving me mad.

AMANDA: You're far too temperamental. Try to control yourself.

ELYOT: Turn it off.

AMANDA: I wont. (ELYOT *rushes at the gramophone.* AMANDA *tries to ward him off. They struggle silently for a moment then the needle screeches across the record.*) There now, you've ruined the record. (*She takes it off and scrutinises it.*)

ELYOT: Good job, too.

AMANDA: Disagreeable pig.

ELYOT (*suddenly stricken with remorse*): Amanda darling—Sollocks.

AMANDA (*furiously*): Sollocks yourself. (*She breaks the record over his head.*)

ELYOT (*staggering*): You spiteful little beast. (*He slaps her face. She screams loudly and hurls herself sobbing with rage on to the sofa, with her face buried in the cushions.*)

AMANDA (*wailing*): Oh, oh, oh——

ELYOT: I'm sorry, I didn't mean it—I'm sorry, darling, I swear I didn't mean it.

AMANDA: Go away, go away, I hate you. (ELYOT *kneels on the sofa and tries to pull her round to look at him.*)

ELYOT: Amanda—listen—listen——

AMANDA (*turning suddenly, and fetching him a welt across the face*): Listen indeed; I'm sick and tired of listening to you, you damned sadistic bully.

ELYOT (*with great grandeur*): Thank you. (*He stalks towards the door, in stately silence.* AMANDA *throws a cushion at him, which misses him and knocks down a lamp and a vase on the side table.*) (ELYOT *laughs falsely.*) A pretty display I must say.

AMANDA (*wildly*): Stop laughing like that.

ELYOT (*continuing*): Very amusing indeed.

AMANDA (*losing control*): Stop—stop—stop— (*she rushes at him, he grabs her hands and they sway about the room, until he manages to twist her round by the arms so that she faces him, closely, quivering with fury*)—I hate you—do you hear? You're conceited, and overbearing, and utterly impossible!

ELYOT (*shouting her down*): You're a vile tempered loose-living wicked little beast, and I never want to see you again so long as I live.

He flings her away from him, she staggers, and falls against a chair. They stand gasping at one another in silence for a moment.

AMANDA (*very quietly*): This is the end, do you understand? The end, finally and forever.

She goes to the door, which opens on to the landing, and wrenches it open. He rushes after her and clutches her wrist.

ELYOT: You're not going like this.

AMANDA: Oh yes I am.

ELYOT: You're not.

AMANDA: I am; let go of me—— (*He pulls her away from the door, and once more they struggle. This time a standard lamp crashes to the ground.* AMANDA, *breathlessly, as they fight.*) You're a cruel fiend, and I hate and loathe you; thank God I've realised in time what you're really like; marry you again, never, never, never. . . . I'd rather die in torment——

ELYOT (*at the same time*): Shut up; shut up. I wouldn't marry you again if you came crawling to me on your bended knees, you're a mean, evil minded, little vampire—I hope to God I never set eyes on you again as long as I live——

At this point in the proceedings they trip over a piece of carpet, and fall on to the floor, rolling over and over in paroxysms of rage. VICTOR *and* SIBYL *enter quietly, through the open door, and stand staring at them in horror. Finally* AMANDA *breaks free and half gets up,* ELYOT *grabs her leg, and she falls against a table, knocking it completely over.*

AMANDA (*screaming*): Beast; brute; swine; cad; beast; beast; brute; devil——

She rushes back at ELYOT *who is just rising to his feet, and gives him a stinging blow, which knocks him over again. She rushes blindly off Left, and slams the door, at the same moment that he jumps up and rushes off Right, also slamming the door.* VICTOR *and* SIBYL *advance apprehensively into the room, and sink on to the sofa——*

THE CURTAIN FALLS

ACT III

The Scene is the same as Act II. It is the next morning. The time is about eight-thirty. VICTOR *and* SIBYL *have drawn the two sofas across the doors* Right, *and* Left, *and are stretched on them, asleep.* VICTOR *is in front of* AMANDA'S *door, and* SIBYL *in front of* ELYOT'S.

The room is in chaos, as it was left the night before.

As the curtain rises, there is the rattling of a key in the lock of the front door, and LOUISE *enters. She is rather a frowsy looking girl, and carries a string bag with various bundles of eatables crammed into it, notably a long roll of bread, and a lettuce. She closes the door after her, and in the half light trips over the standard lamp lying on the floor. She puts her string bag down, and gropes her way over to the window. She draws the curtains, letting sunlight stream into the room. When she looks round, she gives a little cry of horror. Then she sees* VICTOR *and* SIBYL *sleeping peacefully, and comes over and scrutinises each of them with care, then she shakes* SIBYL *by the shoulder.*

SIBYL (*waking*): Oh dear.

LOUISE: Bon jour, Madame.

SIBYL (*bewildered*): What ?—Oh—bon jour.

LOUISE: Qu'est-ce que vous faites ici, madame ?

SIBYL: What—what ?—Wait a moment, attendez un instant—oh dear——

VICTOR (*sleepily*): What's happening ? (*Jumping up.*)

Of course, I remember now. (*He sees* LOUISE.) Oh!

LOUISE (*firmly*): Bon jour, Monsieur:

VICTOR: Er—bon jour—What time is it?

LOUISE (*rather dully*): Eh, Monsieur?

SIBYL (*sitting up on the sofa*): Quelle heure est il s'il vous plait?

LOUISE: C'est neuf heure moins dix madame.

VICTOR: What did she say?

SIBYL: I think she said nearly ten o'clock.

VICTOR (*taking situation in hand*): Er—voulez—er—wake—revillez Monsieur et Madame—er—toute suite?

LOUISE (*shaking her head*): Non, Monsieur. Il m'est absolument defendu de les appeler jusqu'à ce qu'ils sonnent.

She takes her bag and goes off into the kitchen. VICTOR *and* SIBYL *look at each other helplessly.*

SIBYL: What are we to do?

VICTOR (*with determination*): Wake them ourselves. (*He goes towards* AMANDA'S *door.*)

SIBYL: No, no, wait a minute.

VICTOR: What's the matter?

SIBYL (*plaintively*): I couldn't face them yet, really, I couldn't; I feel dreadful.

VICTOR: So do I. (*He wanders gloomily over to the window.*) It's a lovely morning.

SIBYL: Lovely. (*She bursts into tears.*)

VICTOR (*coming to her*): I say, don't cry.

SIBYL: I can't help it.

VICTOR: Please don't, please——

SIBYL: It's all so squalid, I wish we hadn't stayed; what's the use?

VICTOR: We've got to see them before we go back to England, we must get things straightened out.

SIBYL (*sinking down on to the sofa*): Oh dear, oh dear, oh dear, I wish I were dead.

VICTOR: Hush, now, hush. Remember your promise. We've got to see this through together and get it settled one way or another.

SIBYL (*sniffling*): I'll try to control myself, only I'm so . . . so tired, I haven't slept properly for ages.

VICTOR: Neither have I.

SIBYL: If we hadn't arrived when we did, they'd have killed one another.

VICTOR: They must have been drunk.

SIBYL: She hit him.

VICTOR: He'd probably hit her, too, earlier on.

SIBYL: I'd no idea anyone ever behaved like that; it's so disgusting, so degrading, Elli of all people—oh dear——(*She almost breaks down again, but controls herself.*

VICTOR: What an escape you've had.

SIBYL: What an escape we've both had.

AMANDA *opens her door and looks out. She is wearing travelling clothes, and is carrying a small suit-case. She jumps, upon seeing* SIBYL *and* VICTOR.

AMANDA: Oh!—good morning.

VICTOR (*with infinite reproach in his voice*): Oh, Amanda.

AMANDA: Will you please move this sofa, I can't get out.

VICTOR *moves the sofa, and she advances into the room and goes towards the door.*

VICTOR: Where are you going?

AMANDA: Away.

VICTOR: You can't.

AMANDA: Why not?

VICTOR: I want to talk to you.

AMANDA (*wearily*): What on earth is the use of that?

VICTOR: I must talk to you.

AMANDA: Well, all I can say is, it's very inconsiderate. (*She plumps the bag down by the door and comes down to* VICTOR.)

VICTOR: Mandy, I——

AMANDA (*gracefully determined to rise above the situation*): I suppose you're Sibyl; how do you do? (SIBYL *turns her back on her.*) Well, if you're going to take up that attitude, I fail to see the point of your coming here at all.

SIBYL: I came to see Elyot.

AMANDA: I've no wish to prevent you, he's in there, probably wallowing in an alcoholic stupor.

VICTOR: This is all very unpleasant, Amanda.

AMANDA: I quite agree, that's why I want to go away.

VICTOR: That would be shirking; this must be discussed at length.

AMANDA: Very well, if you insist, but not just now, I don't feel up to it. Has Louise come yet?

VICTOR: If Louise is the maid, she's in the kitchen.

AMANDA: Thank you. You'd probably like some coffee, excuse me a moment. (*She goes off into the kitchen.*)

SIBYL: Well! How dare she?

VICTOR (*irritably*): How dare she what?

SIBYL: Behave so calmly, as though nothing had happened.

VICTOR: I don't see what else she could have done.

SIBYL: Insufferable I call it.

ELYOT *opens his door and looks out.*

ELYOT (*seeing them*): Oh God.

He shuts the door again quickly.

SIBYL: Elyot—Elyot—— (*She rushes over to the door and bangs on it.*) Elyot—Elyot—Elyot——

ELYOT (*inside*) : Go away.

SIBYL (*falling on to the sofa*) : Oh, oh, oh.

She bursts into tears again.

VICTOR : Do pull yourself together for heaven's sake.

SIBYL : I can't, I can't—oh, oh, oh——

AMANDA *re-enters.*

AMANDA : I've ordered some coffee and rolls, they'll be here soon. I must apologise for the room being so untidy.

She picks up a cushion, and pats it into place on the sofa. There is a silence except for SIBYL'S *sobs.* AMANDA *looks at her, and then at* VICTOR ; *then she goes off into her room again, and shuts the door.*

VICTOR : It's no use crying like that, it doesn't do any good.

After a moment, during which SIBYL *makes renewed efforts to control her tears,* ELYOT *opens the door immediately behind her, pushes the sofa, with her on it, out of the way, and walks towards the front door. He is in travelling clothes, and carrying a small suitcase.*

SIBYL (*rushing after him*) : Elyot, where are you going?

ELYOT : Canada.

SIBYL : You can't go like this, you can't.

ELYOT : I see no point in staying.

VICTOR : You owe it to Sibyl to stay.

ELYOT : How do you do, I don't think we've met before.

SIBYL : You must stay, you've got to stay.

ELYOT : Very well, if you insist. (*He plumps his bag down.*) I'm afraid the room is in rather a mess. Have you seen the maid Louise?

VICTOR : She's in the kitchen.

ELYOT: Good. I'll order some coffee.

He makes a movement towards the kitchen.

VICTOR (*stopping him*): No, your—er—my—er—Amanda has already ordered it.

ELYOT: Oh, I'm glad the old girl's up and about.

VICTOR: We've got to get things straightened out, you know.

ELYOT (*looking around the room*): Yes, it's pretty awful. We'll get the concierge up from downstairs.

VICTOR: You're being purposely flippant, but it's no good.

ELYOT: Sorry. (*He lapses into silence.*)

VICTOR (*after a pause*): What's to be done?

ELYOT: I don't know.

SIBYL (*with spirit*): It's all perfectly horrible. I feel smirched and unclean as though slimy things had been crawling all over me.

ELYOT: Maybe they have, that's a very old sofa.

VICTOR: If you don't stop your damned flippancy, I'll knock your head off.

ELYOT (*raising his eyebrows*): Has it ever struck you that flippancy might cover a very real embarrassment?

VICTOR: In a situation such as this, it's in extremely bad taste.

ELYOT: No worse than bluster, and invective. As a matter of fact, as far as I know, this situation is entirely without precedent. We have no prescribed etiquette to fall back upon. I shall continue to be flippant.

SIBYL: Oh Elyot, how can you—how can you.

ELYOT: I'm awfully sorry, Sibyl.

VICTOR: It's easy enough to be sorry.

ELYOT: On the contrary. I find it exceedingly

difficult. I seldom regret anything. This is a very rare and notable exception, a sort of red letter day. We must all make the most of it.

SIBYL: I'll never forgive you, never. I wouldn't have believed anyone could be so callous and cruel.

ELYOT: I absolutely see your point, and as I said before, I'm sorry.

There is silence for a moment. Then AMANDA *comes in again. She has obviously decided to carry everything off in a high handed manner.*

AMANDA (*in social tones*): What! Breakfast not ready yet? Really, these French servants are too slow for words. (*She smiles gaily.*) What a glorious morning. (*She goes to the window.*) I do love Paris, it's so genuinely gay. Those lovely trees in the Champs Elysées, and the little roundabouts for the children to play on, and those shiny red taxis. You can see Sacre Cœur quite clearly to-day, sometimes it's a bit misty, particularly in August, all the heat rising up from the pavements you know.

ELYOT (*drily*): Yes, dear, we know.

AMANDA (*ignoring him*): And it's heavenly being so high up. I found this flat three years ago, quite by merest chance. I happened to be staying at the Plaza Athenee, just down the road——

ELYOT (*enthusiastically*): Such a nice hotel, with the most enchanting courtyard with a fountain that goes plopplopplopplopplopplopplopplopplop———

VICTOR: This is ridiculous, Amanda.

ELYOT (*continuing*): Plop plop plop plop plop plop plop plop plop plop——

AMANDA (*overriding him*): Now, Victor, I refuse to discuss anything in the least important until after breakfast. I couldn't concentrate now, I know I couldn't.

ELYOT (*sarcastically*): What manner. What poise. How I envy it. To be able to carry off the most embarrassing situation with such tact, and delicacy, and above all—such subtlety. Go on Amanda, you're making everything so much easier. We shall all be playing Hunt the Slipper in a minute.

AMANDA: Please don't address me, I don't wish to speak to you.

ELYOT: Splendid.

AMANDA: And what's more, I never shall again as long as I live.

ELYOT: I shall endeavour to rise above it.

AMANDA: I've been brought up to believe that it's beyond the pale, for a man to strike a woman.

ELYOT: A very poor tradition. Certain women should be struck regularly, like gongs.

AMANDA: You're an unmitigated cad, and a bully.

ELYOT: And you're an ill mannered, bad tempered slattern.

AMANDA (*loudly*): Slattern indeed.

ELYOT: Yes, slattern, slattern, slattern, and fishwife.

VICTOR: Keep your mouth shut, you swine.

ELYOT: Mind your own damned business.

They are about to fight, when SIBYL *rushes between them.*

SIBYL: Stop, stop, it's no use going on like this. Stop, please. (*To* AMANDA) Help me, do, do, do, help me——

AMANDA: I'm not going to interfere. Let them fight if they want to, it will probably clear the air anyhow.

SIBYL: Yes but——

AMANDA: Come into my room, perhaps you'd like to wash or something.

SIBYL: No, but——

AMANDA (*firmly*): Come along.

SIBYL: Very well.

She tosses her head at ELYOT, *and* AMANDA *drags her off.*

VICTOR (*belligerently*): Now then!

ELYOT: Now then what?

VICTOR: Are you going to take back those things you said to Amanda?

ELYOT: Certainly. I'll take back anything, if only you'll stop bellowing at me.

VICTOR (*contemptuously*): You're a coward too.

ELYOT: They want us to fight, don't you see?

VICTOR: No, I don't, why should they?

ELYOT: Primitive feminine instincts—warring males—very enjoyable.

VICTOR: You think you're very clever, don't you?

ELYOT: I think I'm a bit cleverer than you, but apparently that's not saying much.

VICTOR (*violently*): What?

ELYOT: Oh, do sit down.

VICTOR: I will not.

ELYOT: Well, if you'll excuse me, I will, I'm extremely tired.

He sits down.

VICTOR: Oh, for God's sake, behave like a man.

ELYOT (*patiently*): Listen a minute, all this belligerency is very right and proper and highly traditional, but if only you'll think for a moment, you'll see that it won't get us very far.

VICTOR: To hell with all that.

ELYOT: I should like to explain that if you hit me, I shall certainly hit you, probably equally hard, if not harder. I'm just as strong as you I should imagine. Then you'd hit me again, and I'd hit you again, and we'd go on until one or the other was knocked out. Now if you'll explain to me satisfactorily how all that can possibly improve the situation, I'll tear off my coat, and we'll go at one another hammer and tongs, immediately.

VICTOR: It would ease my mind.

ELYOT: Only if you won.

VICTOR: I should win alright.

ELYOT: Want to try?

VICTOR: Yes.

ELYOT (*jumping up*): Here goes then——

He tears off his coat.

VICTOR: Just a moment.

ELYOT: Well?

VICTOR: What did you mean about them wanting us to fight?

ELYOT: It would be balm to their vanity.

VICTOR: Do you love Amanda?

ELYOT: Is this a battle or a discussion? If it's the latter I shall put on my coat again, I don't want to catch a chill.

VICTOR: Answer my question, please.

ELYOT: Have a cigarette?

VICTOR (*stormily*): Answer my question.

ELYOT: If you analyse it, it's rather a silly question.

VICTOR: Do you love Amanda?

ELYOT (*confidentially*): Not very much this morning

to be perfectly frank, I'd like to wring her neck. Do you love her?

VICTOR: That's beside the point.

ELYOT: On the contrary, it's the crux of the whole affair. If you do love her still, you can forgive her, and live with her in peace and harmony until you're ninety-eight.

VICTOR: You're apparently even more of a cad than I thought you were.

ELYOT: You are completely in the right over the whole business, don't imagine I'm not perfectly conscious of that.

VICTOR: I'm glad.

ELYOT: It's all very unfortunate.

VICTOR: Unfortunate: My God!

ELYOT: It might have been worse.

VICTOR: I'm glad you think so.

ELYOT: I do wish you'd stop about being so glad about everything.

VICTOR: What do you intend to do? That's what want to know. What do vou intend to do?

ELYOT (*suddenly serious*): I don't know, I don't care.

VICTOR: I suppose you realise that you've broken that poor little woman's heart?

ELYOT: Which poor little woman?

VICTOR: Sibyl, of course.

ELYOT: Oh, come now, not as bad as that. She'll get over it, and forget all about me.

VICTOR: I sincerely hope so . . . for her sake.

ELYOT: Amanda will forget all about me too. Everybody will forget all about me. I might just as well lie down and die in fearful pain and suffering, nobody would care.

VICTOR: Don't talk such rot.

ELYOT: You must forgive me for taking rather a gloomy view of everything but the fact is, I suddenly feel slightly depressed.

VICTOR: I intend to divorce Amanda, naming you as co-respondent.

ELYOT: Very well.

VICTOR: And Sibyl will divorce you for Amanda. It would be foolish of either of you to attempt any defence.

ELYOT: Quite.

VICTOR: And the sooner you marry Amanda again, the better.

ELYOT: I'm not going to marry Amanda.

VICTOR: What?

ELYOT: She's a vile tempered wicked woman.

VICTOR: You should have thought of that before.

ELYOT: I did think of it before.

VICTOR (*firmly*): You've got to marry her.

ELYOT: I'd rather marry a ravening Leopard.

VICTOR (*angrily*): Now look here. I'm sick of all this shilly-shallying. You're getting off a good deal more lightly than you deserve; you can consider yourself damned lucky I didn't shoot you.

ELYOT (*with sudden vehemence*): Well, if you'd had a spark of manliness in you, you would have shot me. You're all fuss and fume, one of these cotton wool Englishmen. I despise you.

VICTOR (*through clenched teeth*): You despise me?

ELYOT: Yes, utterly. You're nothing but a rampaging gas bag! (*He goes off into his room and slams the door, leaving* VICTOR *speechless with fury,* AMANDA *and* SIBYL *re-enter.*)

AMANDA (*brightly*): Well, what's happened?

VICTOR (*sullenly*): Nothing's happened.

AMANDA: You ought to be ashamed to admit it.

SIBYL: Where's Elyot?

VICTOR: In there.

AMANDA: What's he doing?

VICTOR (*turning angrily away*): How do I know what he's doing?

AMANDA: If you were half the man I thought you were, he'd be bandaging himself.

SIBYL (*with defiance*): Elyot's just as strong as Victor.

AMANDA (*savagely*): I should like it proved.

SIBYL: There's no need to be so vindictive.

AMANDA: You were abusing Elyot like a pick-pocket to me a little while ago, now you are standing up for him.

SIBYL: I'm beginning to suspect that he wasn't quite so much to blame as I thought.

AMANDA: Oh really?

SIBYL: You certainly have a very unpleasant temper.

AMANDA: It's a little difficult to keep up with your rapid changes of front, but you're young and inexperienced, so I forgive you freely.

SIBYL (*heatedly*): Seeing the depths of degradation to which age and experience have brought you, I'm glad I'm as I am!

AMANDA (*with great grandeur*): That was exceedingly rude. I think you'd better go away somewhere. (*She waves her hand vaguely.*)

SIBYL: After all, Elyot is my husband.

AMANDA: Take him with you, by all means.

SIBYL: If you're not very careful, I will! (*She*

goes over to ELYOT'S *door and bangs on it.*) Elyot—Elyot——

ELYOT (*inside*): What is it?

SIBYL: Let me in. Please, please let me in; I want to speak to you!

AMANDA: Heaven preserve me from nice women!

SIBYL: Your own reputation ought to do that.

AMANDA (*irritably*): Oh, go to hell!

ELYOT *opens the door, and* SIBYL *disappears inside,* AMANDA *looks at* VICTOR, *who is standing with his back turned, staring out of the window, then she wanders about the room, making rather inadequate little attempts to tidy up. She glances at* VICTOR *again.*

AMANDA: Victor.

VICTOR (*without turning*): What?

AMANDA (*sadly*): Nothing.

She begins to wrestle with one of the sofas in an effort to get it in place. VICTOR *turns, sees her, and comes down and helps her, in silence.*

VICTOR: Where does it go?

AMANDA: Over there. (*After they have placed it,* AMANDA *sits on the edge of it and gasps a little.*) Thank you, Victor.

VICTOR: Don't mention it.

AMANDA (*after a pause*): What did you say to Elyot?

VICTOR: I told him he was beneath contempt.

AMANDA: Good.

VICTOR: I think you must be mad, Amanda.

AMANDA: I've often thought that myself.

VICTOR: I feel completely lost, completely bewildered.

AMANDA: I don't blame you. I don't feel any too cosy.

VICTOR: Had you been drinking last night?

AMANDA: Certainly not!

VICTOR: Had Elyot been drinking?

AMANDA: Yes—gallons.

VICTOR: Used he to drink before? When you were married to him?

AMANDA: Yes, terribly. Night after night he'd come home roaring and hiccoughing.

VICTOR: Disgusting!

AMANDA: Yes, wasn't it?

VICTOR: Did he really strike you last night?

AMANDA: Repeatedly. I'm bruised beyond recognition.

VICTOR (*suspecting slight exaggeration*): Amanda!

AMANDA (*putting her hand on his arm*): Oh, Victor, I'm most awfully sorry to have given you so much trouble, really I am! I've behaved badly, I know, but something strange happened to me. I can't explain it, there's no excuse, but I am ashamed of having made you unhappy.

VICTOR: I can't understand it at all. I've tried to, but I can't. It all seems so unlike you.

AMANDA: It isn't really unlike me, that's the trouble. I ought never to have married you; I'm a bad lot.

VICTOR: Amanda!

AMANDA: Don't contradict me. I know I'm a bad lot.

VICTOR: I wasn't going to contradict you.

AMANDA: Victor!

VICTOR: You appal me—absolutely!

AMANDA: Go on, go on, I deserve it.

VICTOR: I didn't come here to accuse you;

there's no sense in that!

AMANDA: Why did you come?

VICTOR: To find out what you want me to do.

AMANDA: Divorce me, I suppose, as soon as possible. I won't make any difficulties. I'll go away, far away, Morocco, or Tunis, or somewhere. I shall probably catch some dreadful disease, and die out there, all alone—oh dear!

VICTOR: It's no use pitying yourself.

AMANDA: I seem to be the only one who does. I might just as well enjoy it. (*She sniffs.*) I'm thoroughly unprincipled; Sibyl was right!

VICTOR (*irritably*): Sibyl's an ass.

AMANDA (*brightening slightly*): Yes, she is rather, isn't she? I can't think why Elyot ever married her.

VICTOR: Do you love him?

AMANDA: She seems so insipid, somehow——

VICTOR: Do you love him?

AMANDA: Of course she's very pretty, I suppose, in rather a shallow way, but still——

VICTOR: Amanda!

AMANDA: Yes, Victor?

VICTOR: You haven't answered my question.

AMANDA: I've forgotten what it was.

VICTOR (*turning away*): You're hopeless—hopeless.

AMANDA: Don't be angry, it's all much too serious to be angry about.

VICTOR: You're talking utter nonsense!

AMANDA: No, I'm not, I mean it. It's ridiculous for us all to stand round arguing with one another. You'd much better go back to England and let your lawyers deal with the whole thing.

VICTOR: But what about you?

AMANDA: I'll be all right.

VICTOR: I only want to know one thing, and you won't tell me.

AMANDA: What is it?

VICTOR: Do you love Elyot?

AMANDA: No, I hate him. When I saw him again suddenly at Deauville, it was an odd sort of shock. It swept me away completely. He attracted me; he always has attracted me, but only the worst part of me. I see that now.

VICTOR: I can't understand why? He's so terribly trivial and superficial.

AMANDA: That sort of attraction can't be explained, it's a sort of a chemical what d'you call 'em.

VICTOR: Yes; it must be!

AMANDA: I don't expect you to understand, and I'm not going to try to excuse myself in any way. Elyot was the first love affair of my life, and in spite of all the suffering he caused me before, there must have been a little spark left smouldering, which burst into flame when I came face to face with him again. I completely lost grip of myself and behaved like a fool, for which I shall pay all right, you needn't worry about that. But perhaps one day, when all this is dead and done with, you and I might meet and be friends. That's something to hope for, anyhow. Good-bye, Victor dear. (*She holds out her hand.*)

VICTOR (*shaking her hand mechanically*): Do you want to marry him?

AMANDA: I'd rather marry a boa constrictor.

VICTOR: I can't go away and leave you with a man who drinks, and knocks you about.

AMANDA: You needn't worry about leaving me, as

though I were a sort of parcel. I can look after myself.

VICTOR: You said just now you were going away to Tunis, to die.

AMANDA: I've changed my mind, it's the wrong time of the year for Tunis. I shall go somewhere quite different. I believe Brioni is very nice in the summer.

VICTOR: Why won't you be serious for just one moment?

AMANDA: I've told you, it's no use.

VICTOR: If it will make things any easier for you, I won't divorce you.

AMANDA: Victor!

VICTOR: We can live apart until Sibyl has got her decree against Elyot, then, some time after that, I'll let you divorce me.

AMANDA (*turning away*): I see you're determined to make me serious, whether I like it or not.

VICTOR: I married you because I loved you.

AMANDA: Stop it, Victor! Stop it! I won't listen!

VICTOR: I expect I love you still; one doesn't change all in a minute. You never loved me. I see that now, of course, so perhaps everything has turned out for the best really.

AMANDA: I thought I loved you, honestly I did.

VICTOR: Yes, I know, that's all right.

AMANDA: What an escape you've had.

VICTOR: I've said that to myself often during the last few days.

AMANDA: There's no need to rub it in.

VICTOR: Do you agree about the divorce business?

AMANDA: Yes. It's very, very generous of you.

VICTOR: It will save you some of the mud-slinging. We might persuade Sibyl not to name you.

AMANDA (*ruefully*): Yes, we might.

VICTOR: Perhaps she'll change her mind about divorcing him.

AMANDA: Perhaps. She certainly went into the bedroom with a predatory look in her eye.

VICTOR: Would you be pleased if that happened?

AMANDA: Delighted.

She laughs suddenly. VICTOR *looks at her, curiously.* SIBYL *and* ELYOT *come out of the bedroom. There is an awkward silence for a moment.*

SIBYL (*looking at* AMANDA *triumphantly*): Elyot and I have come to a decision.

AMANDA: How very nice!

VICTOR: What is it?

AMANDA: Don't be silly, Victor. Look at their faces.

ELYOT: Feminine intuition, very difficult.

AMANDA (*looking at* SIBYL): Feminine determination, very praiseworthy.

SIBYL: I am not going to divorce Elyot for a year.

AMANDA: I congratulate you.

ELYOT (*defiantly*): Sibyl has behaved like an angel.

AMANDA: Well, it was certainly her big moment.

LOUISE *comes staggering in with a large tray of coffee and rolls, etc., she stands peering over the edge of it, not knowing where to put it.*

ELYOT: Il faut le met sur la petite table la bas.

LOUISE: Oui, monsieur.

ELYOT *and* VICTOR *hurriedly clear the things off the side table, and* LOUISE *puts the tray down, and goes back into the kitchen.* AMANDA *and* SIBYL *eye one another.*

AMANDA: It all seems very amicable.

SIBYL: It is, thank you.

AMANDA: I don't wish to depress you, but Victor isn't going to divorce me either.

ELYOT (*looking up sharply*): What!

AMANDA: I believe I asked you once before this morning, never to speak to me again.

ELYOT: I only said "What." It was a general exclamation denoting extreme satisfaction.

AMANDA (*politely to* SIBYL): Do sit down, won't you?

SIBYL: I'm afraid I must be going now. I'm catching the Golden Arrow; it leaves at twelve.

ELYOT (*coaxingly*): You have time for a little coffee surely?

SIBYL: No, I really must go!

ELYOT: I shan't be seeing you again for such a long time.

AMANDA (*brightly*): Living apart? How wise!

ELYOT (*ignoring her*): Please, Sibyl, do stay!

SIBYL (*looking at* AMANDA *with a glint in her eye*): Very well, just for a little.

AMANDA: Sit down, Victor, darling.

They all sit down in silence. AMANDA *smiles sweetly at* SIBYL *and holds up the coffee pot and milk jug.*

Half and half?

SIBYL: Yes, please.

AMANDA (*sociably*): What would one do without one's morning coffee? That's what I often ask myself.

ELYOT: Is it?

AMANDA (*withering him with a look*): Victor, sugar for Sibyl. (*To* SIBYL) It would be absurd for me to call you anything but Sibyl, wouldn't it?

SIBYL (*not to be outdone*): Of course, I shall call you Mandy. (AMANDA *represses a shudder.*)

ELYOT: Oh God! We're off again. What weather! (AMANDA *hands* SIBYL *her coffee.*)

SIBYL: Thank you.

VICTOR: What's the time?

ELYOT: If the clock's still going after last night, it's ten-fifteen.

AMANDA (*handing* VICTOR *cup of coffee*): Here, Victor dear.

VICTOR: Thanks.

AMANDA: Sibyl, sugar for Victor.

ELYOT: I should like some coffee, please.

AMANDA *pours some out for him, and hands it to him in silence.*

AMANDA (*to* VICTOR): Brioche?

VICTOR (*jumping*): What?

AMANDA: Would you like a Brioche?

VICTOR: No, thank you.

ELYOT: I would. And some butter, and some jam. (*He helps himself.*)

AMANDA (*to* SIBYL): Have you ever been to Brioni?

SIBYL: No. It's in the Adriatic, isn't it?

VICTOR: The Baltic, I think.

SIBYL: I made sure it was in the Adriatic.

AMANDA: I had an aunt who went there once.

ELYOT (*with his mouth full*): I once had an aunt who went to Tasmania.

AMANDA *looks at him stonily. He winks at her,*

and she looks away hurriedly.

VICTOR: Funny how the South of France has become so fashionable in the summer, isn't it?

SIBYL: Yes, awfully funny.

ELYOT: I've been laughing about it for months.

AMANDA: Personally, I think it's a bit too hot, although of course one can lie in the water all day.

SIBYL: Yes, the bathing is really divine!

VICTOR: A friend of mine has a house right on the edge of Cape Ferrat.

SIBYL: Really?

VICTOR: Yes, right on the edge.

AMANDA: That must be marvellous!

VICTOR: Yes, he seems to like it very much.

The conversation languishes slightly.

AMANDA (*with great vivacity*): Do you know, I really think I love travelling more than anything else in the world! It always gives me such a tremendous feeling of adventure. First of all, the excitement of packing, and getting your passport visa'd and everything, then the thrill of actually starting, and trundling along on trains and ships, and then the most thrilling thing of all, arriving at strange places, and seeing strange people, and eating strange foods——

ELYOT: And making strange noises afterwards.

AMANDA *chokes violently.* VICTOR *jumps up and tries to offer assistance, but she waves him away, and continues to choke.*

VICTOR (*to* ELYOT): That was a damned fool thing to do.

ELYOT: How did I know she was going to choke?

VICTOR (*to* AMANDA): Here, drink some coffee.

AMANDA (*breathlessly gasping*): Leave me alone.

I'll be all right in a minute.

VICTOR (*to* ELYOT) : You waste too much time trying to be funny.

SIBYL (*up in arms*) : It's no use talking to Elyot like that ; it wasn't his fault.

VICTOR : Of course it was his fault entirely, making rotten stupid jokes——

SIBYL : I thought what Elyot said was funny.

VICTOR : Well, all I can say is, you must have a very warped sense of humour.

SIBYL : That's better than having none at all.

VICTOR : I fail to see what humour there is in incessant trivial flippancy.

SIBYL : You couldn't be flippant if you tried until you were blue in the face.

VICTOR : I shouldn't dream of trying.

SIBYL : It must be very sad not to be able to see any fun in anything.

AMANDA *stops choking, and looks at* ELYOT. *He winks at her again, and she smiles.*

VICTOR : Fun ! I should like you to tell me what fun there is in——

SIBYL : I pity you, I really do. I've been pitying you ever since we left Deauville.

VICTOR : I'm sure it's very nice of you, but quite unnecessary.

SIBYL : And I pity you more than ever now.

VICTOR : *Why* now particularly ?

SIBYL : If you don't see why, I'm certainly not going to tell you.

VICTOR : I see no reason for you to try to pick a quarrel with me. I've tried my best to be pleasant to you, and comfort you.

SIBYL: You weren't very comforting when I lost my trunk.

VICTOR: I have little patience with people who go about losing luggage.

SIBYL: I don't go about losing luggage. It's the first time I've lost anything in my life.

VICTOR: I find that hard to believe.

SIBYL: Anyhow, if you'd tipped the porter enough, everything would have been all right. Small economies never pay; it's absolutely no use——

VICTOR: Oh, for God's sake be quiet!

AMANDA *lifts her hand as though she were going to interfere, but* ELYOT *grabs her wrist. They look at each other for a moment, she lets her hand rest in his.*

SIBYL (*rising from the table*): How dare you speak to me like that!

VICTOR (*also rising*): Because you've been irritating me for days.

SIBYL (*outraged*): Oh!

VICTOR (*coming down to her*): You're one of the most completely idiotic women I've ever met.

SIBYL: And you're certainly the rudest man I've ever met!

VICTOR: Well then, we're quits, aren't we?

SIBYL (*shrilly*): One thing, you'll get your deserts all right.

VICTOR: What do you mean by that?

SIBYL: You know perfectly well what I mean. And it'll serve you right for being weak-minded enough to allow that woman to get round you so easily.

VICTOR: What about you? Letting that unprincipled roué persuade you to take him back again!

Amanda and Elyot are laughing silently. Elyot blows her a lingering kiss across the table.

Sibyl: He's nothing of the sort, he's just been victimized, as you were victimized.

Victor: Victimized! What damned nonsense!

Sibyl (*furiously*): It isn't damned nonsense! You're very fond of swearing and blustering and threatening, but when it comes to the point you're as weak as water. Why, a blind cat could see what you've let yourself in for.

Victor (*equally furious*): Stop making those insinuations.

Sibyl: I'm not insinuating anything. When I think of all the things you said about her, it makes me laugh, it does really; to see how completely she's got you again.

Victor: You can obviously speak with great authority, having had the intelligence to marry a drunkard.

Sibyl: So that's what she's been telling you. I might have known it! I suppose she said he struck her too!

Victor: Yes, she did, and I'm quite sure it's perfectly true.

Sibyl: I expect she omitted to tell you that she drank fourteen glasses of brandy last night straight off; and that the reason their first marriage was broken up was that she used to come home at all hours of the night, screaming and hiccoughing.

Victor: If he told you that, he's a filthy liar.

Sibyl: He isn't—he isn't!

Victor: And if you believe it, you're a silly

scatter-brained little fool.

SIBYL (*screaming*): How dare you speak to me like that! How dare you! I've never been so insulted in my life! How dare you!

AMANDA *and* ELYOT *rise quietly, and go, hand in hand, towards the front door.*

VICTOR (*completely giving way*): It's a tremendous relief to me to have an excuse to insult you. I've had to listen to your weeping and wailings for days. You've clacked at me, and snivelled at me until you've nearly driven me insane, and I controlled my nerves and continued to try to help you and look after you, because I was sorry for you. I always thought you were stupid from the first, but I must say I never realised that you were a malicious little vixen as well!

SIBYL (*shrieking*): Stop it! Stop it! You insufferable great brute!

She slaps his face hard, and he takes her by the shoulders and shakes her like a rat, as AMANDA *and* ELYOT *go smilingly out of the door, with their suitcases, and——*

THE CURTAIN FALLS.

BITTER SWEET

First produced at His Majesty's Theatre, London, (after a preliminary run in Manchester), on 12 July 1929 with the following cast:

THE MARCHIONESS OF SHAYNE (SARAH MILLICK)	Peggy Wood
DOLLY CHAMBERLAIN	Dorothy Boyd
LORD HENRY JEKYLL	William Harn
VINCENT HOWARD	Billy Milton
CARL LINDEN	George Metaxa
MRS. MILLICK	Elaine Inescourt
HUGH DEVON	Robert Newton
VICTORIA	Jose Fearon
HARRIET	Masie Drage
GLORIA	Rose Hignell
HONOR	Isla Bevan
JANE	Eileen Carey
EFFIE	Mary Pounds
LOTTE	Millie Sim
FREDA	Betty Huntley-Wright
HANSI	Marjorie Rogers
GUSSI	Norah Howard
MANON (LA CREVETTE)	Ivy St Helier
CAPTAIN AUGUST LUTTE	Austin Trevor
CAPTAIN SCHENZI	Gerald Nodin
LIEUTENANT TRANISCH	Arthur Alexander
HERR SCHLICK	Clifford Heatherley
THE MARQUIS OF SHAYNE	Alan Napier
VERNON CRAFT	Arthur Alexander
CEDRIC BALLANTYNE	William Harn
BERTRAM SELLICK	Eric Lauriston
LORD HENRY JADE	Penryn Bannerman

Directed by Noël Coward
Designed by G. E. Calthrop and Ernst Stern

ACT ONE: SCENE I

Characters: THE MARCHIONESS OF SHAYNE, DOLLY CHAMBERLAIN, LORD HENRY JEKYLL, VINCENT HOWARD, NITA, HELEN, JACKIE, FRANK, PARKER, GUESTS, MUSICIANS, etc. *The scene is* LADY SHAYNE'S *house in Grosvenor Square. The Year is* 1929.

There is a small dance in progress. At the back of the stage in the centre are large double doors leading into the supper room. On the left-hand side is a small jazz band which is playing in front of the open windows. On the right-hand side a smaller door opens into the library. When the curtain rises the stage is crowded with DANCERS *and the conversation and laughter combined with the band music should give an effect almost of pandemonium. The music comes to an end with the usual flourish and there is a smattering of applause from the* DANCERS. PARKER *throws open the double doors at the back and announces supper. Everyone goes in laughing and talking and can be seen taking their places at small tables. The double doors are closed and the members of the band retire on to the balcony for a little fresh air, with the exception of* VINCENT HOWARD, *who remains at the piano improvising syncopations softly.*

DOLLY CHAMBERLAIN *and* HENRY JEKYLL *come in from the library.* DOLLY *is pretty and attractive, about twenty.* HENRY *is a trifle older and inclined to be faintly pompous.*

DOLLY: They've all gone in to supper—come on.

HENRY: It's damned hot.

DOLLY: You've been grumbling about one thing and another all the evening.

HENRY: Sorry, old darling.

DOLLY: Do you think you love me really?

HENRY: Of course. Don't be an ass.

DOLLY: Enough?

HENRY: Enough for what?

DOLLY: Oh, I don't know—enough to spend your life with me, I suppose.

HENRY: It's a little late to worry about that now—with the wedding next Monday.

VINCENT *strikes a chord with some viciousness.* DOLLY *looks sharply over her shoulder at him.*

DOLLY: You're right, it is hot.

HENRY: Where's Lady Shayne?

DOLLY (*pointing to supper room*): In there, I expect.

HENRY: Strange old girl.

DOLLY: I hope I shall be like that when I'm seventy.

HENRY: She can't be as much as that.

DOLLY: She is—she was at school with my grandmother.

HENRY: Good God!

DOLLY: It must be funny to look back over so many years. I wonder if she minds.

HENRY: Minds what?

DOLLY: Being old, of course—to have led such a thrilling life and then suddenly to realise there's nothing left to look forward to.

HENRY: Well, she certainly is a gay old bird.

DOLLY: Henry! (*She looks at him almost shocked.*)

HENRY: What?

DOLLY: How silly that sounds—A gay old bird.

HENRY: Well, it's true, isn't it?—That's what she is, always travelling around and giving parties and staying up all night—it's almost indecent—I wouldn't like to see my grandmother going on like that.

DOLLY: Well, you needn't worry. (*She laughs.*)

HENRY: How do you mean?

DOLLY: All your relations are too pompous to enjoy anything.

HENRY: Dolly!

DOLLY: Well, they are—they've all got several feet in the grave, there's no life left in them, if ever there was any, which I doubt—you'll probably be like that too in a few years.

HENRY: You think Lady Shayne's life has been thrilling, do you? (*He smiles superciliously.*) That's funny.

DOLLY: Yes, I do—I do—and it isn't so funny either.

HENRY: Now look here, Dolly, if you knew some of the things about Lady Shayne that *I* know——

DOLLY: I know more than you know—I know that she justified her existence—she lived for something——

HENRY: She was thoroughly immoral in her youth—lovers and awful second-rate people round her all the time. It was lucky for her she met Shayne and got back.

DOLLY: Got back to what?

HENRY: Decent people—society.

DOLLY: Oh, dear. I can laugh now.

HENRY: Now, Dolly, my girl—I——

DOLLY (*suddenly with vehemence*): Shut up—shut up—

go away from me—you're pompous and silly and I can't bear it——

HENRY: Dolly!

DOLLY (*wildly*): Go away—go away!

HENRY: You're impossible.

He stamps off into the supper room.

VINCENT: Can I stop playing now?

DOLLY (*in a stifled voice*): No—go on.

VINCENT: I can't bear it much longer—darling.

DOLLY: Vincent—don't.

VINCENT: Please come over here and sit close to me.

DOLLY: I'd better not, I think.

VINCENT: Afraid?

DOLLY: Yes. (*She goes over and sits beside him—he goes on playing.*)

VINCENT: I love you so.

DOLLY: Oh, God! I'm so utterly, utterly miserable. (*She buries her head in her arms.*)

VINCENT: Don't cry—you're going to marry a rich man and have rich friends and a rich house and rich food, and some day if you're really rich enough you'll be able to engage me to come and play for you. (*He laughs bitterly.*)

DOLLY: How can you be so horrid!

VINCENT: You'll be safe anyhow.

DOLLY: I don't want to be safe.

VINCENT: Come away with me then—I've got no money—nothing to offer you--you'd look fine singing my songs in some cheap cabaret somewhere—and living in third-rate hotels and just—well, earning your living——

DOLLY: It sounds marvellous.

VINCENT: Don't be a damned fool!

DOLLY: Vincent——

VINCENT: It's hell—— (*He stops playing and goes towards the window.*)

DOLLY: Where are you going?

VINCENT: To call the boys—we've got to work some more.

DOLLY: I shan't see you again until—until—after I'm married.

VINCENT: Never mind—safety first.

DOLLY: What am I to do?——

VINCENT: Good-bye, you poor little kid——

He suddenly takes her in his arms and kisses her. She twines her arms round his neck and they stand there clasped tight. LADY SHAYNE *enters from the supper room. She watches them silently for a moment. She is seventy years old, but her figure is still slim; her hair is snow-white, and her gown is exquisite.*

LADY S.: Dolly!

DOLLY *and* VINCENT *break away from one another.*

I come on an errand of peace from your fiancé. If it is inopportune, I apologise.

DOLLY: Oh, Lady Shayne.

LADY S. (*to* VINCENT): You are the piano player in the band, aren't you?

VINCENT: I'm the leader of the band.

LADY S.: What a pity! It's not a very good band.

VINCENT: I'm sorry for what happened just now, your ladyship. It—it was an accident.

LADY S.: In what way—an accident?

VINCENT: I—er—we were saying good-bye.

LADY S.: Your drummer is too loud, and I can't bear the man who plays the saxophone.

DOLLY: Lady Shayne—I—let me explain.

LADY S.: When a man plays off key the only explanation is that he is a bad musician.

DOLLY: Lady Shayne—I love Vincent and—and he loves me.

LADY S.: And this is Vincent?

DOLLY: Yes, of course.

LADY S.: And Henry, your future husband, is in there—practically weeping into the cold asparagus.

VINCENT: You're laughing at us—your ladyship.

LADY S.: I laugh at almost everything now—it's only when one is very old indeed that one can see the joke all the way round.

DOLLY: What joke?

LADY S.: Life and death and happiness and despair and love. (*She laughs again.*)

VINCENT: Don't laugh like that, please—your ladyship.

LADY S.: So you're a musician—an amiable, sensitive-looking young man—and you've been making love to this child—or has she been making love to you?—everything seems to have changed round lately.

VINCENT: It just happened—we—at least that is—I don't know.

LADY S.: Are you a married man?

VINCENT: No—of course not.

LADY S.: Well, you needn't be so vehement. I merely thought you might have forgotten——

VINCENT: My intentions are quite honourable, if presumptuous.

DOLLY: Are you angry?

LADY S.: Not in the least, my dear. What do you intend to do?

DOLLY: I don't know.

LADY S.: Well, if I were you I should make up my mind. (*She turns towards the supper room.*)

DOLLY: You *are* angry.

LADY S.: I detest indecision.

DOLLY: I don't understand——

Several people come out of the supper room, including NITA *and* HELEN.

NITA: Dolly—what have you been doing to Henry—he's plunged in gloom.

HELEN: He's sending out thought waves of depression and I got the lot, being next to him.

JACKIE *rushes out of the supper room with* FRANK *and several others.*

JACKIE: What's happened to the band? Oh, Mr. Howard, play something—play something romantic—I want to dance.

LADY S. (*laughing*): Yes—play something romantic.

VINCENT (*savagely*): I'll play anything anybody wants—that's what I'm hired for—— (*He goes to the piano.*) Here's romance for you—how's this——

He plays a swift jazz tune. Everyone begins to dance and jig about. NITA *Charlestons a few steps, while* HELEN *and* JACKIE *clap their hands and sing. Suddenly* LADY SHAYNE *stamps her foot sharply.*

LADY S.: Stop—stop—it's hideous—you none of you know anything or want anything beyond noise and speed—your dreams of romance are nightmares. Your conception of life grotesque. Come with me a little—I'll show you—listen—listen——

FRANK (*softly*): Oh God, what's the old girl up to now.

DOLLY: Be quiet.

LADY SHAYNE *begins to sing—everyone squats down on the floor, some of them giggling furtively.* VINCENT *and* DOLLY *stare at her as though transfixed.*

"THE CALL OF LIFE."

LADY S.: Your romance could not live the length of a day,
You hesitate and analyse,
Betray your love with compromise,
Till glamour fades away;
And all too soon you realise
That there is nothing left to say.

CHORUS: Hey, hey—hey, hey,
How does she get that way;
She'd be more light-hearted
If she started—to Charleston;
She's never danced it,
She's never chanced it;
Perhaps her muscles are disinclined,
Perhaps she hasn't the strength of mind.

LADY S.: Love that's true can mean naught to you but a name,
A thing that isn't part of you;
Can never touch the heart of you;
It's nothing but a game,
A fire without a flame.

MEN: We find it dificult to grasp your meaning.

LADY S.: Maybe the past is intervening.

CHORUS: We very much regret that times have
changed so,
Life is more speedily arranged so.

LADY S.: In your world of swiftly turning wheels
Life must be extremely grey.

CHORUS: We've no time to waste on Love Ideals,
That which to our senses most appeals
Is all we can obey.

LADY S.: No—no. Not so;
There must be something further on,
A vision you can count upon,
To help you to acquire
A memory when Youth is gone
Of what was once your heart's desire.

There is a call that echoes sweetly
When it is Spring and Love is in the air;
Whate'er befall, respond to it completely,
Tho' it may bring you sadness and
despair;
Fling far behind you
The chains that bind you,
That love may find you
In joy or strife;
Tho' Fate may cheat you,
And defeat you,
Your Youth must answer to the Call of
Life.

The lights slowly go out, and through the darkness her voice grows sweeter and younger, until presently the lights go up again and disclose a young girl of about seventeen standing demurely in a prim Victorian room with spring sunlight flooding through the windows behind her. Seated beside her at an Erard grand pianoforte is a young MUSIC MASTER—*he is playing the piano, but his eyes are gazing up at her face and he is smiling a trifle wistfully as she comes to the end of the song.*

ACT ONE : SCENE II

Characters : SARAH MILLICK, CARL LINDEN, MRS. MILLICK, HUGH DEVON. *The scene is the* MILLICK'S *house in Belgrave Square. The Year is* 1875.

When SARAH *finishes singing,* CARL *allows his hands to drop from the keys, and still gazing into her eyes, he speaks :*

CARL : That was excellent, Miss Sarah—you are improving in a very marked manner.

SARAH (*demurely*) : Thank you.

CARL : I wrote that song for you when I was sixteen years old.

SARAH : But Mr. Linden, that cannot be true—we have only known each other during the past year.

CARL : I mean that I wrote it for someone like you.

SARAH (*quickly*) : Oh !

CARL : Not a real person—just an ideal in my mind, someone young and charming—holding out her arms as you did just now—expectantly.

SARAH : Expectant of what, Mr. Linden ?

CARL (*hopelessly turning away*) : I don't know.

SARAH : I think it is the loveliest song I ever heard.

CARL (*looking at her again*) : Do you ?

SARAH (*meeting his eyes*) : Yes—of course.

CARL: You took the high note too much at the back of your throat.

SARAH: I'm sorry.

CARL: It doesn't matter.

SARAH: Oh, but, surely it does.

CARL: Nothing matters but just these few moments.

SARAH: Why do you say that, Mr. Linden?

CARL: Because it's spring, and I—I——

SARAH: Yes?

CARL: I fear I am talking nonsense.

SARAH (*smiling*): Perhaps a little.

CARL: We have festivals in the spring in my country—and the young boys and girls dance and their clothes are brightly coloured, glinting in the sun, and the old people sit round under the trees, watching and tapping their sticks on the ground and reviving in their hearts memories of when they, too, were young and in love.

SARAH: In love?

CARL: Yes—as you are in love with your handsome Mr. Devon.

SARAH: Oh—Hugh—yes, of course. Tell me more about your country, Mr. Linden.

CARL: There is nothing to tell really—it seems so very far away—I've almost forgotten.

SARAH: You're homesick though, I can see you are.

CARL: Can you?

SARAH: Perhaps it's the climate here, it *is* depressing——

CARL: Yes, a little. (*He sings.*)

Tho' there may be beauty in this land of yours,
Skies are very often dull and grey;

If I could but take that little hand of yours,
Just to lead you secretly away.
We would watch the Danube as it gently flows,
Like a silver ribbon winding free;
Even as I speak of it my longing grows,
Once again my own dear land to see.
If you could only come with me,
If you could only come with me.

SARAH: Oh, Mr. Linden.

CARL: Yes.

SARAH: How very strange everything is to-day.

CARL: Will you forgive me, Miss Sarah, when I tell you that I shall be unable to play at your wedding reception.

SARAH (*disappointed*): Oh!

CARL: I must go away on that day—to Brussels.

SARAH: Brussels?

CARL (*hurriedly*): Yes, a concert—I have to play at a concert—it is very important.

SARAH: I understand.

CARL: Do you?

SARAH: Yes—but it is very, very disappointing.

CARL: But I am deeply grateful for the honour you have done me in asking me.

SARAH (*lightly, but turning away*): This is the last time we shall meet then for ever so long.

CARL: To-night—I am playing to-night for the dance.

SARAH: But that is different. There will be so many people——

CARL: This is indeed the last time we shall be alone together.

SARAH (*looking down*): Yes.

CARL: You have been a charming pupil—I shall always look back on these months with happiness.

SARAH: Happiness?

CARL: And sadness too.

SARAH: Oh, dear.

CARL: There are tears in your eyes.

SARAH: In yours also.

CARL: I know—I am sorry to be so foolish.

SARAH: Dear Mr. Linden——

She gives him her hand, he kisses it fervently, then pulls himself together with a tremendous effort.

CARL: Once more now—your exercises—just once more through.

SARAH (*tearfully*): Very well.

CARL *strikes a chord*—SARAH *sings up and down, saying "Ah." Suddenly a barrel organ strikes up in the street outside a sugary sentimental melody.* SARAH *perseveres with her exercises, then* CARL *begins to sing to her, accompanied by the orchestra, with the barrel organ as a background.*

"I'LL SEE YOU AGAIN."

CARL: Now Miss Sarah, if you please,
Sing a scale for me.

SARAH: Ah—Ah—Ah——

CARL: Take a breath and then reprise
In a different key.

SARAH: Ah—Ah—Ah——

CARL: All my life I shall remember knowing you,
All the pleasure I have found in showing you
The different ways
That one may phrase

The changing light, and changing shade;
Happiness that must die,
Melodies that must fly,
Memories that must fade,
Dusty and forgotten by and by.

SARAH: Learning scales will never seem so sweet again
Till our Destiny shall let us meet again.

CARL: The will of Fate
May come too late.

SARAH: When I'm recalling these hours we've had
Why will the foolish tears
Tremble across the years,
Why shall I feel so sad,
Treasuring the memory of these days
Always?

CARL: I'll see you again,
Whenever Spring breaks through again;
Time may lie heavy between,
But what has been
Is past forgetting.

SARAH: This sweet memory,
Across the years will come to me;
Tho' my world may go awry,
In my heart will ever lie,
Just the echo of a sigh,
Good-bye.

MRS. MILLICK *enters with* HUGH DEVON. *During the ensuing scene until* CARL'S *exit, the love theme should be continued in the orchestra very softly.*

MRS. M.: Darling child—your lesson should have been over a quarter of an hour ago. There is so much to be done—I declare I'm nearly frantic—Hugh has been telling me about his aunt—poor Lady Ettleworth, she developed acute gastritis yesterday evening, and it may mean postponing the wedding, and on the other hand it may not. I'm certain it was the peas she ate at lunch here. They were like bullets. Good-afternoon, Mr. Linden.

CARL (*bowing*): Good-afternoon, Mrs. Millick.

HUGH: Good-afternoon.

CARL (*bowing*): Good afternoon.

HUGH: You look tired, Sarah.

SARAH: I am a little—I—it is quite hot to-day.

MRS. M.: I fear I must hurry you away, Mr. Linden—Sarah has a dressmaker at four-thirty—and there is so much to be done.

CARL: I quite understand.

MRS. M.: Doubtless Sarah will resume her lessons with you when she is settled down in her new home.

SARAH: Mother—I——

MRS. M.: It will be an occupation—I always believe in young married women having an occupation.

CARL: I should have thought being married would be sufficient.

MRS. M. (*slightly scandalised*): Mr. Linden——

CARL (*bitterly*): Your daughter must learn from someone else when she is a young married woman, Mrs. Millick. I shall not be here.

MRS. M.: Well, I'm sure I'm very sorry, I——

CARL (*looking fixedly at* SARAH): I shall be far away in my own country—but each year when spring comes round again, I shall remember you, Miss Sarah, and what a charming pupil you were, and how, although you sometimes sang your top notes from the back of your throat, and your middle notes through your nose, you always sang your deep notes from your heart.

MRS. M.: My dear Mr. Linden!

CARL: This is good-bye, Miss Sarah, except for to-night, when there will be so many people—too many people.

He bows abruptly and goes out. The music swells loudly in the orchestra, the theme of The Call of Life. SARAH *begins to sing it brokenly.* HUGH *advances towards her, but she pushes him away and falls weeping into her mother's arms as the lights fade out.*

ACT ONE: SCENE III

Characters: SARAH MILLICK, CARL LINDEN, MRS. MILLICK, HUGH DEVON, LADY DEVON, SIR ARTHUR FENCHURCH, VICTORIA, HARRIET, GLORIA, HONOR, JANE, EFFIE, THE MARQUIS OF STEERE, LORD EDGAR JAMES, LORD SORREL, MR. VALE, MR. BETHEL MR. PROUTIE, FOUR FOOTMEN, GUESTS, MUSICIANS, etc. *The scene is the ballroom of the* MILLICK'S *house in Belgrave Square. The Year is* 1875.

It is the ballroom of the MILLICK'S *house in Belgrave Square. There are three wind ws at the back opening on to a balcony overlooking the Square. On the left at an angle are double doors opening on to the landing and staircase. On the right is a small dais upon which the orchestra is playing, conducted by* CARL LINDEN.

Below this double doors lead into the supper room and on the left below the big doors is a small door leading into the drawing-room. There are coloured lights festooned over the balcony which look charming against the shadowy trees in the Square.

When the curtain rises, the ball is nearly over. A mazurka is in progress: the dresses of the guests are almost entirely pastel shades with the exception of a few chaperons in black and grey and purple, who are seated on small chairs and sofas below the orchestra. At the end of the mazurka most of the couples leave the floor; some go out on to the balcony, some into the supper room, and some into the drawing-room.

LADY DEVON, *an imposing dowager, meets* MRS. MILLICK *as she billows in from the supper room.*

LADY D.: Charming, Violet—quite delightful—I congratulate you.

MRS. M.: The young people seem very happy, I think.

LADY D.: I thought Sarah looked radiant but a trifle flushed when she was waltzing with Hugh a little while ago.

MRS. M.: She has been flushed all the evening. I hope she isn't feverish—I feel quite disturbed about her.

LADY D.: I feel sure you have no cause to be—she was positively hilarious in the supper room.

MRS. M.: Unnaturally so.

LADY D.: She is in love, my dear.

HUGH *enters from the supper room.*

HUGH (*in harassed tones*): Oh, there you are.

LADY D. (*fondly*): Happy boy.

HUGH: I am very worried.

MRS. M.: Why—what has happened?

HUGH: Sarah is behaving in a most peculiar manner—she upset a full glass of claret cup over Sir Arthur Fenchurch and laughed.

MRS. M.: Laughed!

LADY D.: Sir Arthur—Good heavens!

SIR ARTHUR *enters, a pompous-looking old gentleman. He is obviously restraining a boiling fury with a great effort. His shirt-front is claret-stained and his manner frigid.*

SIR A. (*bowing to* MRS. MILLICK *furiously, but politely*): A delightful evening, Mrs. Millick—thank you a thousand times.

MRS. M.: But, Sir Arthur—you mustn't think of going.

SIR A.: I couldn't think of staying—so many fresh young people enjoying themselves so very thoroughly—I feel out of place.

LADY D.: But, Sir Arthur——

SIR A. (*firmly*): Good-night, Lady Devon. Good-night, Mrs. Millick. (*To* HUGH) My boy—I sincerely *hope* your marriage will be a happy one.

MRS. M.: Well!

HUGH: There now.

LADY D.: How very, very unfortunate.

SARAH *enters from the supper room; she looks lovely, but her manner is strained and almost defiant.*

SARAH: Has he gone?

MRS. M.: Sarah—I'm ashamed of you.

SARAH: He patted my hand, mamma, then he patted my head. I detest being patted.

HUGH: He's one of the most influential men in London.

MRS. M.: And so kind.

SARAH: And so pompous.

LADY D.: Sarah!

MRS. M.: The first thing to-morrow morning you shall write him a letter of apology.

She moves away with LADY DEVON.

SARAH: To-morrow is so far away. (*She laughs.*)

HUGH: I don't understand you to-night, Sarah.

SARAH: I don't think I quite understand myself.

HUGH: Why did you cry this afternoon in the music room?

SARAH: Are you glad you are going to marry me, Hugh?

HUGH: Why did you cry like that?

SARAH: And will you be kind to me—always?

HUGH: You haven't answered me.

SARAH: And do you love me?

HUGH (*irritably*): Sarah!

SARAH: Do you?

HUGH: Of course I do—what is the matter with you?

CARL LINDEN *stands up on the orchestra dais where the band have been regaling themselves with refreshments, and very softly plays on the violin "I'll See You Again."* SARAH *starts and then begins to laugh hysterically.*

SARAH: Don't look so solemn, Hugh—I'm in love.

HUGH: My dear girl, that's all very well——

SARAH: Is it?

HUGH: But you really must restrain yourself.

SARAH (*almost rudely*): What a stupid tune, Mr. Linden—so dismal——

HUGH: Sarah!

SARAH (*peremptorily*): Play something gay, please—immediately.

HUGH (*softly*): Sarah, you must not speak like that—have you taken leave of your senses?

SARAH (*vehemently*): Let me alone—please go away—let me alone!

HUGH *goes angrily on to the balcony.* CARL *strikes up a tremendously gay melody.*

"WHAT IS LOVE?"

Play something gay for me,
Play for me, play for me;
Set me free,
I am in a trance to-night,
Can't you see
How I want to dance to-night?
Madly my heart is beating,
Some insane melody possessing me,
In my brain thrilling and obsessing me;
How can I leave it to call in vain?
Is it joy or pain?
Live your life, for Time is fleeting,
Some insistent voice repeating;
Hear me—hear me,
How can I leave it to call in vain?
Is it joy or pain?

Refrain.

Tell me—tell me—tell me, what is love?
Is it some consuming flame;
Part of the moon, part of the sun,
Part of a dream barely begun?
When is the moment of breaking-waking?
Skies change, nothing is the same,
Some strange magic is to blame;

Voices, that seem to echo round me and above,
Tell me, what is love, love, love?

Play something gay for me,
Play for me—play for me;
Tell me why
Spring has so enchanted me;
Why this shy
Passion has been granted me;
Am I awake or dreaming?
Far and near
Every lover follows you,
Swift and clear,
Flying as the swallows do;
Leave me no longer to call in vain,
Are you joy or pain?
Leave me not by Love forsaken,
If I sleep, then let me waken;
Hear me—hear me,
Leave me no longer to call in vain
Are you joy or pain?

Repeat Refrain.

SARAH *begins to waltz round the stage by herself, and as she passes the supper room, the library and the balcony,* GUESTS *join her in her dance, until the whole stage is encircled by a wheel of young people laughing and chattering. At the end of this, the band plays "God save the Queen"; everyone naturally stands still, and then the party breaks up.* SARAH *takes her place at the door with her mother, in order to bid good-bye to the* GUESTS. *The* MUSICIANS *are packing up their instruments, and finally all go out, including* CARL. HUGH *comes in from the balcony.* SARAH *leaves her mother talking to some* GUESTS *and runs up to him.*

SARAH: I'm sorry, Hugh.

HUGH (*stiffly*): It doesn't matter.

SARAH: Oh, but it does—I was unkind and silly.

HUGH: It doesn't matter.

SARAH: Will you please forgive me?

HUGH: There is nothing to forgive.

SARAH: I shall be bad again if you are so polite.

HUGH: My dear Sarah!

SARAH (*desperately*): Are you always going to be like this—after we are married, I mean—cold and unbending?

HUGH: I can only hope you are not often going to behave as you have to-night.

SARAH: Oh, dear.

HUGH: I don't feel that you realise yet the dignity of the position you will hold as my wife.

SARAH: I am not your wife yet.

HUGH: I enjoy being high-spirited as much as anyone.

SARAH: Do you?

HUGH: But there is a time and place for everything.

SARAH: Then I can look forward to us being very high-spirited when we are alone—when no one is looking—you might wear a funny hat at breakfast.

HUGH: I am very fond of you, my dear, but you must remember I am older than you.

SARAH: Not so very much.

HUGH: And it is part of my profession to consider appearances.

SARAH: Diplomatically speaking.

HUGH: Are you laughing at me?

SARAH: No, but I'm looking at you—just as though I had never seen you before.

LADY DEVON *enters*.

LADY D.: Hugh, *dear*.

HUGH: Yes, mother?

LADY D.: I have been waiting for you downstairs. The carriage is at the door. Good-night, Sarah.

SARAH: Good-night. I have been telling Hugh I was sorry to have behaved so badly.

LADY D. (*smiling*): I am afraid you're marrying a tomboy, Hugh.

SARAH: No, no—I won't be one any more.

LADY D.: Dear child. (*She kisses her.*) Come, Hugh. (*She moves over to* MRS. MILLICK *at the door.*)

HUGH: Good-night, Sarah.

SARAH: Good-night, Hugh.

HUGH: Will you drive with me to-morrow afternoon in Regent's Park?

SARAH: Thank you—that will be delightful.

HUGH: Until to-morrow—my dear. (*He looks round carefully and then kisses her chastely and departs with* LADY DEVON.)

MRS. M.: Well, that's over. Where are the girls?

SARAH: Harriet and Gloria?

MRS. M.: Yes.

SARAH: Sitting out somewhere with Lord Edgar and Mr. Proutie.

MRS. M.: And Effie and Jane and Honor and Victoria?

SARAH: They're sitting out, too.

MRS. M.: Come with me—we must find them—

really you modern young people have no sense of behaviour at all.

She goes with SARAH *into the supper room while the music strikes up the introductory bars of a concerted number.* HARRIET *and* LORD EDGAR *peep round the library door and tiptoe out on to the stage.* GLORIA *and* MR. PROUTIE *do the same from the balcony—* EFFIE, JANE, HONOR, VICTORIA, MR. VALE *and* LORD SORREL, LORD STEERE, MR. BETHEL *all join them.*

"THE LAST DANCE."

MEN: They've all gone now—have no fear—
GIRLS: Sarah's mother may be near,
If she should hear
ALL: She might be rather cross with us,
Elderly people make too much fuss.
MEN: Always insist on a chaperone,
Never leave love alone.
GIRLS: We feel frightened, if you please
Don't flirt or tease.
MEN: Gentle and sweet in your purity,
We give our hearts as security.
GIRLS: We shall be scolded a lot for this.
MEN: You won't miss just one kiss.

They all kiss.

GIRLS: Think of the consequences, please, you haven't realised
What an appalling thing for us to be so compromised,
So dreadfully, dreadfully, dreadfully compromised.

MEN: Everything's ending,
The moon is descending,
Behind the tall trees in the park.

GIRLS: Silence falls,
Slumber calls.

MEN: We men together
Were wondering whether
We might have a bit of a lark.

GIRLS: No jokes in the dark, please,
What sort of a lark, please?

ALL: Just a slight dance,
One more dream-of-delight dance;
Just a sort of good-night dance
Would be glorious fun.

MEN: Won't you let us, please let us, just stay for a while,
Won't you, please won't you, be gay for a while?
All we desire is to play for a while
Now the party's done.

GIRLS Just a fast waltz,
Till the world seems a vast waltz
Very often the last waltz
Is the birth of Romance.

ALL: It's a June night,
There's a thrill in the moonlight;
Let's give way to the tender surrender
Of our last dance.

At the end of the number all the men, with the exception of MR. PROUTIE, *creep out, leaving the* GIRLS *seated demurely on gilt chairs at some distance from one another all round the stage.* MR. PROUTIE, *being very smitten with* GLORIA, *hides behind the sofa.* MRS.

MILLICK *re-enters, looking rather agitated, followed by* SARAH.

MRS. M.: Girls—where have you been?

HARRIET: Nowhere, Aunt Violet.

MRS. M.: Where is Lord Edgar?

HONOR: He went hours ago, Mrs. Millick.

MRS. M.: And Lord Steere, Mr. Bethel, Mr. Vale and Lord Sorrel?

VICTORIA (*sighing*): All gone.

MRS. M.: And Mr. Proutie?

GLORIA: He was so tired he left early.

MRS. M.: Come out from behind that sofa, Mr. Proutie.

MR. PROUTIE *comes out, looking very sheepish. All the girls giggle.* MR. PROUTIE *is very young and cherubic.*

MR. P.: I—I—fell asleep—I apologise.

MRS. M.: I quite understand.

MR. P. (*appealingly to* GLORIA): Miss Gloria, I——

MRS. M.: Good-night, Mr. Proutie.

MR. P.: Miss Gloria said that——

MRS. M. (*sternly*): Good-*night*, Mr. Proutie.

MR. P.: Er—er—— Good-night—thank you for having me—er—good-night.

He goes out, covered with embarrassment.

MRS. M.: Gloria—-what does this mean?

GLORIA: Nothing, Aunt Violet.

MRS. M.: If it were not that this was a festive occasion, I should punish you severely for your deceit.

HARRIET: Dear Aunt Violet—don't be cross.

MRS. M.: To bed with the lot of you.

EFFIE: Oh, not yet—just ten minutes more.

MRS. M.: Certainly not—it's nearly one o'clock—

fine bridesmaids you'll make on Thursday, if you stay up so late.

HARRIET: Won't you let us stay up just a little longer?

HONOR: Oh, Mrs. Millick, do—please do.

MRS. M.: No—Sarah's tired——

SARAH: No, I'm not, mother—I know I couldn't sleep for ages.

GLORIA: Just a short while—please!

They all cluster round her and speak at once—finally she breaks away from them.

MRS. M.: Very well—ten minutes then and no more. Sarah, come into my room and say good-night.

SARAH: Yes, mother.

MRS. M.: Remember now—in ten minutes' time I shall tell Parker to come and put out the lights—and don't make too much noise——

HARRIET: We won't, we promise.

GLORIA: Good-night, Aunt Violet.

MRS. MILLICK *goes out amid a chorus of "Good-nights." The moment the door has closed upon her the girls fling aside their demure manner and dance about the stage.* HARRIET *jumps on to the orchestra dais and begins to strum the piano.* EFFIE, HONOR *and* SARAH *sing gaily while* VICTORIA *and* JANE *dance.*

HONOR: Oh, Sarah—I do envy you—being married and going to Paris and everything.

SARAH: Do you?

EFFIE: Aren't you dying of excitement?—I know I should be.

SARAH: No, not exactly—I feel strange somehow.

GLORIA: What sort of strange?

SARAH: I don't know—it's difficult to explain—

perhaps I'm frightened.

JANE: Nobody could be frightened of Hugh.

VICTORIA: When I marry, it must be somebody just like Hugh.

HARRIET: I shall choose someone taller—more robust, you know.

EFFIE: How can you, Harriet—Hugh's just the right size.

GLORIA: I shall marry Mr. Proutie.

ALL: Gloria!—What do you mean?

GLORIA (*calmly*): He adores me.

JANE: Has he asked you?

GLORIA: Of course.

HONOR: And you said yes?

GLORIA: I said no. But that doesn't matter—he'll ask me again.

EFFIE: Are you in love with him?

GLORIA: No—not a bit.

HONOR: How *can* you, Gloria?

GLORIA: I'd much rather marry someone I didn't love really.

ALL: "Gloria!" "Really!" "You're dreadful!" "Why?" etc.

GLORIA: Because I could manage him better.

HARRIET: I agree with Gloria

VICTORIA: So do I.

SARAH: I don't—I want love.

EFFIE (*giggling*): So do I—but you'll get it before I do——

They all laugh.

HONOR: I mean to have a lot of babies——

JANE: I want someone to protect me always—someone strong that I can look up to——

HARRIET: Fiddlesticks!

VICTORIA: Rubbish!

GLORIA: Old-fashioned nonsense!

JANE: Let's play a game.

SARAH: What game?

EFFIE: Yes, yes—any game.

HONOR: Postman's knock.

SARAH: No—no—that means one of us going out——

JANE: How, when and where.

EFFIE: So does that.

SARAH: Let's play an exciting game—a noisy game.

HARRIET: Aunt Violet will hear.

SARAH: No—she's two floors up.

GLORIA: Blind Man's Buff.

EFFIE: Yes—yes.

SARAH: That will do——

VICTORIA: Who'll be it——

JANE: Eeny meeny miny mo—we must do eeny meeny miny mo——

FINALE.

GLORIA: Eeny meeny miny mo
HARRIET: Catch a nigger by his toe
VICTORIA: If he hollers let him go
ALL: O.U.T. spells out and so
GLORIA: Out goes she. (*She points to* EFFIE.)
EFFIE: Out goes me. (*Skipping about.*) This is the loveliest, loveliest part of the party.
GLORIA: Eeny meeny miny mo
HARRIET: Catch a nigger by his toe
VICTORIA: If he hollers let him go
ALL: O.U.T. spells out and so

GLORIA: Out goes she. (*She points to* HARRIET.)
HARRIET: Out goes me.

She and EFFIE *take hands and twirl around.*

HARRIET: }
EFFIE: } Now we're free who knows who'll be he!

GLORIA: Eeny meeny miny mo
VICTORIA: Catch a nigger by his toe
SARAH: If he hollers let him go
ALL: O.U.T. spells out and so
VICTORIA: Out goes she. (*She points to* GLORIA.)
GLORIA: Out goes me. (*She joins* EFFIE *and* HARRIET.)

HARRIET: }
EFFIE: }
GLORIA: } This is the loveliest, loveliest part of the party.

VICTORIA: Eeny meeny miny mo
SARAH: Catch a nigger by his toe
JANE: If he hollers let him go
JANE: Out goes she. (*Points to* VICTORIA.)
VICTORIA: Out goes me. (*She joins* EFFIE, HARRIET *and* GLORIA.)
ALL: This is the loveliest, loveliest part of the party.

EFFIE: }
HARRIET: } Only three of them left now we're excited to see

GLORIA: }
VICTORIA: } Who is going to be blind man, who's it going to be.

SARAH: I have a strange presentiment it's me.
JANE: Eeny meeny miny mo
Out goes she. (*She points to* HONOR, *who joins the others.*)
SARAH: Eeny meeny mo
Out goes she. (*She points to* JANE.)

I'm HE—it's me
It's me—I'm HE

GIRLS: Just get a handkerchief and bind it around her eyes.

SARAH: Not too tight, not too tight.

They blindfold her.

GIRLS: She mustn't see a thing no matter how much she tries.

SARAH: That's all right—that's all right.

GIRLS: She will cheat if she can,
That corner's raised a bit,
Turn her round till she's dazed a bit,
Are you ready now,
One, two, three!

SARAH: Since the party began,
Something's been taunting me,
Some presentiment haunting me,
What can it be?

GIRLS: Start now—start now,
She can see the ground,
She can see the ground.

SARAH: Somehow, somehow,
Some forgotten sound,
Some forgotten sound,
Echoes deep in my heart,
Strangely enthralling me,
Someone secretly calling me,
Like a melody far away.

GIRLS: Oh, for Heaven's sake start,
Here go along with you,
We can see nothing wrong with you
We want to play.

They all dance about and dodge her. The door on the right opens quietly and CARL LINDEN *comes into the room. He moves across to the piano and collects his music and is on his way out when* SARAH *clasps him round the neck. All the* GIRLS *laugh.* CARL *is staggered for a moment, drops his music, and then completely losing all restraint kisses her on the mouth. She snatches the bandage from her eyes and stares into his face. All the other* GIRLS *are watching aghast.*

SARAH (*softly*): It's you I love—now and always.

She kisses him, then draws back and they stand there staring at one another oblivious of everything. EFFIE *giggles suddenly and then stops herself.*

HARRIET: Sarah——

GLORIA: Sarah—don't be silly—Sarah——

Neither CARL *nor* SARAH *turn their heads.*

CARL: Come with me——

SARAH: Now?

CARL: Yes—now—to-night.

SARAH: I'll come with you—whenever you want me to.

CARL: I love you—do you hear—I've loved you for months—for years really—ever since I was a boy I've known you were waiting for me somewhere—I'll take care of you—live for you—die for you.

SARAH: Don't say that, my darling. (*Singing.*)

Should happiness forsake me,
And disillusion break me,
Come what may,
Lead the way,
Take me, take me.
Although I may discover,
Love crucifies the lover,

Whate'er Fate has in store,
My heart is yours for evermore.

CARL (*singing*):

Oh Lady, you are far above me,
And yet you whisper that you love me,
Can this be true or is it just some foolish dream?

SARAH (*speaking*): You know it's true, look in my eyes—can't you see?

CARL (*speaking softly*): Oh, my dear, dear love. (*Singing*)

Now tho' your fears are sleeping,
Look well before the leaping.
Love of me
May be repaid
By weeping.
Life can be bitter learning,
When there is no returning,
Whate'er Fate has in store,
My heart is yours for evermore,
I love you—I love you—I love you.

GLORIA: You cannot realise the things you say.
You quite forget yourself, please go away.

HARRIET: Now leave this all to me, my dear,
It's really too absurd.

EFFIE: It's quite the most romantic thing that I have ever heard!

VICTORIA (*speaking*): Effie, be quiet.

SARAH *kisses him again full on the mouth.* HARRIET *rushes up and drags them apart.*

HARRIET: Sarah—are you mad?—Mr. Linden, please go at once.

CARL (*smiling*): How can I go?

GLORIA: Harriet—leave this to me——

SARAH: Stop—don't say another word.

EFFIE (*rushing up hysterically*): It's the most wonderfully thrilling thing that ever happened in the world.

HARRIET: Don't be an idiot, Effie.

SARAH (*quietly*): Effie's right, Harriet.

HARRIET: I'm going straight upstairs to fetch Aunt Violet.

EFFIE (*struggling with her*): You shan't! You shan't!—They love each other—look at them—Honor, Victoria, Jane, help me!

HONOR, VICTORIA *and* JANE *come to her assistance.*

SARAH *and* CARL (*singing*):

I'll see you again,
Whenever Spring breaks through again,
Always I'll be by your side,
No time or tide
Can part us ever——

VICTORIA: Shhh! Someone's coming—hide—quickly——

They all hide behind sofas and chairs.

FOUR FOOTMEN *enter pompously to music.*

FOOTMEN QUARTETTE.

Now the party's really ended,
And our betters have ascended
All with throbbing heads,
To their welcome beds,
Pity us, who have to be up,
Sadly clearing the debris up,
Getting for our pains,
Most of the remains.

Though the Major-Domo is a trifle tight,
Though the mistress hiccoughed when she said good-night,
We in our secluded garret,
Mean to finish up the claret-
Cup all right.
When we've doused the final candles,
We'll discuss the latest scandals
We have overheard,
Pleasure long deferred.
When the Duke of So and So stares
At his wife, we know below stairs,
While she smirks and struts,
That he hates her guts.
Though we all disguise our feelings pretty well,
What we mean by " Very good " is " Go to hell."
Though they're all so grand and pompous,
Most of them are now non compos,
Serve them right,
Good-night.

They extinguish all the lights and close the windows and go out, closing the doors behind them. All the GIRLS *come out, and lastly* CARL *and* SARAH. SARAH *goes up to* HARRIET. GLORIA *lights two candles.*

SARAH: Harriet—whatever you do won't be the slightest use—I love Carl—I'm going with him—I don't care where or how—but this is my life, you understand—my whole life—so help me—all you can—please—please——

HARRIET: Think of Hugh—you're mad.

SARAH: Perhaps I am mad, but I'm happy—can't you see—I'm really happy——

HARRIET: Mr. Linden, I appeal to you.

GLORIA: It's no use, Harriet.

HARRIET: I feel as if I were in a dream.

CARL: You are.

HARRIET: What are your prospects—have you any money?

CARL: None—no money—but I can earn enough.

SARAH: So can I—I'll sing——

VICTORIA: Sarah!

CARL: Yes—Sarah will sing and I will play and we will make a living—come, Sarah.

SARAH: Like this?

EFFIE: Quickly, Jane—your bedroom is nearest—your hat and cape.

JANE *and* EFFIE *fly out of the room.* "*The Call of Life*" *theme plays softly.* SARAH *runs up to the windows and flings them open, singing.* CARL *joins her.*

SARAH *and* CARL (*singing*):

Fling far behind you
The chains that bind you,
That Love may find you
In joy or strife;
Tho' Fate may cheat you,
And defeat you,
Your youth must answer to the Call of Life.

EFFIE *and* JANE *return with a hat and cape. They dress her in them, and she and* CARL *go out together. As the orchestra crashes out the final chords, the* OTHERS *rush to the balcony to wave.*

CURTAIN

ACT TWO: SCENE I

Characters: SARI LINDEN, CARL LINDEN, MANON (LA CREVETTE), LOTTE, FREDA, HANSI, GUSSI, CAPTAIN AUGUST LUTTE, HERR SCHLICK, WAITERS, CLEANERS, ORCHESTRA, etc. *The scene is* HERR SCHLICK'S *café in Vienna. The Year is* 1880.

The scene is the interior of "SCHLICK'S" *cafe in Vienna. It is about* 12 *o'clock noon, and* WAITERS *in shirt-sleeves are tidying up the tables and polishing brasses. There are also some cleaners and charwomen swabbing the floor.* CARL, *in shirt-sleeves, is rehearsing with the Orchestra on the orchestra platform at the back.* LOTTE, HANSI, *and* FREDA, *three ladies of the town, elaborately dressed, are seated at a table down stage left. The* OPENING CHORUS *is sung in snatches by the* WAITERS, CLEANERS, *etc.*

WAITERS: Life in the morning isn't too bright,
When you've had to hurry round and carry plates all night;
And the evening isn't too gay,
When you know you've got to rise and be at work all day.
This café merely caters
For a horde of drunken satyrs,
Why, oh why, we're waiters nobody can say.

CLEANERS: Oh dear, it's clear to see that cleaners lead a worse life,
Every day we curse life;
More and more
The muscles on our brawny arms like iron bands are
Scrubbing till our hands are sore;
We scour and polish till our fingers ache.

WAITERS (*humming*): Hum—hum——!

CLEANERS: Each hour we feel as tho' our backs would break,

WAITERS: Hum—hum!

CLEANERS: We weep and keep our growing families as well,
Why we're here at all nobody can tell.

WAITERS: Life in the morning isn't too bright,
When you've had to hurry round and carry plates all night.

CLEANERS: Oh dear, it's clear to see that cleaners lead a worse life.

WAITERS: And the evening isn't too gay,
When you know you've got to rise and be at work all day.

CLEANERS: You see the reason why each day we want to curse life.

WAITERS: For this cafe merely caters

CLEANERS: Weary

WAITERS: For a horde of drunken satyrs;

CLEANERS: Dreary

WAITERS: Why, oh why, we're waiters nobody can say.

CLEANERS: Every day.

WAITERS: Ah—Ah—Ah——

CLEANERS: Ah—Ah—Ah——

At the end of it, CARL *rests his orchestra for a moment.*

LOTTE: He left me at half-past ten, my dear, he kissed my hand, à la grand chevalier, which made me laugh, I *must* say.

FREDA: Is that all he left you with—a kiss?

LOTTE: Don't be vulgar, Freda, everything was arranged last night in his carriage—we drove round and round the Ringstrasse.

HANSI: I hope it didn't make you too giddy, dear.

LOTTE: You none of you understand, this is an "affaire de cœur," I'm sure of it.

FRITZ, *a waiter, brings* LOTTE *a bill for the coffee and brioches they have been having.*

LOTTE: It's not my turn—Hansi?

HANSI: I paid yesterday.

LOTTE: Come along, Freda—no fumbling.

FREDA: I wasn't fumbling—I was just trying to count up how many times I've paid during the last month.

HANSI: That oughtn't to take you long.

FREDA (*rather crossly*): Oh, here you are, then. (*She gives him some money.*)

He nods and goes off.

LOTTE: Where was I?

FREDA: Driving round the Ringstrasse, my dear, talking business.

LOTTE: You can all jeer if you like, but just you wait and see. Anyhow, I feel positively exhausted, having had to get up so early.

HANSI: I'm tired too.

GUSSI *enters, elaborately dressed and wearing a fur tippet and muff.*

GUSSI: Hallo, girls.

FREDA: Oh, my God, look at Gussi.

HANSI (*fingering the tippet*): Where did you get it?

GUSSI: Here, leave off, surely you've seen a bit of mink before?

HANSI: Not on you.

GUSSI: Well, have a good look now and enjoy it.

LOTTE: Who gave it to you?

GUSSI (*with great coyness*): I hardly like to tell you, it was such a delightful surprise—I had been spending the night with my dear old grandmother——

HANSI: I hope she took her spurs off.

They all laugh. GUSSI *sits down at the table.*

LOTTE: Do you want some coffee?

GUSSI: No thanks, it would spoil my lunch.

FREDA: I'm lunching at Sacher's—I can bring a friend—Hansi?

HANSI: No thank you, dear.

FREDA: Lotte?

LOTTE: Who are you lunching with, the old ostrich?

FREDA: No, he's gone to Warsaw. This is a banker—quite young, but common, no use for dinner—do you want to come?

LOTTE: I don't mind.

HANSI: I can't imagine, Freda, why you waste your time with small fry.

FREDA: I don't consider any free meal small fry.

LOTTE, FREDA *and* HANSI *sing a trio:*

"LADIES OF THE TOWN"

Though we're often accused of excessively plastic,
drastic sins,
When we're asked to decide on the wrong or the
right life,
Night life wins,
We know that destiny will never bring
A wedding ring about.
Our moral sense may really not be quite the thing
To fling about, sing about;
We'll achieve independence before it's too late, and
Wait and see.
What care, what care we?

Refrain

Ladies of the town,
Ladies of the town,
Though we've not a confessional air,
We have quite a professional flair,
Strolling up and down, strolling up and down,
We employ quite an amiable system
Of achieving renown,
Though the church and state abuses us,
For as long as it amuses us,
We'll remain, no matter how they frown,
Naughty, naughty, ladies of the town.

We can often behave in a very disarming, charming
way,
Which can frequently add to the money we lay by,
Day by day.
If we are told of something on the Stock Exchange
We pry a bit,

And if it's safe we get some kindly banker
To supply a bit, buy a bit,
And if later our helpers may wish to forget us
Set us free,
What care, what care we ?

Refrain

Ladies of the town, ladies of the town,
 Though we're socially under a cloud,
 Please forgive us for laughing aloud,
Strolling up and down, strolling up and down,
Disapproval may sometimes submerge us,
But we none of us drown,
We have known in great variety
Members of the best society,
And should we decide to settle down,
We'll be wealthy ladies of the town.

When LOTTE, FREDA *and* HANSI *have gone off* CARL *addresses his orchestra on the dais.*

CARL: It is lacking in colour. Strings, when you take the theme in the first refrain, bring it out, let it live and breathe, and mean something. In the last four bars I've marked a rallentando—Now then——

He raises his baton and the orchestra begins La Crevette's Song—as the music swells MANON *enters briskly. She is, naturally, in day clothes and a hat ; she listens for a moment, and then stamps her foot.* CARL *stops the orchestra.*

MANON: No, Carl—it must be quicker there.

CARL: When we were working yesterday that was the exact spot you wanted it slower.

MANON: Listen—it starts so—— (*She sings.*)

" Lorsque j'étais petite fille en marchant parmi les prés "—swift, staccato like that, then " J'entendis la voix d'ma tante, qui murmura à côté "—just a leetle slower—not much, you understand——

CARL : Very well. (*He starts the music again.*)

MANON *stops him.*

MANON : No, no, no—you are so stubborn.

CARL : Stubborn ?

MANON : Yes—you are a musician, yes, but you know nothing about singers, especially when they have no voice like me.

CARL (*coming down to her*) : You have a beautiful voice, Manon.

MANON (*laughing suddenly*) : Now you are being earnest and sincere, it is so many years since I saw that solemn look in your eyes——

CARL : You can't expect me to pay you compliments often, when you try to quarrel with me all the time.

MANON : I quarrel ! Don't be a fool.

CARL (*turning away*) : It's you who are a fool——

MANON (*touching his arm, softly*) : No, Carl—I was once—but I'm not any more.

CARL : What do you mean ?

MANON : Where is Sari—your little English Sarah ?

CARL : She will be here soon.

MANON (*mockingly*) : How exciting !

CARL : You do hate her, don't you ?

MANON (*gaily*) : Passionately—I should like to scratch her eyes out and pull her nose off and wring her neck——

CARL : Manon !

MANON : ——in a friendly way. (*She laughs again.*)

CARL: Don't laugh like that.

MANON: You used to love my laughter—it was so gay and charming, you said—I think you mentioned once that it reminded you of a bird chirruping, that was a very pretty thought, Carl——

CARL: Please go away now—I must continue my rehearsal.

MANON: Carl——

CARL: Yes.

MANON: I'm only teasing you and irritating you because I'm jealous——

CARL: But, Manon——

MANON (*holding up her hand*): No, don't protest and say I have no right to be jealous! I know that well—ours was such a silly little affair really, and so long ago, but somehow it was very sweet and it left a small sting behind——

CARL: It was your fault that it ended.

MANON: I know that too—and I'm glad—I was very proud of myself finishing it all suddenly like that—because it was for the best—I'm no good for you really—not faithful enough, and you should be free always, because you're an artist. (*She turns away.*) But now you'll never be free, so my beautiful little sacrifice was all in vain. (*She laughs.*) Go back to your work—I'll run through my words here——

CARL: Manon—I——

MANON: Please—play my music for me—I'm not sure of it yet—I'm not sure of anything.

> CARL *looks at her silently for a moment, and then goes thoughtfully back to the orchestra.* MANON *calls* FRITZ *and orders herself a drink. He brings it immediately and she sings her song quietly.*

"IF LOVE WERE ALL"

Life is very rough and tumble,
For a humble
  Diseuse,
One can betray one's troubles never,
Whatever
  Occurs,
Night after night,
Have to look bright,
Whether you're well or ill
People must laugh their fill.
You mustn't sleep
Till dawn comes creeping.
Though I never really grumble
Life's a jumble.
Indeed——
And in my efforts to succeed
I've had to formulate a creed——

Refrain

I believe in doing what I can,
In crying when I must,
In laughing when I choose.
Heigho, if love were all
I should be lonely,
I believe the more you love a man,
The more you give your trust,
The more you're bound to lose.
Although when shadows fall

I think if only——
Somebody splendid really needed me,

Someone affectionate and dear,
Cares would be ended if I knew that he
Wanted to have me near.
But I believe that since my life began
The most I've had is just
A talent to amuse.
Heigho, if love were all!
Tho' life buffets me obscenely,
It serenely
Goes on.
Although I question its conclusion,
Illusion
Is gone.
Frequently I
Put a bit by
Safe for a rainy day.
Nobody here can say
To what, indeed,
The years are leading.
Fate may often treat me meanly,
But I keenly
Pursue
A little mirage in the blue.
Determination helps me through.

Repeat Refrain

MANON *goes off after song.* CARL, *at the end of* MANON'S *song, dismisses the orchestra, who go off. He comes down from the dais, putting on his coat, when* GUSSI *enters.*

GUSSI: Hallo, Carl.

CARL (*absently*): Hallo.

GUSSI: Like a drink?

CARL: No, thanks.

GUSSI: Are you lunching with anyone?

CARL: Yes, my wife.

GUSSI: I might have known it. (*She slips her arm through his.*) Let me know when you feel like being unfaithful to her, won't you?

CARL (*smiling*): You're bad, Gussi, thoroughly bad—go along with you.

GUSSI: Here listen, you know that dark red coat of mine?

CARL: Yes.

GUSSI: Would your Sari like it? I've had this given to me. (*She waves her muff.*) I shan't need it any more.

CARL: It's very, very sweet of you, Gussi.

GUSSI: You both look so pinched—it depresses me to look at you—bring Sarah along to lunch at my flat——

CARL: Very well.

CAPTAIN AUGUST LUTTE *enters.* CAPTAIN AUGUST *is a debonair, imposing-looking man.*

GUSSI: Just a moment, some good news has come in—come at 1.30, if I'm not back tell Liza to serve you.

CARL: But, Gussi——

GUSSI (*firmly*): *Good*-bye, *dear* Carl——

CARL *goes off laughing.* GUSSI *sidles up to* CAPTAIN AUGUST.

GUSSI: Good morning.

CAPTAIN (*bowing stiffly*): Good morning.

GUSSI: Can I do anything for you?

CAPTAIN: I wish to see Herr Schlick.

GUSSI (*grimacing*): How nice.

CAPTAIN (*abruptly*): You are very pretty.

GUSSI (*shrinking away*): Oh, Captain—my salts—my salts.

CAPTAIN: Perhaps you will make a rendezvous with me for next week?

GUSSI: I may be dead next week, what's the matter with now?

CAPTAIN: I fear that I am otherwise engaged.

HERR SCHLICK *enters, oily and ingratiating.*

HERR S.: Captain—forgive me please—I—— (*Sees* GUSSI.) What are you doing here?

GUSSI: Just feeding the swans—— Good-bye.

She goes off.

CAPTAIN: Herr Schlick, I have a complaint to make.

HERR S.: It shall be rectified—before you say it, whatever is wrong is rectified.

CAPTAIN: Among your professional dancing partners you have been careless enough to engage an iceberg.

HERR S.: Good God!

CAPTAIN: A beautiful, alluring, unsociable iceberg—her name is Sari.

HERR S.: She is new, Captain; she has only been here a few weeks.

CAPTAIN: Even a few weeks is surely time enough to enable her to melt sufficiently to sup with me——

HERR S.: She is English, Captain, one must make allowances.

CAPTAIN: I do not come to a café of this sort to make allowances—I come to amuse myself and to pay for it.

MANON *re-enters on the dais just above them. She*

is looking for CARL, *but stops on hearing their voices.*

HERR S. (*very flurried*): Captain—I assure you—anything that you wish—I will arrange as soon as possible.

CAPTAIN: I wish for this Sari, to sup with me—to-night.

HERR S.: She shall, Captain, she shall.

CAPTAIN: You will please have a special supper laid ready in a quiet room—No. 7 is the best, I think—

HERR S.: You are sure that you would not rather have Lotte or perhaps Hansi——

Captain: Quite sure.

HERR S.: You see this English girl is the wife of my orchestra leader—they are said to be in love—it will be a little difficult——

CAPTAIN (*rising*): I hope I have made myself quite clear——

HERR S.: But, Captain——

CAPTAIN: You will please arrange things as I have suggested—to-night I wish no allowances to be made.

He bows as he is about to go out, meets SARI *coming in. She has grown more poised and mature during the years spent with* CARL. *She starts visibly on seeing* CAPTAIN AUGUST—*he clicks his heels and bows.*

Good morning.

SARI: Good morning.

CAPTAIN: It is a beautiful morning.

SARI: Beautiful.

CAPTAIN: But chilly.

SARI: It is very warm out.

CAPTAIN: Would you honour me by lunching with me?

SARI: I'm so sorry, but I am already engaged.

CAPTAIN: Perhaps a drive, a little later on; we might go up to Cobenzil——

SARI: Please forgive me, but to-day it is impossible.

CAPTAIN: I quite understand. (*He bows again.*) Until to-night, madame.

He goes off.

HERR S. (*furiously*): It may interest you to know that you are losing me one of my most valued clients—I'll deal with you later. Captain—a moment, please—Captain——

He rushes off. SARI *looks after him pensively for a moment and then sighs.* MANON *comes down from the dais.*

MANON: Sari.

SARI: Oh!

MANON: Don't look so startled——

SARI: I came to find Carl. Have you seen him?

MANON: Yes, I've just been rehearsing with him.

SARI: Oh!

MANON: He's about somewhere.

SARI: I'll find him. (*She turns to go.*)

MANON: I want to speak to you.

SARI (*coldly*): Yes? What is it?

MANON: Oh, why do you always look at me like that?

SARI: Like what?

MANON: Aloof and superior.

SARI: I wasn't conscious of being either of those things.

MANON: Yes, you were—you know you were—you always are with me. But, listen, never mind about that now—I heard Schlick arranging for you to have supper in a private room with Captain August to-night

SARI: What!

MANON: So be careful.

SARI (*incredulously*): You heard Schlick arranging for *me*——

MANON: Yes—yes, yes—I thought you might like to know.

SARI: How horrible!

MANON: Not so horrible as all that; lots of the girls here would be glad of the chance, but as Carl is in love with you and you are apparently in love with him, I thought——

SARI (*rather stiffly*): Thank you, Manon.

MANON: Not at all. (*She turns to go.*)

SARI: Manon——

MANON (*stopping*): Yes?

SARI: I'm sorry.

MANON: What for?

SARI: If my manner is—well, unkind——

MANON (*patting her arm*): All is well, my dear—I don't love him any more, really, at least I don't think I do, and anyhow you have no reason to be jealous, nothing to be afraid of. Look at me, and then look in the glass. (*She kisses her lightly, and goes off humming a reprise of her former song.*)

CARL *enters from left.*

SARI: Carl.

CARL: Darling! (*He kisses her fondly.*) How quick you've been dressing. I crept out without waking you.

SARI: Yes, I know; you must never do that again.

CARL: Why—what's the matter?

SARI: I dreamt—something dreadful. I awoke terrified—I came straight here without any coffee or anything—to see if you were safe.

CARL: I safe? Why, of course I'm safe—why shouldn't I be?

SARI: I don't know, I'm frightened. I hate this place—let's go away. I'd rather go back to singing in the streets again, at least we were independent then and together.

CARL: We're together now—always.

SARI (*wildly*): No, no—not here we're not—we're separated by hundreds of things and people—you're the chef d'orchestre and I'm a professional dance partner. I hate it, I tell you—I can't be gay and enjoy it like the other girls, because I love you—I can't feel happy when the cavalry officers put their arms round my waist and dance and flirt with me, because I love you, and because I'm scared.

CARL: Why are you scared?

SARI: Something horrible will happen if we stay here. I know it, I feel it——

CARL: Come along and have a little lunch, then you'll feel better. We're going to Gussi's flat—she's got a present for you—you know that red coat——

SARI: Oh, Carl, Carl, you won't understand!——

CARL *takes her in his arms.*

CARL: You must take hold of your courage, my sweet—we must both put up with things now in order to be secure later on—no more street singing—it broke my heart to see you hungry—that's all past—you've been so splendid and brave all through—just hold on for a few weeks more until we have enough to start that little café——

SARI (*hysterically*): Laugh at me then—laugh everything away, stop me being solemn—we're both too young to be dreary and sentimental—make me forget the present in planning for the future—where will our café be? How shall we manage it? Shall I be able to sing your songs there?—one day I might make them famous—I love your music so very much—I want it to be known all over the world, and one day it will be, I'm sure of it—do you think I could help—do you?

CARL (*kissing her*): Darling.

"LITTLE CAFE"

CARL: We share a mutual ambition
Which naught can disarrange,
SARI: Based on the hopeful supposition
That soon our luck will change.
CARL: Tho' we very often wonder whether
Poverty will win the day,
SARI: Just as long as we remain together
Troubles seem to fade away.
BOTH: However hard the bed one lies on
The same old dreams begin,
We're always scanning the horizon
For when our ship comes in.

Refrain

CARL: We'll have a sweet little café
In a neat little square,
SARI: We'll find our fortune
And our happiness there.
CARL: We shall thrive on the vain and resplendent
SARI: And contrive to remain independent.
CARL: We'll have a meek reputation
And a chic clientele.
SARI: Kings will fall under our spell.

BOTH : We'll be so zealous
That the world will be jealous
Of our sweet little café in our square.

SARI : Can you imagine our sensations
When we've security ?
CARL : And all our dreary deprivations
Are just a memory.
SARI : Tho' we're very often driven frantic,
Peace is very hard to find.
CARL : All these dreadful days will seem romantic
When we've left them far behind.
BOTH : Fate needn't be quite such a dragon,
He knows how tired we are.
We'll hitch our hopeful little wagon
On to a lucky star.

Refrain

CARL : We'l lhave a sweet little café
In a neat little square,
SARI : We'll find our fortune
And our happiness there.
CARL : We shall thrive on the vain and resplendent
SARI : And contrive to remain independent.
CARL : We'll have a meek reputation
And a chic clientele.
SARI : Kings will fall under our spell.
BOTH : We'll be so zealous
That the world will be jealous
Of our sweet little café in our square.

At the end of the last refrain CARL *takes* SARI *in his arms and the curtain falls.*

ACT TWO: SCENE II

Characters: SARI LINDEN, CARL LINDEN, MANON (LA CREVETTE), CAPTAIN AUGUST LUTTE, LIEUTENANT TRANISCH, HERR SCHLICK, LOTTE, FREDA, HANSI, GUSSI, SIX SPECIAL DANCERS, OFFICERS, GUESTS, WAITERS, MUSICIANS, etc. *The scene is the same as* ACT TWO, SCENE I.

The Scene is the same, except that the atmosphere has changed from a frowsy daylight squalor to a tinselled gas-light gaiety.

It is about 2 a.m.

When the curtain rises everyone is waltzing. CARL *is conducting the orchestra on the dais. Some of the* GIRLS *have* MALE PARTNERS *and some are dancing with one another. The stage should look as hot and crowded as possible. At the end of the opening waltz* CARL *stops his orchestra and the theatre orchestra takes up the* OFFICERS' *entrance music. About a dozen smart* OFFICERS *come marching on in attractive undress uniform. They sing a concerted introductory number with the* GIRLS.

OFFICERS' CHORUS

OFFICERS: We wish to order wine, please,
Expressly from the Rhine, please,
The year we really don't much care.

LADIES: Oh dear,
Now that you're here
Think of the wear and tear.

OFFICERS: We hope without insistence
To overcome resistance
In all you little ladies fair.

LADIES: Oh well,
How can we tell
Whether you'd really dare?

OFFICERS: We sincerely hope it's really not a thankless task
Amusing us,
Won't you please agree?

LADIES: Ah, me!

OFFICERS: You could quickly break our hearts by everything we ask
Refusing us;
Cruel that would be
Ladies, can't you see!
We're officers and gentlemen,
Reliable and true,
Considerate and chivalrous
In everything we do.

Though we're gay and drunk a trifle,
All our laughter we should stifle,
Were we summoned by a bugle call.
We're amorous and passionate,
But dignified and stern,
Which if you play us false you'll quickly learn.
Do not let our presence grieve you,
When we've loved you we shall leave you,
For we're officers and gentlemen, that's all!

After song, CAPTAIN AUGUST *and* TRANISCH *enter, and* CAPTAIN AUGUST *and the* OFFICERS *sing "Tokay," of which everyone joins in the last Refrain.*

"TOKAY"

OFFICERS: Tokay!
CAPTAIN A.: When we're thoroughly wined and dined,
And the barracks are left behind,
We come down to the town to find
Some relief from the daily grind.
Love is kind,
Love is blind.
OFFICERS: Tokay!
CAPTAIN A.: When the thoughts of a man incline
To the grapes of a sunlit vine,
On the banks of the golden Rhine,
Slowly ripening pure and fine,
Sweet divine,
Lover's wine.
Lift your voices till the rafters ring,
Fill your glasses to the brim and sing:

Refrain

Tokay!
The golden sunshine of a summer day,
Tokay!
Will bear the burden of your cares away.
Here's to the love in you,
The hate in you,
Desire in you.
OFFICERS: Wine of the sun that will waft you along
Lifting you high on the wings of a song.

CAPTAIN A.: Dreams in you,
The flame in you,
The fire in you,
Tokay—Tokay.

OFFICERS: So while forgetfulness we borrow,
Never minding what to-morrow has to say,

CAPTAIN A.: Tokay!

ALL: The only call we all obey,
Tokay—Tokay—Tokay!

Some go off to the bar, others seat themselves at tables and order wine. SARI *and* MANON *come in and sit at a table below the balcony to the right.* SARI *is simply dressed in white.* MANON *is very gay in scarlet sequins.*

SARI: I'm so tired.

MANON: Well, for heaven's sake don't look as if you were.

SARI: I'm sick of pretending.

MANON: So am I, but it's no use worrying about that. The whole business is pretending. Life's pretending.

SARI: That hateful Captain August—he smiled at me in the bar—an odious smile.

MANON: I hope you smiled back.

SARI: I certainly did not.

MANON: Well, that was very foolish of you—there's nothing so alluring to that type of man as snowy chastity.

SARI: How can you, Manon. (*She smiles.*) I'm so miserable really, it's horrid of you to laugh at me.

MANON: That's better—you're smiling yourself now.

LIEUTENANT TRANISCH *enters from the bar, comes to their table and bows to* MANON.

TRANISCH: Mademoiselle la Crevette.

MANON: Yes?

TRANISCH: We have never spoken before, but I wish to say you are an admirable artiste—you sing like an angel.

MANON (*laughing very loudly*): You Viennese are so gallant. I sing like a frog.

TRANISCH: Will you come to the bar and take a drink with me?

MANON: What is this now—what does this mean? Is it the birth of a romance? I feel so flattered.

TRANISCH (*slightly embarrassed*): Mademoiselle—I——

MANON: Never mind, Lieutenant, I am not deceived—you think I sing well, that is very kind—now tell me—cards on the table—to which of the more attractive women here do you want me to introduce you?

TRANISCH: Really—you misunderstand me—I——

MANON: Come now—tell me—I have no sensibilities.

TRANISCH: There is a small blonde lady like a kitten in yellow—I will admit to you frankly—she enthrals me strangely.

MANON: That would be Gussi. (*She rises.*) Excuse me for a moment, Sari.

SARI: Of course.

TRANISCH (*clicking his heels and bowing to* SARI): Fraulein.

MANON: Come along—but let me warn you—Gussi is a collector.

TRANISCH: Collector?

MANON: Yes, of antiques—very enthusiastic—old jewellery for preference. If your acquaintance ripens, let me advise you when walking to keep to the more modern thoroughfares. (*She looks at* SARI *smilingly.*) Heigho—if love were all!

She and TRANISCH *go off to the bar.* CAPTAIN AUGUST *enters and comes to* SARI'S *table, but as he does so* CARL *sees him and comes down from the orchestra.*

CAPTAIN A. (*bowing*): Madame——

CARL: Sari, I want to talk to you. You remember the second movement in the concerto I was scoring yesterday, I have had the most magnificent idea—instead of using strings alone, I shall strengthen it with the zimbale just towards the end where it goes—tum tum tum tum—— (*He hums.*)

SARI: Yes, I know—*what* a good idea. (*She also hums.*) Tum tum—tum tum tum——

They both hum together, and finally CAPTAIN AUGUST, *finding himself completely ignored, turns on his heel and marches back into the bar.*

(*Half laughing.*) Oh, Carl—that was wonderful of you.

CARL: I was watching—I'm always watching to see that no harm comes to you.

SARI: I hate him so—he won't leave me alone—he embarrasses me.

CARL: Cheer up, my dearest.

SARI: I'll try. (*She smiles.*) Oh, Carl, there's something so heavy weighing down on my heart—I felt it this morning, and it's there again now.

CARL (*looking at her*): You're very strange to-night—you've been strange all day—eager and tense like a frightened child. Is there anything the matter really?

SARI: Yes—no—I don't know. I feel as though fate were too strong for us, as though our love for one another and our happiness together was making the gods angry. I feel suddenly insecure.

CARL: We'll go away, then, to-morrow.

SARI: Carl!

CARL: We have a little money saved anyhow. I hate Schlick and this place as much as you do really. To-night is the end of it. We'll go to Frankfort. Heinrich is there, he'll help us.

SARI: To-night is the end of it.

CARL: You remember Heinrich—with the long brown beard—you laughed at him.

SARI: Yes, he was funny, but I liked him.

CARL: Do you feel happier now?

SARI: Oh yes, much, much happier.

CARL: So do I—we'll be free again—independent—I must get back. Au revoir, my dear love.

SARI: Au revoir.

She kisses her hand to him and goes off. GUSSI *and* LIEUTENANT TRANISCH *come on, followed by* HANSI *and* FREDA, *who are giggling.*

GUSSI: Louis Quinze—of course it was only paste, but definitely Louis Quinze.

TRANISCH: How interesting.

GUSSI: I'll show it to you to-morrow—we can drive there after luncheon.

TRANISCH: We haven't had supper yet.

GUSSI: No, but we will—we'll sit here—I shall have to dance in a minute—Fritz—Hans——

She sits down with TRANISCH *at a small table and calls the* WAITERS. FREDA *and* HANSI *sit down also, but on the opposite side of the stage, at the same table at which* CARL *and* SARI *played the preceding scene.*

HANSI: I'll tell you one thing here and now, whatever Gussi is talking about is *not* paste.

FREDA: I doubt if it's even Louis Quinze.

SARI *comes in.*

HANSI: Here comes the snow queen.

FREDA: Hullo, Sari.

SARI: Hullo.

HANSI: Any offers to-night

FREDA: Don't tease her, Hansi—she's in love.

SARI (*smiling*): No, no offers so far.

HANSI: Do you want a drink?

SARI: Yes—I'd love one.

HANSI: Fritz——

She calls the waiter and orders wine.

FREDA: That's pretty, that dress—is it new?

SARI: Yes. I made it myself from a pattern.

FREDA: It sags a little bit behind—here—look—give me a pin, Hansi.

HANSI: You can have this brooch for the time being, but give it back, it's not valuable, but lucky.

She gives SARI *a brooch.* SARI *stands up while* FREDA *fixes the brooch on to the dress.* CAPTAIN AUGUST *comes in and bows ironically to* SARI.

CAPTAIN A.: Will you honour me with this dance, please?

SARI (*jumping slightly*): Oh—no, I'm sorry—I'm engaged.

CAPTAIN A.: I fear that is not strictly true.

FREDA: I'll dance with you, if you like.

CAPTAIN A.: Please do not think me impolite, but I have set my heart on dancing with Fraulein Sari.

SARI: Forgive me, Captain, but it's quite impossible.

CAPTAIN A.: We shall see. (*He bows abruptly and walks across the stage to where* SCHLICK *is standing talking to two other officers. He is obviously very angry. He speaks to* SCHLICK *swiftly and angrily.*

SARI: I hate him—he's always tormenting me.

FREDA: You're unwise, my dear—it's best to humour them a little.

SARI: I've tried—I've danced with him, but he presses me too close and whispers horrible things to me.

HANSI: He's very rich and, I believe, generous.

SARI: Yes, but that doesn't interest me.

HANSI (*wistfully*): There's no doubt about it—love is very bad for business.

SCHLICK *comes to their table.*

SCHLICK: Sari——

SARI: Yes, Herr Schlick.

SCHLICK: You are engaged and paid by me as a dancing partner for my clients, are you not?

SARI: Yes.

SCHLICK: I have received several complaints from Captain August Lutte—he says you persistently refuse to dance with him.

SARI: He takes advantage of my position.

SCHLICK: It would be better if you realised once and for all that you have no position—after to-night you may consider your engagement at an end.

SARI (*with spirit*): It is at an end anyhow—my husband and I are leaving Vienna to-morrow.

SCHLICK: Oho—I see. Well, I should like to remind you that you both have a week's salary owing to you, and unless you dance willingly and agreeably with Captain August or any other of the officers when they ask you to, neither you nor your husband will receive a penny of your salary—I run my café on business lines, you understand.

SARI: But, Herr Schlick, that is unfair—my behaviour has nothing to do with my husband.

SCHLICK: That is enough. I am sick to death of your stupid mincing airs and graces—unless you behave yourself to-night, you will both leave to-morrow without your money, and be damned to you!

He leaves SARI, *who sinks miserably into her chair.* HANSI *and* FREDA *try to comfort her and give her some wine.* SCHLICK *advances to the middle of the floor to announce the commencement of the entertainment.*

Ladies and Gentlemen, I crave your kind attention for the most superb musical entertainment ever offered in Vienna.

Everyone applauds.

Thank you. Thank you. My first number will be my six magnificent dancing girls—trained exclusively in the finest ballet schools in the world. Lise, Trude, Fritz, Toni, Greta and Elsa.

SIX GIRLS *rise from their various tables and make a line in the middle of the floor. There is a lot of applause.* CARL *strikes up their music and they dance, after which they return to their tables amid cheers.* SCHLICK *again takes the floor.*

Gentlemen—Ladies and Gentlemen—I beg attention for my favourite, your favourite, the world's favourite star—Manon la Crevette.

He steps aside and MANON *comes running on. She is greeted with vociferous applause. She sings a very saucy French song: "Bonne Nuit, Merci!" interspersed with a good deal of back-chat and ogling.*

"BONNE NUIT, MERCI!"

MANON: Lorsque j'étais petite fille
En marchant parmi les prés
J'entendit la voix d'ma tante
Qui murmura à côté,
'N'oublie pas la politesse
Lorsque viendra un amant
Car tout la bonheur réside là dedans.'

Refrain

C'est pourquoi dans mes affaires,
Soit de cœur ou soit d'esprit,
C'est pourquoi je tâche de plaire
Toute la foule de mes amis,
Soit qu'ils m'offrent pied-à-terre
Ou me montrent une bonne affaire
J'leurs réponds, 'Vas-y. Bonne Nuit Merci!'

Lorsque je suis v'nue à Paris
J'étais sage de nature,
Mais que faire dans la vie
Etant jeune pour rester pure!
Quand ma politesse m'obligea
Lorsqu'je suivais par hasard
Une adventure dans les boîtes des boulevards.

Refrain

Et j'ai rencontré en ville
Un monsieur bien comme il faut,
Il m'a dit, 'ma petite fille,
Veux-tu faire un p'tit do-do?'

Lorsqu' j'arrive chez lui toute de suite
I'me dit 'Deshabilles-toi vite!'
J'me suis dis 'Vas'y. Bonnie Nuit.
Merci!'

As encore she sings a waltz song in which everybody ioins.

WALTZ SONG

'Tis time that we were parted,
You and I,
However broken-hearted,
'Tis good-bye!
Although our love has ended
And darkness has descended,
Icall to you with one last cry:

Kiss me
Before you go away!
Miss me
Through every night and day.
Though clouds are grey above you,
You'll hear me say I love you!
Kiss me
Before you go away!

Parmi les chansons tristes
De l'amour,
Joies et chagrins existent
Tour à tour,
Et presqu'avec contrainte
On risque la douce étreinte
Qui nous sépare enfin toujours.

Refrain

Je t'aime,
Tes baisers m'ont grisée
Même
A l'heure de t'en aller,
La volupté troublante
Brise mes lèvres brûlantes,
Je t'aime,
A l'heure de t'en aller.

At the end of this CARL *strikes up another waltz and everybody begins to dance.* SCHLICK *comes over to* SARI'S *table and stands behind it. After a moment* CAPTAIN AUGUST *approaches and bows.*

CAPTAIN A.: Fraulein Sari has perhaps by now forgotten her other engagement.

SARI (*rising agitatedly*): I—please—I——

SCHLICK: You are quite right, Captain, she has forgotten.

SARI: Captain August—I am very tired—will you please forgive me just this once?

CAPTAIN A.: One dance, please.

SCHLICK: I think you would be well advised to grant Captain August's request.

SARI (*pulling herself together*): Certainly, Captain, I shall be charmed.

She gives one despairing look at CARL *on the dais—he is watching anxiously—then she surrenders herself to the* CAPTAIN'S *arms and they begin to waltz.* CARL *watches all the time. As the dance progresses* CAPTAIN AUGUST *is obviously becoming more and more aggressively amorous.* CARL, *with obvious agitation, perceptibly quickens the tempo of the music. Finally the* CAPTAIN *waltzes* SARI *into the centre of the floor—stops dead, tightens his arms round her and kisses her on the mouth passionately, bending her right back as he does so. She gives one cry,* CARL *stops the music dead with a crash and leaps over the railing of the dais on to the middle of the floor. He drags* SARI *away from* CAPTAIN AUGUST, *then, springing at him, strikes him in the face. Immediately the buzz of excitement dies down into dead silence.*

CARL (*wildly*): Swine—filthy, ill-mannered drunken swine!

SARI (*in a whisper*): Carl!

MANON (*rushing forward*): Carl—don't be a fool.

CAPTAIN AUGUST *gives an unpleasant laugh and draws his sword.*

CAPTAIN A.: Tranisch—look after our foolhardy young friend here, will you?

TRANISCH: Not now—not now—wait.

CAPTAIN A.: I regret—I cannot wait.

TRANISCH *draws his sword and hands it to* CARL—MANON *clutches his arm.*

CARL: Stand back, Manon—look after Sari—please.

The CAPTAIN *attacks him and they fight a brief duel, the crowd making a large ring round them. Suddenly* CAPTAIN AUGUST *knocks* CARL'S *sword from his hand and runs him through. There is a general scream and everyone crowds forward.* SARI *silently and madly fights through the crowd and sinks to the ground, taking* CARL *in her arms.* TRANISCH *motions the crowd back. There is silence except for* MANON, *who is crying loudly and hopelessly.*

SARI (*softly—she is dry-eyed*): I'll love you always—always—do you hear?

CARL (*weakly*): Sari—Sari—my sweet, sweet Sari——

His head falls back in her lap, and she kneels there staring before her dazed and hopeless as the curtain falls.

ACT THREE: SCENE I

Characters: MADAME SARI LINDEN, THE MARQUIS OF SHAYNE, LADY JAMES (HARRIET), MRS. PROUTIE (GLORIA), MRS. BETHEL (EFFIE), LADY SORREL (HONOR), MRS. VALE (JANE), THE DUCHESS OF TENTERDEN (VICTORIA), LORD JAMES, MR. PROUTIE, MR. BETHEL, LORD SORREL, MR. VALE, THE DUKE OF TENTERDEN, THE HON. HUGH DEVON, MRS. DEVON, VERNON CRAFT, CEDRIC BALLANTYNE, BERTRAM SELLICK, LORD HENRY JADE, ACCOMPANIST (to MADAME LINDEN) BUTLER, GUESTS, etc.
The scene is LORD SHAYNE'S *house in London. The Year is* 1895.

It is the drawing-room of the MARQUIS OF SHAYNE'S *house in London. Fifteen years have passed since Act II, and it is now* 1895. *When the curtain rises,* LORD SHAYNE, *a distinguished old man, is standing a little to the right receiving his guests, who are announced by the* BUTLER. LADY JAMES (HARRIET) *and* MRS. PROUTIE (GLORIA) *are announced with their husbands, likewise* MRS. BETHEL (EFFIE), LADY SORREL (HONOR), MRS. VALE (JANE), *and lastly the* DUCHESS OF TENTERDEN (VICTORIA). *They are all by now smart middle-aged society matrons. Their entrance and* LORD SHAYNE'S *reception of them is all part of the opening chorus.*

OPENING CHORUS

ALI: Tarara boom-de-ay,
Tarara boom-de-ay,
We are the most effectual,
Intellectual
Movement of the day.
Our moral standards sway
Like Mrs. Tanqueray,
And we are theoretically
Most æsthetically
Eager to display
The fact that we're aggressively
And excessively
Anxious to destroy
All the snobbery
And hob-nobbery
Of the hoi-polloi.
Tarara boom-de-ay.
It's mental washing day,
And come what may
We'll scrub until the nation's morals shrink away.
Tarara boom-de-ay!

EXQUISITES: Though we are languid in appearance,
We're in the vanguard.
We feel we can guard
The cause of Art.
We shall ignore all interference,
For our complacence
With this renaissance
Is frightfully smart.
Please do not think us unrelenting,
Our charming frolic

With the symbolic
Is meek and mild.
We merely spend our time preventing
Some earnest stripling
From liking Kipling
Instead of Wilde.
Now that we find the dreary nineteenth century is closing,
We mean to start the twentieth in ecstasies of posing.

ALL
Tarara boom-de-ay,
It's mental washing day,
And come what may
We'll scrub until the tiresome bourgeois shrink away.
Tarara boom-de-ay!

Which is concluded by a SEXTETTE *by* HARRIET, GLORIA, HONOR, JANE, EFFIE *and* VICTORIA. *Everyone else retires into the supper room, leaving them on the stage.*

"ALAS THE TIME IS PAST"

Alas, the time is past when we
Could frolic with impunity.
Secure in our virginity,
We sometimes look aghast
Adown the lanes of memory,
Alas, the time is past.
Ah, then the world was at our feet,
When we were sweet-and-twenty,
We never guessed that what we'd got,
Tho' not a lot—was plenty.

We gaily sought some Abelard
To cherish, guard and own us,
But all we know of storm and strife
Our married life—has shown us.
Alas, the time is past when we
Could frolic with impunity.
Secure in our virginity,
We sometimes look aghast
Adown the lanes of memory.
Alas, the time is past.
Alack-a-day me—alack-a-day me!
Ah, then the world was at our feet,
Alas, the time is past.

HARRIET: What have you done to your hair, Effie?—it strikes me as peculiar.

EFFIE: Nothing in particular.

GLORIA: I'm afraid you're becoming a little pernickety, Harriet; you must guard against it.

HONOR: Where's your late husband, Victoria?

VICTORIA: Later than ever, my dear—he's at Boodles, I expect.

JANE: Talking too much.

HARRIET: And drinking much too much.

VICTORIA: You can't upset me by saying that, Harriet dear. I find alcohol one of the greatest comforts of matrimony!

HONOR: Victoria!

VICTORIA: In a husband, I mean—it leaves one free for one's charities.

JANE: A little too free sometimes, my pet.

HARRIET: Who is this woman?

EFFIE: Which woman?

HARRIET: The one we've been invited to meet.

VICTORIA: Some strange Hungarian singer—probably very glittering and rather stout.

HONOR: Oh, I shouldn't think so—Lord Shayne has been pursuing her for ages from capital to capital.

HARRIET: Central Europe is far too musical, there can be no two opinions about that.

JANE: I hear she's very beautiful.

LORD SHAYNE *has entered unobserved from the supper room.*

LORD S.: She is——

VICTORIA: Good heavens, how you made me jump!

LORD S.: She is one of the few really beautiful people in the world.

HARRIET: How very disconcerting!

HONOR: Do you think we shall like that?

LORD S.: I shall be very interested to see the effect she has on you—you are all—if I may say so—so very representative.

VICTORIA: Of what, dear Lord Shayne?

LORD S.: Shall we say "fin de siècle"?

HARRIET: I was afraid somebody would say that before the evening was over.

The BUTLER *announces the* HON. HUGH DEVON *and* MRS. DEVON. LORD SHAYNE *moves over to greet them.* HUGH *has developed along the exact lines that one would have expected; he has become a good deal more pompous with the years, and has a tremendously diplomatic manner. His wife is fat and vague.*

VICTORIA: Margaret dear, how are you?

MRS. D.: Shattered, completely shattered! Our cabby was raving mad. He kept saying the oddest things to his horse, at least I hope they were to his horse. I pretended not to understand, one has to think of prestige——

LORD S.: I hear you're going to Vienna.

HUGH: Yes, next week, thank God! I believe Mullins has been making a fearful hash of everything.

MRS. D.: Isn't it exciting! I was so afraid we were going to be sent to Riga or Christiania or somewhere draughty like that.

HARRIET: Hugh generally gets what he wants.

MRS. D.: As it is, I don't know what I shall do with the children. I can't help feeling that Eva is the wrong age for Vienna.

LORD S.: No one is the wrong age for Vienna—it's a city of enchantment—magnificent.

HUGH: I'm told the plumbing is appalling.

VICTORIA: Lord Shayne has fallen in love again—haven't you, my dear?

LORD S.: I am always in love with beauty.

HUGH: Admirably put, Shayne. I quite agree with you.

JANE: We're all on tenterhooks to see Madame Linden—she's due at any moment.

MRS. D.: What are tenterhooks, I never know.

The BUTLER *throws open the doors and announces* MADAME SARI LINDEN. SARAH *enters, exquisitely gowned and radiantly beautiful, carrying herself with tremendous poise; her jewels are superb, and the years have invested her with a certain air of decision which is almost metallic as compared with the tremulous diffidence of her youth.* LORD SHAYNE *goes forward and kisses her hand.*

LORD S.: My dear, how enchanting to see you

again. (*He turns with a smile.*) I think you know everyone here.

HARRIET: Good heavens, Sarah!

VICTORIA (*astounded*): Sarah!

EFFIE: It can't be—it can't be——

She rushes up and kisses her. There is a babel of surprised and excited conversation. HUGH *stands a little apart, looking a trifle embarrassed.*

HONOR: We heard that you had died, ages and ages ago.

SARI: I did die. Fifteen years ago to be exact. Things happened and I couldn't come back. I didn't want to come back, so I thought I'd better die, vaguely and obscurely. It was the only thing to do—it sort of rounded everything off so satisfactorily.

JANE: It's unbelievable, Sarah, dear Sarah.

SARI: Please don't be quite so pleased to see me. It makes me feel ashamed, particularly with Hugh standing there, looking so stern. How do you do, Hugh?

HUGH: I'm delighted to see you again. Margaret, I want you to meet Sarah—Sarah——? (*He looks questioningly at her.*)

SARI: Linden—don't say you've forgotten Carl Linden, the man I eloped with, practically under your nose, Hugh?

HUGH: I remember perfectly—how is he?

SARI: He's dead—I'm so glad to meet you, Mrs. Devon. I do hope Hugh is a charming husband and not too embittered—I treated him abominably, you know.

MRS. D. (*shaking hands with her*): It's all so very surprising—very, very surprising—Hugh told me the whole story, when he heard of your death in Prague or somewhere. He was dreadfully upset, weren't you, Hugh?

HUGH: Yes, indeed, I was.

SARI (*smiling and tapping him lightly with her fan*): Dear Hugh, never mind—everything always turns out for the best, doesn't it? At least, almost everything.

LORD S.: Won't you have a little supper—Sari?

HONOR: "Sari"—it does sound pretty, doesn't it—"Sari."

SARI: Only a very little, if you want me to sing for you.

They all go into the supper room, chattering and laughing, while the ORCHESTRA *very softly and lightly plays a reprise of the "Blindman's Buff Finale" in Act I. When the supper room doors close behind them, the other doors open and four over-exquisitely dressed young men enter. They all wear in their immaculate buttonholes green carnations.* VERNON CRAFT, *a poet,* CEDRIC BALLANTYNE, *a painter,* LORD HENRY JADE, *a dilettante, and* BERTRAM SELLICK, *a playwright.*

BERTIE: It's entirely Vernon's fault that we are so entrancingly late.

VERNON: My silk socks were two poems this evening and they refused to scan.

HENRY: It's going to be inexpressibly dreary, I can feel it in my bones.

CEDRIC: Don't be absurd, Henry, your whole charm lies in the fact that you have no bones.

They sing a quartette: "We all Wore a Green Carnation."

"WE ALL WORE A GREEN CARNATION."

Blasé boys are we,
Exquisitely free
From the dreary and quite absurd
Moral views of the common herd.
We like porphyry bowls,
Chandeliers and stoles,
We're most spirited,
Carefully filleted "souls."

Refrain.

Pretty boys, witty boys, too, too, too
Lazy to fight stagnation,
Haughty boys, naughty boys, all we do
Is to pursue sensation.
The portals of society
Are always opened wide,
The world our eccentricity condones,
A note of quaint variety
We're certain to provide.
We dress in very decorative tones.
Faded boys, jaded boys, womankind's
Gift to a bulldog nation,
In order to distinguish us from less enlightened minds,
We all wear a green carnation.

We believe in Art,
Though we're poles apart
From the fools who are thrilled by Greuze.
We like Beardsley and Green Chartreuse.

Women say we're too
Bored to bill and coo,
We smile wearily,
It's so drearily true:

Refrain.

Pretty boys, witty boys, you may sneer
At our disintegration,
Haughty boys, naughty boys, dear, dear, dear!
Swooning with affectation.
Our figures sleek and willowy,
Our lips incarnadine,
May worry the majority a bit.
But matrons rich and billowy,
Invite us out to dine,
And revel in our phosphorescent wit.

Faded boys, jaded boys, come what may,
Art is our inspiration,
And as we the reason for the 'Nineties' being gay,
We all wear a green carnation.

Refrain.

Pretty boys, witty boys, yearning for
Permanent adulation,
Haughty boys, naughty boys, every pore
Bursting with self-inflation,
We feel we're rather Grecian,
As our manners indicate,
Our sense of moral values isn't strong.
For ultimate completion
We shall really have to wait
Until the Day of Judgment comes along.

Faded boys, jaded boys, each one craves
Some sort of soul salvation,
But when we rise reluctantly but gracefully from our graves,
We'll all wear a green carnation.

They go off. LORD SHAYNE *and* SARI *come in from the supper room.*

LORD S.: I want to talk to you.

SARI: I know.

LORD S.: You can guess what I am going to say?

SARI: Yes, I think so.

LORD S.: I love you.

SARI (*smiling*): I was right.

LORD S.: Will you honour me by becoming my wife? You've now refused me in practically every capital in Europe—London is the last on the list.

SARI: Why should London prove the exception?

LORD S.: It's home.

SARI (*sighing*): Yes—I suppose it is.

LORD S.: It has charm, London—a very peaceful charm, particularly for anyone who is tired like you. You can drive in the Park in the Spring and look at the crocuses.

SARI: Please don't talk of Spring.

LORD S.: Then there's the Autumn, when the leaves fall in the Square, and you can sit on a rickety iron chair and watch the children searching for horse chestnuts.

SARI (*wistfully*): Whose children?

LORD S.: Just anybody's.

SARI: The fogs come in November.

LORD S.: Fogs can be delightful.

SARI: Can they? (*She smiles.*)

LORD S.: Particularly when you're warm and snug by a crackly fire drinking tea, while from the yellow gloom outside the trees look in at you like ghosts.

SARI: I don't like tea or ghosts.

LORD S.: You're very hard to please.

SARI: How do you know I'm tired?

LORD S.: By your voice, and your eyes.

SARI: I'm afraid I don't love you—actually! I think you're kind and understanding and gay and very dear, but you know I've only really loved one man all my life. I know it's tiresome to be so faithful, particularly to a mere memory, but there it is.

LORD S.: I think perhaps I could make you happy—anyhow happier.

SARI: May I think it over a little? I'll let you know a little later.

The supper room doors open and everyone comes noisily into the room.

VICTORIA: Sarah—aren't you going to sing soon?

HONOR: Do you remember our singing lessons at Madame Claire's before you met Carl Linden—I mean—Oh dear——

SARI (*smiling*): I remember! I do hope my voice has improved since then.

LORD S.: Silence, please! Madame Sari Linden will sing us some of Carl Linden's enchanting songs, the songs she has made so famous.

Everyone applauds and arranges themselves comfortably.

SARI: Where is my accompanist, is he here?

A foreign-looking YOUNG MAN *detaches himself from the crowd.*

YOUNG MAN: Here I am.

SARI: What shall we start with?

YOUNG MAN: "The River Song"?

SARI: No, that's too difficult to begin with.

YOUNG MAN: "Zigeuner?"

SARI: That will do. Ladies and Gentlemen, this song needs a slight preface. My husband wrote it when he was only sixteen. He visited Germany for the first time and sailed down the Rhine past forests and castles and gipsy encampments, and they fired his imagination so much that he wrote this song of a lovely flaxen-haired German Princess who fell in love with a Zigeuner gipsy.

The YOUNG MAN *starts the introduction and* SARI *takes her stand by the piano.* LORD SHAYNE *stands pensively near her, gazing at her. She sings "Zigeuner."*

"ZIGEUNER."

Once upon a time
Many years ago,
Lived a fair Princess,
Hating to confess
Loneliness was torturing her so.
Then a gipsy came,
Called to her by name.
Woo'd her with a song,
Sensuous and strong,
All the summer long;
Her passion seemed to tremble like a living flame.

Is taken up after the first verse by the ORCHESTRA.

Bid my weeping cease,
Melody that brings
Merciful release,
Promises of peace;

Through the gentle throbbing of the strings.
Music of the plain,
Music of the wild,
Come to me again,
Hear me not in vain,
Soothe a heart in pain,
And let me to my happiness be reconciled.

Refrain.

Play to me beneath the summer moon,
Zigeuner !—Zigeuner !—Zigeuner!
All I ask of life is just to listen
To the songs that you sing,
My spirit like a bird on the wing
Your melodies adoring—soaring,
Call to me with some barbaric tune,
Zigeuner !—Zigeuner !—Zigeuner !
Now you hold me in your power,
Play to me for just an hour,
Zigeuner !

At the end of it everyone applauds. She silences them by raising her hand.

This is a very simple, sentimental little song. I do hope you won't laugh at it—it means a very great deal to me.

She unpins a bunch of white violets from her waist and throws them to LORD SHAYNE. *Then she begins to sing the refrain of " I'll See You Again."*

Reprise.

I'll see you again,
I live each moment through again.

Time has lain heavy between,
But what has been
Can leave me never;
Your dear memory
Throughout my life has guided me.
Though my world has gone awry,
Though the years my tears may dry,
I shall love you till I die,
Good-bye!

At the end the lights dim and the ORCHESTRA *crashes out the melody. When the lights go up again, it is the present day, the same as Act I, Scene I, and she is an old woman singing to a lot of young people sprawling on the floor. When she finishes singing,* DOLLY CHAMBERLAIN *springs to her feet.*

DOLLY: It is the most thrilling, divine, marvellous thing I've ever heard—Vincent, I'm mad about you—d'you hear—I love you.

She flings herself into his arms, he gently and rather absently disengages himself.

VINCENT: What a melody—my God, what a melody!

He goes to the piano and begins to play "I'll See You Again," softly as a fox-trot. The rest of the band join in and then the ORCHESTRA. *Everyone gets up "hey-heying" and Charlestoning and finally, led by* DOLLY, *they all go jazzing out through the double doors, followed by* VINCENT *and the members of the dance band.* LADY SHAYNE *is left alone, standing quite still. Suddenly she begins to laugh, a strange, cracked, contemptuous laugh; she rises to her feet, and then, suddenly holding out her arms wide, she sings:*

SARI: Though my world has gone awry,
Though the end is drawing nigh,
I shall love you till I die,
Good-bye!

THE CURTAIN FALLS

THE MARQUISE

First produced at the Criterion Theatre, London, on 16 February 1927 with the following cast:

THE MARQUISE ELOISE DE KESTOURNEL	Marie Tempest
ALICE, *her maid*	Lilian Cavanagh
THE COMPTE RAOUL DE VRIAAC	W. Graham Browne
ADRIENNE, *his daughter*	Eileen Sharp
JACQUES RIJAR, *his secretary*	Robert Harris
FATHER CLEMENT	Colin Johnston
ESTEBAN EL DUCO DE SANTAGUANO	Frank Cellier
MIGUEL, *his son*	Godfrey Winn
HUBERT, *servant in the Château de Vriaac*	Rupert Lister

Directed by W. Graham Browne
Designed by William Nicholson

The action of the play passes in the main living-room of the Château de Vriaac, a few hours from Paris.

ACT I

Evening.

ACT II

The following morning.

ACT III

The same evening.

The period is eighteenth century, and the time autumn.

ACT I

The scene is the main living-room of the Château de Vriaac, a few hours away from Paris. It is about ten o'clock on a September evening in the year 1735. The room is almost completely round, being at the base of a tower. On the left-hand side are two windows opening on to a terrace, over which little can be seen save sky and the tops of trees. Towards the centre above the windows are double doors opening into a large stone hall, and then the main door of the château. Immediately next to these is a wide shallow staircase which disappears in the symmetry of the room. A little way beyond the stairs is a small door leading to the library, and below this, on the right, a large open fire-place with, hanging above it, a full-length portrait of the late Comptesse de Vriaac in black and looking very depressed. A scarlet velvet curtain half conceals the staircase; there are also scarlet velvet curtains at the windows, but to-night, owing to the brilliance of the moon, they are drawn back. The furniture is old and rather ponderous; there has been no innovation of those spindly Parisian pieces which have lately become the rage, the only concession to modernity being a gaily painted spinet upon which ADRIENNE *is encouraged to practise unaffected little "Bergerettes".*

When the curtain rises, supper is almost over, and round the table in the centre are seated on the right, profile to the audience, RAOUL, *and on his right* MIGUEL. *Facing* RAOUL *is seated* ESTEBAN *with, on his right,* ADRIENNE,

with her back to the audience. Next to her is JACQUES, *and next to* MIGUEL, FATHER CLEMENT.
HUBERT *has just served the coffee, and he goes out. There is an air of solemnity hanging over the party which* ESTEBAN *has been doing his utmost to alleviate with light conversation and mild anecdotes.* RAOUL *rises with a glass of wine in his hand.*

RAOUL (*with slight pomposity*): This is a very auspicious occasion.

ESTEBAN (*heartily*): Splendid, Raoul! I entirely agree with you!

RAOUL (*frowning faintly*): I wish to propose a toast.

ESTEBAN: Adrienne, your father has certainly changed these last years. I notice it especially at meal-times.

RAOUL: What do you mean by that?

ESTEBAN: Nothing—please go on.

RAOUL: Miguel.

MIGUEL: Yes, sir.

RAOUL: I am giving my daughter into your keeping.

At this ADRIENNE *looks down demurely and* JACQUES *furtively presses her hand.*

MIGUEL (*politely*): Thank you, sir.

ESTEBAN (*with a sudden laugh*): Good.

RAOUL (*irritably*): Really, Esteban——!

ESTEBAN: I'm sorry.

RAOUL: You are both young and on the threshold of life—and your mutual happiness can only be assured by clarity of purpose and humility of spirit.

ESTEBAN: I agree with the first, anyhow.

RAOUL (*crossly*): I drink to you both. (*He sits down abruptly*): I have nothing more to say.

ADRIENNE: Don't be cross, Father.

RAOUL: I am not cross—a little hurt, perhaps. I resent that the sincerity of my affection for you both should be laughed at.

ESTEBAN: No one was questioning your sincerity, Raoul.

RAOUL: If I may say so, Esteban, you have been facetious and annoying the whole evening.

ESTEBAN: You misjudge my mild efforts to enjoy myself.

RAOUL: This *is* a serious moment, is it not?

ADRIENNE (*with feeling*): Oh, yes, indeed, it is.

RAOUL: Well then?

ESTEBAN: I merely felt, Raoul, that as such it would be a pity to overweight it with serious behaviour.

RAOUL: I don't understand.

ESTEBAN: A few years ago you would have. (*Looking at* FATHER CLEMENT.) But as I said before, you've changed.

RAOUL: We all change as we grow older.

ESTEBAN: Very well, that shall excuse you.

MIGUEL (*rising*): Anyhow, sir, I wish to thank you for your toast—you may rest assured that I will guard and protect Adrienne to the best of my ability—always. (*He sits down.*)

ESTEBAN: Very nicely put, Miguel. I feel that it now devolves upon me to murmur something appropriate.

RAOUL (*irritably*): Esteban——

ESTEBAN (*politely, with a smile*): Yes, Raoul?

RAOUL: Nothing.

ESTEBAN (*rising*): Children, my very dear children, if I were a magician the gift I would bestow upon you would be Lightness of Touch. But being just an ordinary man, I can only whisper to you a little advice—

enjoy yourselves as much as possible, it will pass the time pleasantly and lead you into old age with a few gay memories to cheer you—and don't ask any more than that.

JACQUES: Splendid—and so easy! (*He rises abruptly and goes out of the room.*)

ADRIENNE (*before she can stop herself*): Jacques——!

RAOUL: Is he ill?

ADRIENNE: Yes—no—I don't know.

RAOUL: I apologise, Esteban.

ESTEBAN (*charmingly*): Please—such an estimable secretary can afford to be a little eccentric—where was I?

MIGUEL: "Don't ask any more than that".

ESTEBAN: Any more than what? I've forgotten.

MIGUEL: Memories—nice memories when we're very, very old.

ESTEBAN: Oh, yes, yes, of course—that's the thing—do try and remember it, won't you?

MIGUEL (*laughing*): Yes, Father.

ADRIENNE: Thank you.

ESTEBAN: I think that is really all I have to say.

RAOUL: Poor advice, Esteban—very poor advice.

ESTEBAN: On the contrary—sound sense.

RAOUL: Immoral into the bargain.

ESTEBAN: Nonsense.

RAOUL: I am ashamed of you.

ESTEBAN: You have no right to be.

RAOUL: I am not surprised that Monsieur Rijar left the room. He was probably shocked.

ESTEBAN: Moonstruck—like as not.

ADRIENNE: Father.

RAOUL: Yes, Adrienne?

ADRIENNE: May I go out on to the terrace for a

little—it's very hot in here—if Miguel would escort me?

RAOUL: By all means—Father Clement?

FATHER CLEMENT *rises sullenly and confers an inaudible blessing, at the end of which* ADRIENNE *and* MIGUEL rise.

MIGUEL: Have you a wrap?

ADRIENNE: Yes, a shawl—on that chair.

MIGUEL (*placing it round her shoulders*): Come then. (*Softly as they go out*) Cheer up. (*They go out on to the terrace.*)

FATHER CLEMENT: I will bid you both good-night.

ESTEBAN (*cheerfully*): Good-night.

FATHER CLEMENT (*putting his hand on* RAOUL'S *shoulder*): My son!

RAOUL: Good-night, Father Clement.

FATHER CLEMENT *goes out sadly.*

ESTEBAN: The presence of Father Clement invariably constrains me to drink too much.

RAOUL: Obviously.

ESTEBAN (*laughing*): You're growing old so beautifully.

RAOUL: You never will—you're a shallow man, Esteban. I always suspected it.

ESTEBAN (*agreeably*): A babbling brook.

RAOUL: Exactly.

ESTEBAN: You used to babble too once upon a time—so prettily.

RAOUL (*rising, irritably*): I have done many foolish things.

ESTEBAN (*appealingly*): Raoul?

RAOUL: What is it?

ESTEBAN: Nothing. I should like some more wine.

RAOUL: Here. (*He passes the wine to him.*)

ESTEBAN: Thank you. Will you drink with me?

RAOUL: No—no more for me.

ESTEBAN: Then *I* won't.

RAOUL: Very well then.

ESTEBAN *fills both glasses.*

ESTEBAN (*holding up his glass*): Seviglia, 1712.

RAOUL: Why?

ESTEBAN: I love remembering.

RAOUL: Have it your own way. (*He raises his glass.*) Seviglia, 1712.

ESTEBAN: Madrilena!

RAOUL (*putting down his glass with a bang*): Really, Esteban.

ESTEBAN: She loved you more than me.

RAOUL: Be quiet.

ESTEBAN (*dreamily*): A lovely face but bad legs.

RAOUL: Her legs were admirable.

ESTEBAN: Ha ha!

RAOUL: Why are you behaving like this?

ESTEBAN: Because there is a harvest moon—and youth is so near us.

RAOUL: You're mistaken—youth is far away.

ESTEBAN: It need not be.

RAOUL: Autumn is a melancholy season.

ESTEBAN: It need not be.

RAOUL: You refuse to face unpleasant truths, Esteban.

ESTEBAN: What, for instance?

RAOUL: Life is nearly over for us both.

ESTEBAN: It need not be.

RAOUL (*irritably*): Do stop saying "it need not be".

ESTEBAN: Come to Paris with me for a little.

RAOUL: I hate Paris—it is so noisy.

ESTEBAN: Do you remember the Masked Ball at Madame de Flomard's?

RAOUL: Yes.

ESTEBAN: How abominably you behaved!

RAOUL: No worse than you.

ESTEBAN: I can see you now sailing your shoes in the fountain at the end of the garden.

RAOUL: Why do you try so hard to disturb me?

ESTEBAN: Do memories of the past disturb you?

RAOUL: Very much.

ESTEBAN: How strange. They amuse me.

RAOUL: I regret so many things.

ESTEBAN: I, nothing.

RAOUL: If my wife had lived, perhaps you would not find me such a depressing companion.

ESTEBAN: I doubt it—it is she who is responsible for this dreary change in you, and she left behind her Father Clement to carry on the good work.

RAOUL: Father Clement is here at my own request.

ESTEBAN: My poor friend, you have been bored into religion.

RAOUL: What do you mean?

ESTEBAN: Your wife began it; she bored you.

RAOUL (*outraged*): Esteban!

ESTEBAN: To distraction—now Father Clement bores you—until gradually everything in life is beginning to bore you—you indulge yourself in a good deal of rather smug hypocrisy in order to hide the truth from yourself. You're a miserable man, Raoul. Have some more wine. (*He brandishes the bottle gaily.*)

RAOUL (*loudly*): No!

ESTEBAN: Shh!—not so loud. Father Clement will come down and scold you.

RAOUL: How dare you talk to me like this!

ESTEBAN: It has been brewing up in my mind for ages.

RAOUL: No friendship, however great, could warrant the things you've said.

ESTEBAN: Nonsense. (*He drinks.*) To your re-degeneration, Raoul!

RAOUL (*rising and wandering about the room*): You're a man of deplorably loose character.

ESTEBAN: Yes.

RAOUL: You have a Pagan soul.

ESTEBAN: You helped to mould it.

RAOUL: I—in what way?

ESTEBAN: All through our youth—you led the way to folly with the greatest determination. Take, for example, that little episode at the opera in Madrid.

RAOUL: Stop! Stop!

ESTEBAN: It was you who were arrested—and rightly.

RAOUL: Stop, I tell you—enough!

ESTEBAN: Fate will have the laugh of you yet—I know it.

RAOUL: Well, until that time comes I should be grateful if you would hold your peace.

ESTEBAN: Why don't you marry again?

RAOUL: I don't wish to.

ESTEBAN: Why not take a mistress?

RAOUL: Esteban!

ESTEBAN: Now that Adrienne is betrothed you will be very lonely.

RAOUL: I shall have Father Clement.

ESTEBAN: He's so unattractive.

RAOUL: He is a good and worthy friend.

ESTEBAN: Scheming old money-grubber.

RAOUL: Once and for all, will you be quiet?

ESTEBAN (*counting on his fingers*): Juliette, Madrilena, Suzanne Montieux, Therese, Marthe du Cros, Felice—where are they all now, I wonder.

RAOUL: I don't care.

ESTEBAN: How callous, when you loved them all so much.

RAOUL: Love—that wasn't love.

ESTEBAN: Have you never loved them?

RAOUL: No—yes—no.

ESTEBAN (*ruminatively*): No—yes—no—he has loved—he hasn't loved—how perplexing.

RAOUL (*bitterly*): I loved once—once only, and I shall never love again. Now are you satisfied?

ESTEBAN: No. Merely curious.

RAOUL: That's all you shall know of it.

ESTEBAN: Why did you never tell me?

RAOUL: We parted in Spain in 1713, my friend, and I never saw you again until you came here ten years ago.

ESTEBAN: We met at Court.

RAOUL: Casually.

ESTEBAN: That was your fault—you were haughty and unforgiving.

RAOUL: For heaven's sake, let the past die!

ESTEBAN: And during that twelve years—while our friendship was laid aside, then, Raoul, you met your fate?

RAOUL: No more.

ESTEBAN: What happened to her?

RAOUL: No more, I tell you.

ESTEBAN (*smiling*): My poor friend——

MIGUEL *and* ADRIENNE *enter from the terrace.*

ADRIENNE: It grows chilly out there after a while.

ESTEBAN: It was fortunate that you came in—your father and I have been quarrelling.

ADRIENNE: Quarrelling?

RAOUL: Nothing of the sort.

ESTEBAN: A few minutes later and you would have heard a clash of swords.

ADRIENNE: Father!

RAOUL: He is joking, Adrienne.

MIGUEL: I apologise for my father, sir, if he has annoyed you.

ESTEBAN (*making a dive at him*): Impudent young pup!

RAOUL (*placing a fatherly hand on* ADRIENNE'S *head*): Adrienne, I wish so deeply that your dear mother were alive to-night.

ADRIENNE (*looking down*): Yes, Father.

ESTEBAN: Come into the library, Raoul.

RAOUL (*ignoring him*): She would have been so happy in your happiness.

ESTEBAN (*plaintively*): *Do* come into the library—you're becoming pompous again.

RAOUL (*angrily*): Esteban.

ADRIENNE (*kissing him gently*): Dear Father.

RAOUL (*disentangling himself*): You must go home soon, Esteban.

ESTEBAN: I wish to talk to you first.

RAOUL (*suspiciously*): What about?

ESTEBAN: A subject that by rights should have been occupying our thoughts for some time past—our children's future.

RAOUL: Very well.

ESTEBAN: If you hadn't been so eager to discuss your past misdemeanours——

RAOUL: You must go home *very* soon, Esteban.

They both go off into the library.

ADRIENNE: Oh, Miguel. (*She sinks into a chair.*)

MIGUEL: What is it?

ADRIENNE: I feel very strange.

MIGUEL: Quite naturally.

ADRIENNE: I hope I haven't caught cold—out there on the terrace.

MIGUEL: You should have let me hold you in my arms.

ADRIENNE (*wearily*): Oh, don't be so silly.

MIGUEL: My beloved.

ADRIENNE: It's no use going on like that.

MIGUEL: We're betrothed, dear heart.

ADRIENNE: Dear heart—how ridiculous—dear heart.

MIGUEL: You're not making things very easy for me.

ADRIENNE: I'm sorry.

MIGUEL: I love you.

ADRIENNE: No you don't.

MIGUEL: Don't contradict me. Of course I do.

ADRIENNE: You will persist in this absurd pretence.

MIGUEL: Adrienne.

ADRIENNE: Yes?

MIGUEL: What is the matter with you?

ADRIENNE: You know perfectly well.

MIGUEL: No, I don't.

ADRIENNE: You say you love me.

MIGUEL: Certainly I do.

ADRIENNE: With passion—burning, thrilling passion?

MIGUEL: Adrienne—please.

ADRIENNE: Answer me.

MIGUEL (*sullenly*): Yes, with burning, thrilling passion.

ADRIENNE: I wish I had a mirror.

MIGUEL: Why?

ADRIENNE: To show you your face when you say that.

MIGUEL: How can you expect me to be passionate when you are so cold?

ADRIENNE: It isn't that.

MIGUEL: You repulse every effort I make.

ADRIENNE: Passion should be effortless.

MIGUEL: Oh, you're hopeless.

ADRIENNE (*wistfully*): Yes, I am—utterly. (*She bursts into tears.*)

MIGUEL: Adrienne, my dear.

ADRIENNE: Leave me alone.

MIGUEL: Don't be unhappy—please don't be unhappy—there's no need.

ADRIENNE: There is—you don't know.

MIGUEL: Don't let either of our fathers find you weeping—to-night of all nights.

ADRIENNE: I can't help it.

MIGUEL (*offering her a handkerchief*): Here, please try.

ADRIENNE: Tell me the truth, Miguel—you don't love me really, do you?

MIGUEL: Yes, I do.

ADRIENNE: With affection, yes—with sweetness and understanding—that I need so badly, but—but——

MIGUEL: But what?

ADRIENNE: Not the other way—please, not the other way.

MIGUEL: That will come—in time.

ADRIENNE: I don't want it to.

MIGUEL: You love someone else?

ADRIENNE: Yes.

MIGUEL: Why didn't you tell me?

ADRIENNE: I didn't dare—it's all so wretched.

MIGUEL: Who?

ADRIENNE: You know—you must know.

MIGUEL: Jacques Rijar?

ADRIENNE: Yes.

MIGUEL: Well, there's nothing to cry about. Does he love you?

ADRIENNE: Yes.

MIGUEL: We must talk it all over. Do stop crying.

ADRIENNE: I'll try.

MIGUEL: You haven't let him be your lover, have you?

ADRIENNE: No—oh, no.

MIGUEL: Your father would never hear of your marrying him.

ADRIENNE: Of course not.

MIGUEL: No money?

ADRIENNE: None—except what he earns by being a secretary.

MIGUEL: Good family?

ADRIENNE: Yes, but poor—terribly poor. Father's set his heart on my marrying you, and your father has, too—if I refuse I shall be sent to a convent or something dreadful. (*She weeps again.*)

MIGUEL (*wisely*): Some convents are very accommodating, you know—an aunt of mine had heaps of lovers when *she* was in a convent.

ADRIENNE: They'd never send me to one like that.

MIGUEL: No, perhaps not. Anyhow, the risk is too great.

ADRIENNE: If you don't love me properly, it makes things much easier.

MIGUEL: I'll confess something to you.

ADRIENNE: What?

MIGUEL: I'm in love, too.

ADRIENNE: Miguel!

MIGUEL: She's a dancer—in Paris.

ADRIENNE: Oh, Miguel—dear, dear Miguel.

MIGUEL: I thought I should have to say good-bye to her for ever.

ADRIENNE: Oh, no—never—whatever happens you must go on loving her always. We must think of a plan.

MIGUEL: Our marriage could be one of convenience only. And then we could go on loving whom we liked?

ADRIENNE: I wouldn't care for that really.

MIGUEL: No, I don't suppose I should either. We must both think hard.

ADRIENNE: Don't say a word to anyone, will you?

MIGUEL: Not a word.

ADRIENNE: Oh, my dear, you'll never, never know how grateful I am to you.

MIGUEL (*putting his finger to his lips*): Shh!

ADRIENNE: There's lots of time after all, isn't there?

MIGUEL: Yes.

ADRIENNE: Come over to-morrow.

MIGUEL: Of course.

Enter JACQUES RIJAR. *He looks from one to the other and then turns to go out again.*

Monsieur Rijar.

JACQUES (*turning*): Sir?

MIGUEL: Will you do me the favour of keeping Mademoiselle company for a few moments. I dropped my snuff-box on the terrace.

JACQUES: I shall be charmed.

MIGUEL: A thousand thanks. (*He bowes, kisses his*

hand lightly to ADRIENNE *and goes out, closing the window behind him.*)

ADRIENNE (*going to him*): Jacques.

JACQUES: Dear heart.

ADRIENNE (*kissing him on the mouth*): I love you.

JACQUES (*with a quick look towards the terrace*): Shhh!

ADRIENNE: He knows.

JACQUES (*astounded*): *He knows?*

ADRIENNE: Yes, I told him.

JACQUES: Adrienne!

ADRIENNE: I told him everything, and he told me everything. He loves someone else, too.

JACQUES: It's not possible.

ADRIENNE: He has been so sweet and understanding.

JACQUES (*falling at her feet*): Oh, my dear love—my dear love.

ADRIENNE: Jacques, someone will hear.

JACQUES (*rising and crushing her in his arms*): I love you so.

ADRIENNE: And I you.

JACQUES: Dear heart.

ADRIENNE: Say that again, dear heart. How sweet it sounds.

JACQUES: Dear heart.

ADRIENNE: All is not lost yet. You see, you need not have been so sad. I should really scold you for the way you behaved at supper.

JACQUES: I couldn't bear it—any of it.

ADRIENNE: You must go now.

JACQUES: Why?

ADRIENNE: Father is in the library with the Duke—they may come out——

JACQUES: Kiss me.

ADRIENNE: Once only.

JACQUES (*kissing her wildly*): Once, twice, thrice——

ADRIENNE (*surrendering herself*): Jacques—Jacques!

ESTEBAN *and* RAOUL *re-enter.* ADRIENNE *and* JACQUES *have just time to break away.*

RAOUL: Where is Miguel?

ADRIENNE: On the terrace, Father.

ESTEBAN: By himself?

ADRIENNE: Yes.

RAOUL: How very odd.

ADRIENNE: He dropped his snuff-box.

ESTEBAN: Oh, I see. I'll call him. (*He goes to the window and calls*) Miguel! Miguel!

MIGUEL (*off*): Coming, Father.

ESTEBAN: Adrienne, my child, I bid you an affectionate good night.

ADRIENNE (*curtseying*): Good-night.

MIGUEL *re-enters.*

ESTEBAN (*kissing her*): Sleep well and dream happily.

ADRIENNE: I'll try.

MIGUEL: Good-night, sweetheart. (*He kisses her.*)

ADRIENNE: Good-night, dear Miguel.

ESTEBAN: It has been a delightful evening, Raoul.

RAOUL: I will see you to the door.

ESTEBAN: There is no need really. Good-night.

RAOUL: Good-night.

ESTEBAN: On second thought, I take that back. I hope your night is stormy and alive with mocking ghosts of the past.

RAOUL (*austerely*): You have done your best to make it so.

ESTEBAN: So good for you.

MIGUEL: Come, Father.

ESTEBAN: Very well—until to-morrow, Raoul. I'm almost certain to ride over to-morrow.

RAOUL (*dryly*): How delightful!

ESTEBAN *and* MIGUEL *go out.*

ADRIENNE: You look perturbed, Father.

RAOUL: His sins will find him out.

ADRIENNE: I don't think he will mind if they do.

RAOUL: That remark sounds unseemly in a child of your age.

ADRIENNE (*going to window*): What a lovely night.

JACQUES (*joinimg her*): See the pattern the trees make with the moon shining through them.

RAOUL: It is time you were in bed, Adrienne.

ADRIENNE (*looking at* JACQUES): I feel so happy.

JACQUES: Look, there are lights on the high road.

ADRIENNE: Where?

JACQUES: There—just before the bridge.

ADRIENNE: It must be a coach.

RAOUL (*joining them*): It's too late for the Diligence.

JACQUES: They're not moving.

RAOUL: Gypsies perhaps—in a caravan. To bed, Adrienne.

ADRIENNE: Very well. (*To* JACQUES.) Good-night, Monsieur.

JACQUES (*kissing her hand*): Mademoiselle, I wish you every happiness with the man you love.

ADRIENNE: Happiness is certain as long as he continues to love me. Thank you, Father. (*She suddenly flings her arms round his neck.*)

RAOUL: Good-night, dear.

ADRIENNE (*passionately*): You'll never be very, very angry with me, will you?

RAOUL: Angry with you? I don't understand.

ADRIENNE: Whatever happens?

RAOUL: You're over-excited and tired.

ADRIENNE: Yes, yes, I am very tired—good-night. (*She curtseys and goes off upstairs.*)

RAOUL: Why did you behave so strangely at supper, my boy?

JACQUES (*looking after* ADRIENNE): Did I behave strangely?

RAOUL: You left the table abruptly while Monsieur le Duc was speaking.

JACQUES: I felt ill.

RAOUL: I'm sorry. What is wrong?

JACQUES: My head ached—my heart ached too.

RAOUL: How very peculiar—indigestion?

JACQUES: Perhaps.

RAOUL: I have some powders upstairs.

JACQUES: Please don't trouble, sir. I feel better now.

RAOUL: Wind, doubtless.

JACQUES (*dreamily*): The wind in the trees——

RAOUL: I beg your pardon.

JACQUES (*exultantly*): He's right, sir—he's right.

RAOUL: Who's right—what do you mean?

JACQUES: Monsieur le Duc—he advocates love, happiness, brightness of touch—in God's name, sir, stop blundering.

RAOUL: Blundering—are you mad?

JACQUES: I apologise—there's something strange in the air to-night.

RAOUL: What do you mean?

JACQUES: Nothing, sir—nothing.

RAOUL: Blundering—how dare you accuse me of blundering!

JACQUES: It slipped out, sir.

RAOUL: Please explain yourself.

JACQUES: I suddenly lost consciousness of all the things I should remember—my position in this house, my youth as opposed to your age, my respect for you as an employer. I said you were blundering because you're afraid.

RAOUL: Afraid?

JACQUES: Afraid of youth—afraid of life—afraid of suffering—afraid of happiness—but I'm not—I'm young—and there's a harvest moon. I want to shout and sing and dance. You wouldn't care to dance with me, would you?

RAOUL (*sternly*): Go to bed, sir, immediately.

JACQUES: I shall hang out of my window and listen to the nightingale.

RAOUL: There are no nightingales at this time of year.

JACQUES: Then I shall listen to the owls.

RAOUL: Have you taken leave of your senses?

JACQUES: Yes, thank God, before it's too late.

RAOUL: I shall talk to you in the morning.

JACQUES: I shall be a poet in the morning.

JACQUES *rushes upstairs laughing, leaving* RAOUL *staring after him in amazement. Then with an irritable shrug of his shoulders, he blows out four candles which are standing on the spinet, and he is on the way to extinguish those which are on the table when he halts abruptly before his wife's portrait. As he is standing there gazing up at it pensively there comes a sharp tap at the window behind him. He is so lost in thought that he doesn't hear it. Then, after a brief pause, there comes a second louder tap. He turns sharply, and starts violently on observing a figure on the terrace. He goes over to the window and opens it, whereupon* ELOISE *steps into the room. She is exquisitely dressed for travelling, her face bears traces of great beauty, and her eyes are glinting as youthfully as ever they did.* RAOUL *stands still, staring at her foolishly.*

ELOISE (*crossing to the fire*): Do close the window, dear. It's cold.

RAOUL (*incredulously*): Eloise!

ELOISE: My dear. (*She turns from warming her hands.*) Do close the window.

RAOUL (*closing it mechanically*): Where have you come from?

ELOISE: What does that matter?

RAOUL: I thought you were dead.

ELOISE: I should never have died without writing to you.

RAOUL (*still dazed with surprise*): Eloise!

ELOISE: Yes.

RAOUL: Eloise!

ELOISE: Yes, dear, Eloise.

RAOUL: After all these years.

ELOISE: Have they seemed so long?

RAOUL: It's incredible.

ELOISE: The way you've managed to retain your looks, Raoul, is nothing short of magnificent.

RAOUL: Where have you been?

ELOISE: When?

RAOUL: Since you went away.

ELOISE: Everywhere. I think I should like a little wine.

RAOUL: I'm so sorry. (*He pours her out a glass of wine.*)

ELOISE: Thank you. It was damp coming up through the woods. You ought to have those stones painted white where the paths cross. I nearly fell flat on my face.

RAOUL: Is that your coach on the high road?

ELOISE: Yes. I left it there because I wished to surprise you.

RAOUL: You've succeeded.

ELOISE: I'm so glad. (*There is a slight pause while she glances round the room.*) It all looks the same as ever. (*Her eyes arrive at the portrait of Madame la Comptesse.*) Who's that?

RAOUL (*stiffly*): My wife.

ELOISE: Poor dear; she looks wretched.

RAOUL: She's dead.

ELOISE: Perhaps that's why.

RAOUL (*frowning*): Eloise!

ELOISE: The spinet is new.

RAOUL: Yes.

ELOISE: And the curtains—I like the curtains.

RAOUL: I'm glad.

ELOISE: Where's my child?

RAOUL: How dare you come back like this?

ELOISE: Like what?

RAOUL: Suddenly—without warning.

ELOISE: I told you—it was a surprise.

RAOUL (*turning away*): It's—it's—infamous.

ELOISE: Don't be silly.

RAOUL (*almost wildly*): Silly!

ELOISE: Yes, silly—you're behaving like an idiot.

RAOUL: I can't believe it possible.

ELOISE: That's quite natural.

RAOUL: You have the effrontery——

ELOISE: Where is my child?

RAOUL: Why should you care?

ELOISE: You've deteriorated, Raoul.

RAOUL: What do you mean by that?

ELOISE: You always used to be so beautifully poised. I admit you had the temper of a fiend, but your self-control was admirable. You seem to have lost it.

RAOUL: I'm outraged by your presence here.

ELOISE: Never mind.

RAOUL: I do mind. I mind more than I've ever minded anything before. Will you please go.

ELOISE: Certainly not.

RAOUL: I insist.

ELOISE: Quite useless. Where's my child?

RAOUL: Your child is dead.

ELOISE (*with sudden violence*): Dead! What do you mean? It's not true!

RAOUL: I mean she is dead as far as you are concerned!

ELOISE (*relieved*): Oh, I see. (*With fury.*) How dare you frighten me like that.

RAOUL: You renounced all claims on her.

ELOISE: Never. I renounced all claims on you.

RAOUL: That's the same thing.

ELOISE: Oh, no, it isn't.

RAOUL: She's mine.

ELOISE: And mine.

RAOUL: She has been brought up as belonging to my wife—and I don't intend her to know the truth ever.

ELOISE: And what if I tell her?

RAOUL: You wouldn't dare.

ELOISE: She's well and happy?

RAOUL (*defiantly*): Yes.

ELOISE: Splendid. (*She sits down.*)

RAOUL: What is the object of this—this surprise?

ELOISE: Don't you know?

RAOUL: I'm waiting to be enlightened.

ELOISE: I've come back to you, dear.

RAOUL: So I see.

ELOISE: For good.

RAOUL: What!

ELOISE: Aren't you going to kiss me?

RAOUL: No.

ELOISE: Very well. There's lots of time. I'm only forty-two.

RAOUL: I don't wish you to come back to me.

ELOISE: How inhospitable.

RAOUL: Go away.

ELOISE: I will not.

RAOUL: I'm completely unaware of your existence.

ELOISE: That's ridiculous with me sitting plump in front of you.

RAOUL: You should be ashamed.

ELOISE: I am—bitterly ashamed—of you.

RAOUL: I can't help that.

ELOISE: Yes, you can. You're behaving disgracefully. You haven't even offered me anything to eat.

RAOUL: I didn't know you were hungry.

ELOISE: I'm not.

RAOUL: Would you like a little fruit to take away with you?

ELOISE: I've told you several times I am not going away.

RAOUL: Your coming here at all was in the worst possible taste.

ELOISE (*delving in her bag*): Wait a moment. Ah! (*She finds what she was looking for.*) Do you remember this? (*She brandishes a letter in his face.*)

RAOUL: What is it?

ELOISE: I'll read it to you.

RAOUL: I don't wish to hear it.

ELOISE: That doesn't matter; you're going to.

RAOUL: Eloise, once and for all——

ELOISE (*reading*): "Beloved—oh, my beloved"—bla bla bla bla—wait here—"If ever in life you are in trouble—if ever in life you are weary and alone—come back to me—I shall always, always be waiting—you have broken my heart, but—bla bla bla—I love you—now and for ever. Raoul." There!

RAOUL: *Are* you in trouble?

ELOISE: No.

RAOUL: Weary and alone?

ELOISE: Yes.

RAOUL: Nonsense.

ELOISE: Can't you see how weary and alone I am?

RAOUL: No, I can't.

ELOISE: Well then, old age has obviously dulled your perceptions.

RAOUL: You've never been alone before.

ELOISE: That's beside the point.

RAOUL: I refuse to wrangle with you any further.

ELOISE: I don't want you to wrangle with me. I want you to be loving and chivalrous and sweet.

RAOUL (*sinking into a chair and burying his face in his hands*): Oh, my God!

ELOISE (*softly*): Raoul.

RAOUL: Go away, please.

ELOISE (*rising and approaching him*): Raoul.

RAOUL: What is it?

ELOISE: Aren't you pleased to see me again—at all?

RAOUL (*his face still hidden*): I don't know what to do.

ELOISE: Look at me.

RAOUL: No.

ELOISE: Please. (*She lifts his head up.*) Have I changed so very much?

RAOUL: You left me—when I needed you—I'll never forgive you.

ELOISE: You had already forgiven me when you wrote that letter.

RAOUL: That letter was a moment of insanity.

ELOISE: You wrote it because you loved me.

RAOUL: Why did you leave me—knowing that?

ELOISE: I'll tell you—one day.

RAOUL: You were tired of me.

ELOISE: No.

RAOUL: Now I'm tired of you. I've been tired of you for years—tired of the memory of you.

ELOISE (*smiling*): Dear Raoul—I'm so glad my memory worried you.

RAOUL: You've come back too late.

ELOISE: Why?

RAOUL: I am a very different man from the one you knew.

ELOISE: Not so very different.

RAOUL: I am, I tell you.

ELOISE: Very well, very well, don't jump at me.

RAOUL: I am absolutely contented—my life is peaceful and happy—I don't wish to be disturbed.

ELOISE: My dear. I wouldn't disturb you—much.

RAOUL: You'd disturb a saint.

ELOISE: That can only be proved when I meet one.

RAOUL: Won't you listen to reason?

ELOISE: By all means.

RAOUL: The past is dead.

ELOISE: I'm not concerned with the past, but with the future.

RAOUL: Your own future?

ELOISE: Certainly.

RAOUL: What have I to do with that?

ELOISE: I have reached an age when I desire to be cherished.

RAOUL: Why should I cherish you?

ELOISE (*meekly*): I thought you might like to.

RAOUL: You were wrong.

ELOISE: There is no need to be so vehement.

RAOUL: If I loved you still it would be different.

ELOISE: But you don't?

RAOUL: No.

ELOISE: Are you sure?

RAOUL: Quite sure.

ELOISE (*fumbling for her handkerchief*): How sad life is.

RAOUL: Don't cry.

ELOISE (*crying*): I'm not really crying—it's the shock of seeing you again.

RAOUL: You don't love me any more?

ELOISE: Yes, I do.

RAOUL: Eloise!

ELOISE: Madly.

RAOUL: What!

ELOISE: Violently—that's why I came back.

RAOUL: You're lying.

ELOISE: How distrustful you've grown!

RAOUL (*bitterly*): With every reason.

ELOISE: Why? Did your wife desert you, too?

RAOUL: No, but she changed me.

ELOISE: Oh, she did, did she?

RAOUL: She was a good woman.

ELOISE: Thank you.

RAOUL: Why do you say thank you?

ELOISE: For the charming implication in your tone.

RAOUL: I didn't mean that.

ELOISE: Yes you did. She certainly changed you—you were never ungallant before.

RAOUL: I was immoral and loose-living—a miserable sinner.

ELOISE: And I your partner?

RAOUL (*after a pause*): If you will have it, yes.

ELOISE: Again I thank you.

RAOUL: I'm sorry.

ELOISE: Did you tell her about me?

RAOUL: No—I never told anyone.

ELOISE: How did you explain Adrienne?

RAOUL: I merely said she was my daughter by someone who had died.

ELOISE: And that satisfied her?

RAOUL: Yes.

ELOISE: Did you love her?

RAOUL: Yes.

ELOISE: Passionately?

RAOUL (*defiantly*): Yes!

ELOISE (*looking at the picture*): Oh, Raoul—you *couldn't* have! (*She laughs.*)

RAOUL: How dare you laugh.

ELOISE: I can't help it.

RAOUL: Have you no decency?

ELOISE (*still looking at the picture and laughing louder*): Not passionately—dutifully, yes—but never passionately. Oh, no—— Oh dear, no——

RAOUL: Stop—stop—you wicked woman.

ELOISE (*laughing helplessly*): I can't—I can't——

RAOUL (*furious*): I command you to stop.

ELOISE: Oh, Raoul—Raoul—my poor Raoul.

RAOUL: Get out of my sight.

ELOISE: Never—it would be inhuman to leave you again.

RAOUL: I don't want you—you're vile——

ELOISE: Shhh!—please—you mustn't shout like that.

RAOUL (*beside himself*): Get out—get out—get out! ! !

ELOISE (*suddenly going close to him*): You fool.

RAOUL: I don't care what you say.

ELOISE: It's me you love—you always have.

RAOUL: No, I tell you. No.

ELOISE: Be careful.

RAOUL: Why should I be careful!

ELOISE (*growing angry at last*): I might take you at your word.

RAOUL: I never wish to see you again.

ELOISE: You were always insanely stubborn.

RAOUL: I cast you out of my mind years ago.

ELOISE: Liar.

RAOUL: It's true—my wife died and left me a heritage——

ELOISE (*contemptuously*): Heritage.

RAOUL: Yes—I'm not afraid to say it—she showed me the error of my ways—I've already told you—I am no longer the man you once knew. She bequeathed me Faith and Peace and Nobility of purpose.

ELOISE: Did she take the heart out of you, too?

RAOUL: She made me realise the truth.

ELOISE: What truth?

RAOUL: That the renunciation of all light living and shallow pleasure was the only way in which to atone for my sins in the past.

ELOISE: And you relegated me among the sins of the past?

RAOUL: Yes.

ELOISE: You see no noble qualities in me anywhere—because I gave myself to you and loved you and bore you a daughter.

RAOUL: Our union was unblessed by the Church!

ELOISE: And whose fault was that?

She walks straight out through the windows into the night. RAOUL *gazes after her, stupefied, then he follows her as far as the windows and calls.*

RAOUL (*calling*): Eloise!—Eloise——

He goes out on to the terrace and after a moment returns. He closes the windows and proceeds to stride about the room, muttering furiously to himself, then with sudden determination he unlocks a cabinet in the corner, from which he takes a small tin box. He bangs it down on the table regardless of broken glass and noise, wrenches it open, and from it takes a bundle of letters tied up with faded ribbon. He flings the entire package into the fire.

At last—at last I have the courage! (*He takes from the box a fan, a small gold locket on a chain, a snuff-box and a miniature and hurls them viciously one by one after the letters.*) How dare she!—How dare she! (*Finally he takes from the box a gaily coloured garter; he regards it tremblingly for a moment.*) Ridiculous—obscene—to be forgotten utterly. (*He flings it after the rest and stands defiantly staring up at his wife's picture.*) There—no more—nothing left! Are you satisfied? There's nothing left!

ADRIENNE *enters hurriedly downstairs in her night-gown and a wrapper.*

ADRIENNE (*alarmed*): Father—what's happening—is anything the matter?

RAOUL: Go back to bed.

ADRIENNE: Father!

RAOUL: Go back to bed, I say.

ADRIENNE: You're trembling.

RAOUL: Do as I tell you, Adrienne.

ADRIENNE: Here—take some wine—quickly. (*She pours out a glass of wine and hands it to him.*)

RAOUL (*taking it*): Do you defy me?

ADRIENNE: Drink it, Father, and calm yourself. Won't you tell me what has happened?

RAOUL (*drinking*): Nothing has happened. Where is Father Clement?

ADRIENNE: In bed.

RAOUL: Call him.

ADRIENNE: My Father?

RAOUL: Call him, I tell you.

ADRIENNE: I want to talk to you—that's why I came down.

RAOUL: Not now.

ADRIENNE: Something *is* wrong—why won't you tell me?

RAOUL (*suddenly clutching her*): Look, Adrienne, look there—— (*He points to the picture.*)

ADRIENNE (*obediently*): Yes, Father.

RAOUL: Your noble mother.

ADRIENNE: Yes, Father.

RAOUL: Guard her memory in your heart always.

ADRIENNE: Very well, Father.

RAOUL: She loved you.

ADRIENNE: No, Father.

RAOUL: What do you mean?

ADRIENNE: She was always quite kind, but she never loved me.

RAOUL: Adrienne! Do you know what you are saying?

ADRIENNE: Yes, Father.

RAOUL: You wicked, ungrateful girl.

ADRIENNE: Father, what *is* the matter?

RAOUL: I'm shocked—immeasurably shocked.

ADRIENNE: *You're* the only one I have ever had to turn to—and even you don't seem to have cared for me so much lately.

RAOUL: I don't understand.

ADRIENNE: But I'm turning to you now in the hope that you *will* understand.

RAOUL: What are you talking about?

ADRIENNE: I don't wish to marry Miguel.

RAOUL: What!

ADRIENNE: I don't love him—as much as I should. He's kind and affectionate and I'm very fond of him, but I don't love him.

RAOUL: Why have you never said this before?

ADRIENNE: I have—but you would never listen. I've grown afraid of you lately.

RAOUL: Is everybody crazed to-night?

ADRIENNE: I don't love him.

RAOUL: What do you know of love?

ADRIENNE: A good deal, Father.

RAOUL: Adrienne—what do you mean by that?

ADRIENNE: I love Jacques Rijar and he loves me.

RAOUL: Wretched girl!

ADRIENNE (*with spirit*): I'm not a wretched girl.

RAOUL: He shall leave my service immediately.

ADRIENNE: Father!

RAOUL: Young puppy—upstart.

ADRIENNE (*appealingly*): You wouldn't—you couldn't be so unkind—it isn't his fault.

RAOUL: He goes to-morrow.

ADRIENNE: Oh, Father—please——

RAOUL: Enough—I'll hear no more of this. You were betrothed this very night to the son of my oldest friend, and you shall marry him, and, what is more, love him! I wish it—his father wishes it—your dear dead mother wished it——

ADRIENNE: She wouldn't mind one way or another.

RAOUL (*outraged*): Adrienne!

ADRIENNE (*wildly*): She wouldn't—she wouldn't—you know she wouldn't—she never cared for me—she never cared for you, she only loved herself and God and Father Clement. You keep on pretending all the time and it's not fair. You pretend that mother adored me, and she didn't. You pretend that Miguel and I love each other, and we don't. And you pretend that *you* love me and have my happiness at heart, and you don't—you don't—you can't have—otherwise you wouldn't insist on making me marry when I don't want to. You used to be so kind and dear—and you used to laugh and make jokes, but now you never do—you only frown and pray and pretend. I *won't* guard mother's memory in my heart—I hated her—and I *won't* marry Miguel. You can send me to a convent if you like, and you'll pretend it's for my good, and I shall die—and it will serve you right!

She flings herself, sobbing hysterically, on to the couch; suddenly, as RAOUL *is about to speak, there comes the most tremendous clanging of the great bell in the hall.* RAOUL *jumps as if he had been shot.* ADRIENNE *sits up.*

ADRIENNE (*tearfully*): What's that?

RAOUL (*half to himself*): It *can't* be——

ADRIENNE: Father——

RAOUL: Go to bed at once.

ADRIENNE: I'm frightened.

RAOUL: I'll talk to you in the morning.

ADRIENNE: Who is it—at this time of night?

RAOUL (*pulling her up off the couch*): Go to bed—you must go to bed.

ADRIENNE: But, Father——

RAOUL (*looking anxiously towards the door*): Do what I tell you—immediately.

ADRIENNE: Father—forgive me—I didn't mean all I said—I'm so unhappy——

RAOUL (*pushing her towards the stairs*): Go to bed!

HUBERT *flings open the double doors.*

HUBERT (*announcing*): Madame La Marquise de Kestournel.

ELOISE *sweeps in with great sang-froid, followed discreetly by* ALICE, *her maid, who stands in the doorway.*

ELOISE (*curtseying*): Monsieur le Compte de Vriaac?

RAOUL (*completely at a loss*): I—I——

ELOISE (*swiftly*): Please forgive this sudden intrusion of a complete stranger—but I am in great distress—the wheel has come off my coach—I crave your hospitality for the night—for myself and my maid.

RAOUL: Madame—I——

ELOISE: I understand that it is several miles to the nearest village. I am a stranger in these parts and extremely weary—please have pity on me.

RAOUL (*pulling himself together*): Madame—I am exceedingly sorry, but I cannot do what you ask.

ADRIENNE (*horrified*): Father!

RAOUL: We have no room at all.

ADRIENNE: Father!

RAOUL: Be quiet, Adrienne. Accept my humblest apologies.

ELOISE: But of course, Monsieur—I *quite* understand.

ADRIENNE (*firmly*): Madame.

RAOUL: Be *quiet*, Adrienne!

ADRIENNE: You must be mad, Father.

ELOISE: Please, Mademoiselle, I will walk to the village—or perhaps my coachman can procure help.

ADRIENNE: Forgive my father, Madame, he is not very well this evening.

ELOISE: I see that clearly. I would never have intruded had I known.

RAOUL: We have no room, Madame.

ELOISE: The château seemed so large from the outside; but there, moonlight is very deceptive, is it not?

ADRIENNE: The château *is* large—we have ample room. Hubert!

HUBERT: Mademoiselle?

ADRIENNE: Conduct Madame la Marquise to the guest-chamber beneath mine—and wake my maid.

RAOUL: I forbid it.

ADRIENNE (*sternly*): Hubert!

ELOISE (*smiling at* HUBERT): I am so very sorry to trouble you.

HUBERT (*looking at her strangely*): For Madame la Marquise nothing is a trouble. (*He bows.*)

ELOISE: Thank you.

HUBERT: This way, Madame.

ELOISE: Alice—will you go on up, please—I will follow in a moment!

ALICE: Yes, Madame. (*She follows* HUBERT *upstairs.*)

RAOUL (*stiffly*): My daughter is perfectly right—I apologise, Madame.

ELOISE: Please don't. There's nothing so upsetting as being taken by surprise, is there? Mademoiselle, will you lead the way?

ADRIENNE (*looking defiantly at* RAOUL): Certainly—I will have some refreshment sent up to you.

ELOISE: No, please—I am not in the least hungry. (*As she vanishes upstairs with* ADRIENNE *she turns to* RAOUL *and deliberately smiles sweetly.*)

CURTAIN

ACT II

SCENE: *It is the next morning sunlight is streaming in through the windows.*

ADRIENNE *is standing gazing out on to the terrace, she has obviously been crying. She crosses over to the library door and listens for a moment, and then goes back to the window.* MIGUEL *enters from the hall.*

MIGUEL: Adrienne!

ADRIENNE (*running to him*): Oh, Miguel!

MIGUEL: I got your note and rode over at once. What's happened?

ADRIENNE: The worst. Father knows everything.

MIGUEL: How does he know?

ADRIENNE: I told him.

MIGUEL: You?

ADRIENNE: Yes—last night—I lost my head—I thought he'd understand.

MIGUEL: It was very, very foolish.

ADRIENNE: I know. Oh, what am I to do?

MIGUEL: What did he say?

ADRIENNE: He was terribly angry, and then a strange lady arrived asking shelter for the night, and he refused, and I defied him and gave her the guest-room, and now he'll never forgive me. He's ordering Jacques out of his service now. They're both in the library—I shall never see him again. Oh, Miguel, I'm desperate—desperate—— (*She bursts into tears on his shoulder.*)

MIGUEL: I'll go in and talk to him.

ADRIENNE: No, no. That would only make matters worse.

MIGUEL: You say he's sending Jacques away?

ADRIENNE: Yes—immediately—to-day.

MIGUEL: I shall talk to father.

ADRIENNE: Oh, no, no—he wouldn't understand either.

MIGUEL: He might. He can manage your father better than anyone else.

ADRIENNE: No one can manage him when he's in a temper like this.

MIGUEL: It's your only chance. I'll ride straight back now.

ADRIENNE: But *he* wants us to be married, too.

MIGUEL: Yes—but he's not hard-hearted—I think I could talk him round.

ADRIENNE (*crying again*): Oh, Miguel!

MIGUEL: There—there—cheer up.

ADRIENNE: I can't bear it.

MIGUEL: I won't marry you—I promise you—whatever happens.

ADRIENNE: How kind you are.

MIGUEL: I mean it—I'm far, far too fond of you.

ADRIENNE: And I of you.

MIGUEL: Don't cry any more now.

ADRIENNE: Very well—I'll try not to.

MIGUEL (*kissing her*): Courage—be brave.

ADRIENNE: Dear Miguel.

MIGUEL: Leave it to me—everything will be all right.

He goes out quickly. ADRIENNE *runs out on to the terrace to wave him good-bye.* JACQUES *comes out of the library utterly despondent.* ADRIENNE *comes back into the room and meets him.*

ADRIENNE: Jacques!

JACQUES: I'm going away.

ADRIENNE: To-day?

JACQUES: Yes.

ADRIENNE (*flinging her arms round him*): You mustn't—you can't.

JACQUES (*gently disentangling himself*): I must—your father's right.

ADRIENNE: What do you mean?

JACQUES: I'm nobody.

ADRIENNE: Jacques!

JACQUES: I'm an upstart—to dare—even to look at you.

ADRIENNE: Don't talk like that.

JACQUES: It's true—I have nothing to offer you—no money—no position—nothing——

ADRIENNE: What does that matter? You love me.

JACQUES: I'm not going to love you.

ADRIENNE: Jacques, don't—please don't say that.

JACQUES: You'll never see me again.

ADRIENNE: I shall love you until I die.

JACQUES: No—when I'm gone—you'll forget me and marry Miguel, and live happily ever after.

ADRIENNE: Never. Never.

JACQUES: Your father made me see—what a fool I've been.

ADRIENNE: How can you be so weak!

JACQUES: It's your happiness that counts.

ADRIENNE: Happiness!

JACQUES: Yes—in the future—now doesn't matter—it's only the future that matters.

ADRIENNE: That's not true.

JACQUES: Don't make it so dreadfully difficult for me.

ADRIENNE: Jacques! (*She kisses him.*)

JACQUES (*crushing her to him*): My dear—oh, my dear——

ALICE *comes downstairs with a tray of fruit and hot chocolate which she places on a small table.* ADRIENNE *and* JACQUES *break away from one another.*

ALICE: Good morning, Mademoiselle.

ADRIENNE (*in a stifled voice*): Good morning.

ALICE: Madame la Marquise wishes to take her breakfast down here.

ADRIENNE: I hope Madame slept well.

ALICE: Excellently, thank you, Mademoiselle. (*She curtseys and returns upstairs.*)

JACQUES: She's coming down at once then.

ADRIENNE: Yes—I suppose so.

JACQUES: This is good-bye.

ADRIENNE: Oh, no—no.

JACQUES: It must be.

ADRIENNE: Not yet—wait a little.

JACQUES: After what your father said—I couldn't wait.

ADRIENNE: Please—oh, please——

JACQUES: What use is it?

ADRIENNE: We'll think of a plan—Miguel will help.

JACQUES: There's no way he can help.

ADRIENNE: Yes, yes there is—he's talking to his father now—go upstairs, pack your things and have everything in readiness if you must—but don't—don't go——

JACQUES: Adrienne—you don't understand—my pride forbids——

ADRIENNE: Someone's coming—come out on to the terrace—quickly.

She drags him out on to the terrace. ELOISE *enters gracefully down the stairs, followed by* ALICE *carrying a cushion and a footstool.*

ELOISE (*selecting a chair*): This one—I think.

ALICE: Yes, Madame.

ELOISE: It looks more comfortable than the others.

ALICE: A little, Madame.

ELOISE (*settling herself*): The house is a trifle old-fashioned, I'm afraid.

ALICE: Yes, Madame. (*She arranges cushion and foot-stool.*)

ELOISE: Thank you—no modern improvements.

ALICE (*bringing up the breakfast table*): Here is your breakfast, Madame.

ELOISE: You're a great comfort to me, Alice. I do hope you're going to be happy here.

ALICE: Are we going to stay long, Madame?

ELOISE: Indefinitely. Ring that bell, will you. I wish to speak to the major-domo.

ALICE (*ringing bell*): Anything further, Madame?

ELOISE: No—that will be all. You might unpack a little more.

ALICE: Yes, Madame.

She curtseys and goes upstairs. ELOISE *pours out some chocolate and drinks a silent toast to Madame la Comptesse over the fireplace.* HUBERT *enters from the hall.*

HUBERT: You rang, Madame?

ELOISE: Yes, Hubert. There are several things I

wish to know. You haven't written to me for ages.

HUBERT: I didn't know where you were, Madame.

ELOISE: I sent you my address in St. Cloud.

HUBERT: I mislaid it, Madame.

ELOISE: How careless. But never mind. Your master seems sadly changed.

HUBERT: Yes, Madame.

ELOISE: Is he happy?

HUBERT: No, Madame.

ELOISE: He needs cheering up. I think it's high time I came back.

HUBERT: I have missed you very much, Madame.

ELOISE: Thank you, Hubert. And Mademoiselle Adrienne—is *she* happy?

HUBERT: Well, yes—and no.

ELOISE: What do you mean by that?

HUBERT: She is too young to be completely happy.

ELOISE: I see—in love?

HUBERT: Yes, Madame.

ELOISE: May I be guilty of remarking that time seems to pass surprisingly quickly.

HUBERT: It certainly does, Madame.

ELOISE: I feel so very, very strange.

HUBERT: I hope pleasantly so, Madame.

ELOISE: Oh, yes—quite—thank you.

FATHER CLEMENT *comes downstairs.* ELOISE *jumps visibly.*

Good gracious!

FATHER CLEMENT (*bowing austerely*): Madame la Marquise—Monsieur le Compte told me you were here.

ELOISE: How kind. That will do, Hubert, for the present.

HUBERT (*bowing*): Thank you, Madame. (*He goes out.*)

ELOISE: Will you have a little chocolate?

FATHER CLEMENT: No, thank you.

ELOISE: It's extremely good. Are you permanent here or only temporary?

FATHER CLEMENT (*stiffly*): I am Monsieur le Compte's confessor.

ELOISE: I'm sure he has deplorably little to confess. It must be so discouraging for you.

FATHER CLEMENT: I trust you slept well.

ELOISE: Beautifully, thank you. I hope my late arrival last night didn't disturb you.

FATHER CLEMENT: Not at all.

ELOISE: Splendid. Will you have some fruit?

FATHER CLEMENT: No, thank you.

ELOISE: Won't you sit down?

FATHER CLEMENT: No, thank you.

ELOISE (*patiently*): What *would* you like to do?

FATHER CLEMENT: You are an old acquaintance of Monsieur le Compte?

ELOISE: What a leading question.

FATHER CLEMENT: I beg your pardon.

ELOISE: Pray don't apologise. (*She peels an apple in silence.*)

FATHER CLEMENT: Have you any news of your coach?

ELOISE: None—I'd forgotten all about it.

FATHER CLEMENT: Perhaps it is repaired by now.

ELOISE: Who knows!

FATHER CLEMENT: Your coachman?

ELOISE: He's very unreliable.

FATHER CLEMENT: Have you ever visited these parts before.

ELOISE: Several times—I am an insatiable traveller.

FATHER CLEMENT: Shall I despatch a groom to the village to make enquiries?

ELOISE: What sort of enquiries?

FATHER CLEMENT: About your coach?

ELOISE: Oh, my coach!

There is another silence. She pours out some more chocolate.

FATHER CLEMENT: Monsieur le Compte asked me to see that you had everything you desired.

ELOISE: How charming of him.

FATHER CLEMENT: He deeply regrets being unable to bid you good-bye.

ELOISE: Is he still unwell?

FATHER CLEMENT: Yes.

ELOISE: I'm so sorry—perhaps he will be better by the time I leave.

FATHER CLEMENT: I doubt it, Madame.

ELOISE: How unfortunate. What is he suffering from exactly?

FATHER CLEMENT: A bad headache.

ELOISE: Then we must all be very quiet, mustn't we?

FATHER CLEMENT (*angrily*): At your service, Madame.

He bows and goes into the library. ELOISE *makes a slight grimace after him.* ADRIENNE *and* JACQUES *re-enter from the terrace.*

ELOISE (*gaily*): What a lovely morning, isn't it?

ADRIENNE: Beautiful.

ELOISE: I was awakened quite early by the birds.

ADRIENNE: I'm so sorry.

ELOISE: Not at all—I love birds. (JACQUES *makes a movement to go.*) Won't you present me?

ADRIENNE: Monsieur Rijar—Madame la Marquise de Kestournel.

ELOISE (*holding out her hand*): I'm charmed to meet you, Monsieur.

JACQUES (*kissing it*): Enchanted.

ADRIENNE: Monsieur Rijar is my father's secretary.

ELOISE (*smiling*): How dreadful.

ADRIENNE: You mustn't be angry with father—he was not himself last night.

ELOISE: Your own personal sweetness made up for everything.

ADRIENNE: Thank you, Madame.

JACQUES (*bowing*): If you will excuse me, Madame—I have some business to attend to.

ELOISE: Certainly.

ADRIENNE (*suddenly*): Jacques!

JACQUES(*turning*): Yes?

ADRIENNE: Nothing—nothing.

She lowers her eyes. ELOISE *watches them both carefully.* JACQUES *looks hopelessly at* ADRIENNE *for a moment, then bows and goes upstairs.*

ELOISE: Come and sit by me a little, won't you?

ADRIENNE: If you will forgive me, I——

ELOISE: Please! (*She smiles pleadingly.*)

ADRIENNE: Very well.

ELOISE: You are the only one who has not made me feel an outrageous intruder. I want to know about you.

ADRIENNE (*half smiling*): What do you wish to know?

ELOISE: Lots of absurd trivial things—for instance, how old are you?

ADRIENNE: Eighteen.

ELOISE: Do you like me?

ADRIENNE (*surprised*): Like you? Why, yes—of course.

ELOISE: I'm so glad. I want you to. (*She glances up at the picture.*) Was that your mother?

ADRIENNE: Yes.

ELOISE: She died?

ADRIENNE: Yes—two years ago.

ELOISE: You're not very like her.

ADRIENNE: No—I sometimes think I must be a changeling.

ELOISE (*startled*): What!

ADRIENNE: I don't know what made me say that!

ELOISE: Do you miss her?

ADRIENNE (*hesitatingly*): Yes—one always misses people when they die.

ELOISE: I suppose you think I'm impertinent, don't you?

ADRIENNE: Impertinent—no—no, not at all.

ELOISE: I'm very interested in you.

ADRIENNE: In me? It's very, very kind of you.

ELOISE: You're unhappy, aren't you?

ADRIENNE: Why do you ask that?

ELOISE: I feel you are, somehow.

ADRIENNE: How strange.

ELOISE: Is it?

ADRIENNE: I like you being interested in me.

ELOISE: It must be lonely for you here with only your father and that priest.

ADRIENNE: Yes, it is—sometimes.

ELOISE: Of course, there's that charming young secretary.

ADRIENNE: Yes, Jacques Rijar—he's very nice.

ELOISE: You love him terribly, don't you?

ADRIENNE (*rising*): Madame!

ELOISE: Please forgive me.

ADRIENNE (*trying to control herself*): But I—I——

ELOISE (*holding her hand*): Oh, my dear—don't be unhappy.

ADRIENNE (*gallantly*): I'm not unhappy—I—I—— (*She turns away.*)

ELOISE: There—there—I'm so very sorry—I trespassed too far.

ADRIENNE: It's all right, really—I'm very silly—I've been silly all the morning.

ELOISE: It isn't silly to be in love.

ADRIENNE: I'm betrothed.

ELOISE (*surprised*): Betrothed?

ADRIENNE: Yes.

ELOISE: To whom?

ADRIENNE: Miguel di Santaguano. His father is an old friend of my father's, and I love Jacques—and, oh dear—— (*She cries a little.*) I keep on crying—it's so ridiculous. What's the use of tears, anyhow? I'm ashamed of being so stupid. Please forgive me——

ELOISE: Tears are wonderfully comforting sometimes.

ADRIENNE: They're humiliating.

ELOISE: You mustn't feel that with me—I'm your friend.

ADRIENNE: Are you—are you really?

ELOISE: Didn't you know?

ADRIENNE: Yes. I think I did—from the first. I'd never have defied father like that if I hadn't felt——

ELOISE (*swiftly*): What did you feel?

ADRIENNE: I don't know—you seemed familiar—I felt a sort of pang, it was strange—I couldn't have borne it if father had turned you away.

ELOISE: My dear! (*She draws her to her and kisses her.*)

ADRIENNE: Don't—don't go away just yet.

ELOISE: Do you hate this Miguel?

ADRIENNE: No—he's a dear—and he's promised me secretly not to marry me—but father's sending Jacques away to-day.

ELOISE: Shh!—don't cry any more——

RAOUL *enters from the library, followed by* FATHER CLEMENT, *who bows stiffly to* ELOISE *and goes off into the hall.* ADRIENNE *rises.*

RAOUL: Adrienne!

ELOISE (*brightly*): Good morning.

RAOUL (*ignoring her*): Adrienne—will you come into the library, please—I want to talk to you.

ELOISE: Adrienne is upset. I think it would be better for her to go and lie down.

RAOUL: Adrienne——

ELOISE (*unmoved*): I wish to speak to *you*, anyhow. Run along, Adrienne.

RAOUL (*icily*): Do you realise, Madame, that you are deliberately suggesting that my daughter should disobey me?

ELOISE: Perfectly. If she hadn't disobeyed you last night I should have languished in the road. It's a habit that should be encouraged.

RAOUL (*sarcastically*): I bow to your better judgment.

ELOISE: That is uncommonly polite of you. Come and talk to me later, Adrienne.

ADRIENNE: Yes, I will—I will—thank you. (*She curtseys and runs off upstairs.*)

RAOUL (*after a pause*): Well!

ELOISE: Good morning.

RAOUL: Good morning.

ELOISE: You will be pleased to hear that I slept excellently.

RAOUL: Did you?

ELOISE: Now that I see you in the daylight you appear to have aged considerably.

RAOUL: I don't intend to lose my temper.

ELOISE: I didn't know you'd found it.

RAOUL: Will you please leave this house?

ELOISE: No.

RAOUL: I'm afraid I must insist.

ELOISE: Very well, go on.

RAOUL: I *do* insist.

ELOISE (*gaily*): Well, now that's failed—try something else.

RAOUL (*in gentler tones*): Eloise.

ELOISE: Aha!

RAOUL: I beg of you.

ELOISE: That's better.

RAOUL: I implore you.

ELOISE: Don't overdo it.

RAOUL: Please go away.

ELOISE: Why should I?

RAOUL: You went out of my life for ever fifteen years ago.

ELOISE (*gently*): Sixteen.

RAOUL: Fifteen.

ELOISE: I went out of your life for ever in September, 1719. I remember perfectly—that's why I came back in September—it rounds it all off so nicely.

RAOUL: Why did you never come back before?

ELOISE: You were married and I was married.

RAOUL: What!

ELOISE: Your amazement is not very flattering.

RAOUL: Whom did you marry?

ELOISE: The Marquis de Kestournel—he was very

sweet—we lived at St. Cloud; a delightful house overlooking the river. Are you fond of the river?

RAOUL: In what way?

ELOISE: Just fond of it?

RAOUL: No—not particularly.

ELOISE: What a pity.

RAOUL: Where is your husband now?

ELOISE: With your wife, I expect.

RAOUL: Please don't speak like that.

ELOISE: I didn't mean it indelicately.

RAOUL: Did you love him?

ELOISE: Mind your own business.

RAOUL: You've no right to force your way into my house after all these years.

ELOISE: Why not?

RAOUL (*inarticulately*): It's—it's—abominable.

ELOISE: I have a perfect right to come back here—if only to see my child, and I intend to stay just as long as I choose.

RAOUL: Very well—I shall take Adrienne away.

ELOISE: I shall come too.

RAOUL: I shall send Father Clement to reason with you.

ELOISE: You've already sent him once this morning and it was a dismal failure.

RAOUL: What do you hope to gain by all this?

ELOISE: That's my affair.

RAOUL: You said last night you loved me.

ELOISE: Passionately. (*She sits down again.*)

RAOUL: That's a lie.

ELOISE: You're very modest.

RAOUL: I suppose you think I love you too.

ELOISE: Madly.

RAOUL: Well, I don't.

ELOISE: How little we know ourselves.

RAOUL: What do you want?—tell me, what do you want?

ELOISE: I told you last night—I want to be cherished.

RAOUL: You can seriously sit there and say you want to be cherished?

ELOISE: Yes, dear.

RAOUL: Well, you're mad—that's all—stark staring mad.

ELOISE: Why don't you give up the struggle, Raoul, and be pleasant?

RAOUL: You want to break up my home and my happiness and my peace of mind?

ELOISE: You don't appear to have much happiness or peace of mind, and your home is extremely uncomfortable.

RAOUL: Leave it.

ELOISE: That would be ungracious.

RAOUL (*losing control*): Leave it—leave it—I command you!

ELOISE: It never *used* to be uncomfortable—I'm afraid you've let things slide rather since your marriage. There is a great patch of wet on the guest-room ceiling.

RAOUL: How dare you!

ELOISE: Some of these chairs appear to me to be falling apart.

RAOUL: How dare you, I say—how dare you!

ELOISE: You should learn to accept criticism without losing control. I'm only mentioning these things out of sheer good-will.

RAOUL: You're a she-devil!

ELOISE: Shhh! Not so loud.

RAOUL (*walking about the room*): It's shameful—infamous.

ELOISE: I haven't examined the gardens yet—I expect everything is overgrown with weeds.

RAOUL (*insultingly*): What is your object in all this? What do you want—money?

She gives him a swift look, then smiles charmingly.

ELOISE: I should love some—money is always useful.

RAOUL: May God forgive you.

ELOISE: What for?

RAOUL: Your wickedness.

ELOISE: I'm not wicked.

RAOUL: You've come to torture me.

ELOISE: You're torturing yourself by being so obstinate—you're really delighted to see me.

RAOUL: I'm not.

ELOISE: You were always far too tenacious—you should have learnt to give in more by this time—you can't beat me down—I know you too well.

RAOUL: I *will* beat you down. You're shallow and frivolous and sinful—you shan't enter my life again.

ELOISE: I have entered your life again.

RAOUL: You shall leave it—I have the Church behind me now.

ELOISE: Meaning Father Clement? Come, come, Raoul!

RAOUL: Father Clement stands between me and the world I detest.

ELOISE: Father Clement knows when he is well off. He'll stand between you and the world just as long as he gets good food and lodging.

RAOUL: The baseness you see in others is nothing

but the reflection of your own soul.

ELOISE: I never thought of that. Oh, Raoul!

RAOUL: It's high time you began to think of it.

ELOISE: Am I so very vile and depraved?

RAOUL: Yes, you are.

ELOISE: You used not to think so.

RAOUL: You can atone by leading a better life.

ELOISE: My life is a model of restraint as it is.

RAOUL: I doubt it.

ELOISE: How do you know that the baseness you see in me is not the reflection of *your* soul?

RAOUL: Not very convincing, I am afraid.

ELOISE: Why not? We can never judge ourselves—it's silly to try.

RAOUL: What do you hope to gain ultimately by this prevarication?

ELOISE: Shelter from the world I detest.

RAOUL (*furiously*): Oh, you're impossible.

ELOISE: It's you who are impossible—you wish to toss me aside like a worn-out glove.

RAOUL: Nothing of the sort.

ELOISE: Drive me out of your house alone—bereft of my child—bereft of your protection—no one to turn to. How can you be so cruel? (*She dabs her eyes with her handkerchief.*)

RAOUL: That doesn't deceive me at all.

ELOISE: It wasn't meant to, really—it is merely my view of the situation.

RAOUL: You can go back to St. Cloud.

ELOISE: I've sold the house. You see, I made sure you would welcome me with open arms.

RAOUL: Why should you imagine that?

ELOISE (*fumbling in her bag*): Wait a moment.

RAOUL: Give me that damned letter!

ELOISE (*meekly*): Yes, Raoul. (*She hands it to him.*)

RAOUL (*tearing it up and throwing it into the fire*): There!

ELOISE (*still fumbling*): Oh dear—I'm so sorry—that was a dressmaker's bill. Here. (*She hands him another letter.*)

RAOUL (*enraged*): Keep it—keep it—and to hell with you!

He stamps angrily out on to the terrace. ELOISE *enacts for her own benefit a pathetic little scene in which she re-reads the letter, looks forlornly after* RAOUL, *and weeps gently.* JACQUES *enters downstairs. He is dressed for travelling, and carries a large bag. He is creeping towards the hall when* ELOISE *sees him.*

ELOISE: Young man—what are you creeping about like that for?

JACQUES: I'm going away.

ELOISE: Without saying good-bye?

JACQUES: I'm sorry, Madame. It's urgent that I leave quickly.

ELOISE: Come here a moment—let me look at you.

JACQUES (*advancing reluctantly*): Madame—I——

ELOISE: How old are you?

JACQUES: Twenty-four.

ELOISE: Where are you going?

JACQUES: Paris.

ELOISE: To work?

JACQUES: I hope so.

ELOISE: You believe in self-sacrifice?

JACQUES (*surprised*): Madame—I——

ELOISE: Answer me. Do you?

JACQUES: Yes, I do.

ELOISE: You're wrong then. It's one of the most

sterile forms of self-indulgence in the world.

JACQUES (*stiffly*): I would prefer not to discuss it if you don't mind.

ELOISE: Will you do me a great favour?

JACQUES (*apprehensively*): What sort of favour?

ELOISE: Don't go away just yet.

JACQUES: Madame—I very much regret—but I must.

ELOISE: Well, go and say good-bye to Adrienne first.

JACQUES (*astonished*): I don't understand—I——

ELOISE: You understand perfectly well—it is cruel and cowardly to leave her without a word.

JACQUES: Madame, if you will forgive my saying so——

ELOISE: It is no affair of mine—I quite see your point—but I happen to have Adrienne's interest very much at heart—I don't wish her to be made needlessly unhappy.

JACQUES: Monsieur le Compte has ordered me to go.

ELOISE: He has ordered me to go too—several times. You mustn't worry about that.

JACQUES: My pride forbids——

ELOISE: Rubbish. Love is more important than pride.

JACQUES: Love!

ELOISE: Yes—you love Adrienne and she loves you—she told me all about it. You seem sincere and honest, but incurably romantic. Romance is all very well in its place, but not when you allow it to stand between you and your heart's desire. You'll be far more useful staying here with Adrienne than gallivanting about the world eating your heart out.

JACQUES: No, no, you don't understand. I could only bring her unhappiness. I have nothing to offer her—it's better she should forget me.

ELOISE: You distrust her love for you?

JACQUES: What do you mean?

ELOISE: Will you forget her?

JACQUES: Never—never—as long as I live.

ELOISE: Well then—she won't forget you either if she loves you enough, and you'll both be miserable. What's the good of that?

JACQUES: Please, Madame—let me go now.

ELOISE: Listen to reason.

JACQUES: What you ask is impossible.

ELOISE: I'm only asking you to wait a little. Everything may turn out quite differently from what you imagine. I may be able to help you both, if only you'll do what I tell you. Go upstairs and wait, please.

JACQUES: But, Madame——

ELOISE: Please—someone is coming. Promise me you won't go without letting me know—promise me. (*She pushes him towards the stairs.*)

JACQUES: Very well—I promise.

ELOISE: That's right—now be off with you.

He goes upstairs again just as HUBERT *enters.*

HUBERT (*announcing*): Monsieur le Duc de Santaguano.

ESTEBAN *enters briskly and* HUBERT *withdraws.* ESTEBAN *stops short on seeing* ELOISE. *They stand for a moment staring at one another.*

ELOISE: Esteban!

ESTEBAN: You! You!

They fall into one another's arms.

ELOISE: Oh, my dear. After all these years—I thought you were in Spain—or dead!

ESTEBAN: I can't believe it.

ELOISE: Tell me—Esteban dear—tell me—how is my child?

ESTEBAN: Well and happy—he's grown into a splendid young man—he's here—near by—my château is just across the valley.

ELOISE: And your wife—what of her?

ESTEBAN: She died—years ago.

ELOISE (*disentangling herself from his arms*): My dear—forgive me—I must sit down—I feel quite upset.

He leads her to the couch.

ESTEBAN: What are you doing here?

ELOISE: I—I don't know exactly.

ESTEBAN: I never realised that you and Raoul knew one another.

ELOISE (*faintly*): My coach broke down last night—late—Monsieur de Vriaac sheltered me for the night.

ESTEBAN: If only I'd known.

ELOISE: Tell me more about François.

ESTEBAN: Miguel.

ELOISE: Miguel!

ESTEBAN: Yes, my family and my wife insisted that he should be called Miguel, after my great-uncle—my wife refused to acknowledge him unless I agreed—I was so dazed and unhappy when they forced us apart—I didn't care what happened.

ELOISE (*intensely*): Miguel!

ESTEBAN: Yes. Are you angry? I've tried to find you—several times—but it was useless.

ELOISE: You have betrothed my son to Mademoiselle Adrienne?

ESTEBAN: Yes—they are old playmates.

ELOISE: Oh—oh—oh!—This is too much. (*She goes off into gales of hysterical laughter.*)

ESTEBAN: What on earth is the matter?

ELOISE: Don't—don't come near me—I shall be better soon. Oh dear!

ESTEBAN: But, Eloise——

ELOISE: It's the shock of seeing you again—so unexpectedly—so very, very unexpectedly. (*She continues to laugh.*)

ESTEBAN: Please try to control yourself.

ELOISE (*pulling herself together*): How long—how long have you known Monsieur de Vriaac?

ESTEBAN: For years—nearly all my life—longer than I've known you. He was sent to Spain in 1711. I was only a sub-lieutenant. We were in Seviglia together, and afterwards Toledo and Barcelona. Then he went back to France, and I met you.

ELOISE: Did you ever tell him—about me?

ESTEBAN: Never. I told no one. The memory of you has been my life's secret.

ELOISE: Oh, Esteban.

ESTEBAN: How long ago it all seems.

ELOISE: I expect it was for the best—our parting.

ESTEBAN: I've often wondered.

ELOISE: Your family were right—according to their lights—I was only a second-rate actress.

ESTEBAN: Never—you were wonderful.

ELOISE: I married, too, you know.

ESTEBAN: When?

ELOISE: Not for years afterwards. I am the Marquise de Kestournel.

ESTEBAN: We might have met at Court—just think.

ELOISE: Unlikely. My husband was dreadfully retiring. Santaguano—I can never see you as anything but Esteban Largo—Hell's Blood Largo.

ESTEBAN: A violent nickname.

ELOISE: You were a violent man.

ESTEBAN: Is your husband dead now?

ELOISE: Yes, quite.

ESTEBAN: Alone in the world?

ELOISE: Yes.

ESTEBAN: So am I—or at least I shall be when Miguel marries.

ELOISE: I must see him.

ESTEBAN: You shall—to-day.

ELOISE: He doesn't know—either?

ESTEBAN: No.

ELOISE: I see. He never shall. I do hope I'm not going to be unhappy.

ESTEBAN: It would be different if you had brought him up—but you went away. I've been very, very fond of him.

ELOISE: Dear Esteban.

ESTEBAN: I think he'd be happier—not knowing.

ELOISE: Was your wife kind to him?

ESTEBAN: Yes—she had to be.

ELOISE: Poor dear.

ESTEBAN: Why? It was a marriage of convenience—she was quite intelligent about it.

ELOISE: Have you loved anyone since me?

ESTEBAN: Hundreds.

ELOISE: Did she have lovers, too?

ESTEBAN: I expect so—I never asked.

ELOISE: How comfortable.

ESTEBAN: When are you leaving here?

ELOISE: I don't know.

ESTEBAN: Do you like Raoul?

ELOISE: Monsieur de Vriaac. Oh, yes, enormously.

ESTEBAN: How strange to find you again like this—in his house.

ELOISE: It is odd, isn't it?

ESTEBAN: Have you met Adrienne?

ELOISE: Yes—she seems a charming girl.

ESTEBAN: She is.

ELOISE: I'm so glad.

ESTEBAN: This is rather a difficult situation really.

ELOISE: Just a little.

ESTEBAN: Where are you going?

ELOISE: When?

ESTEBAN: When you leave here?

ELOISE: I don't know quite.

ESTEBAN: I mean where were you travelling to when your coach broke down?

ELOISE: Oh then—Paris, I suppose.

ESTEBAN: Suppose?

ELOISE: Don't cross-examine me.

ESTEBAN: I'm sorry.

ELOISE: I think—I think it would be as well if one didn't tell Monsieur de Vriaac that we had met before—it might lead to complications.

ESTEBAN: What sort of complications?

ELOISE: I don't know. Fate is very tricky.

ESTEBAN: Very well.

ELOISE: How far is your château from here?

ESTEBAN: About seven miles by road.

ELOISE: I may visit you.

ESTEBAN: I should be charmed.

ELOISE: I love visiting people.

ESTEBAN: Eloise——

ELOISE: Yes.

ESTEBAN: Are you pleased to see me again?

ELOISE: Of course.

ESTEBAN: How pleased?

ELOISE: Very pleased.

ESTEBAN: Had you forgotten me?

ELOISE: No—I never forget—besides, I've got your letter.

ESTEBAN: You received it then?

ELOISE (*fumbling in her bag*): Yes—I have it here somewhere.

ESTEBAN: Why did you never answer it?

ELOISE: I thought it best to leave things as they were. (*She finds it.*) Ah! (*She reads.*) "Beloved—bla bla bla bla —I wonder if my heart will ever mend." That was a lovely phrase, Esteban—bla bla bla—— "If ever you are in trouble—if ever you are lonely——" Oh dear! (*She folds it up.*) I always carry it about with me.

ESTEBAN: I meant it—every word.

ELOISE: Dear Esteban—you're as gallant as ever.

ESTEBAN: Are you in need of protection?

ELOISE: No, dear, thank you.

ESTEBAN: You can always rely on me.

ELOISE: I know—but I won't—it would be tiresome.

ESTEBAN: No it wouldn't.

ELOISE: You got over your love for me years ago.

ESTEBAN: Why do you think that?

ELOISE: Come now—it's the truth, isn't it?

ESTEBAN: I shall always be fond of you.

ELOISE: I said love.

ESTEBAN (*aggrieved*): Well, after all you can't expect——

ELOISE: I don't, dear—you mustn't upset yourself—I don't love you either.

ESTEBAN: There you are then.

ELOISE: It's much more easy to manage—this.

ESTEBAN (*smiling*): Quite—you look enchanting.

ELOISE: Do I?

ESTEBAN: Superb.

ELOISE: So do you.

ESTEBAN: No—I'm grizzly and old and debauched.

ELOISE: Not a bit of it—your figure is as youthful as ever.

ESTEBAN: I flatter myself I *have* kept my figure more or less.

ELOISE: Has it been a strain?

ESTEBAN: Yes—at moments.

ELOISE: I too have had my struggles.

ESTEBAN: I should never suspect it.

ELOISE: I must have been lovely as a girl.

ESTEBAN: You were—slim and radiant.

ELOISE (*regarding herself ruefully*): I've always hoped I was plump.

ESTEBAN: No—I'm very sorry—slim.

ELOISE: It doesn't matter.

ESTEBAN: *How* I loved you.

ELOISE: And I you. First love. I should have made a splendid courtesan.

ESTEBAN: Why didn't you?

ELOISE: I was too emotional—I allowed my heart to lead me instead of my head.

ESTEBAN: Do you regret it?

ELOISE: No—I've been very happy—I've travelled everywhere. Russia—Norway—England.

ESTEBAN: Before you married?

ELOISE: Oh, yes—long before. I sang in London.

ESTEBAN: Successfully?

ELOISE: Not very—they expected me to be naughty all the time—being French—it was very wearying trying not to disappoint them.

ESTEBAN: I always thought the English a very proper nation.

ELOISE: Not theatrically—their drama is extremely coarse. Really those Elizabethans!

RAOUL *enters from the terrace. He has controlled his temper and is austerely polite.*

RAOUL: Ah, Esteban! Good morning.

ESTEBAN: Good morning, Raoul. I rode over casually to chat with you and had the honour of meeting Madame la Marquise.

RAOUL: I have made enquiries about your coach, Madame—it is in perfect condition.

ELOISE: How charming of you.

RAOUL: I myself am leaving for Paris within the hour.

ESTEBAN: Leaving for Paris?

RAOUL: Yes, I am taking Adrienne to visit some dressmakers.

ESTEBAN: A very sudden decision.

RAOUL: Perhaps—Madame—my house is at your service for as long as you desire it.

ELOISE: Are you taking Father Clement with you?

RAOUL: No.

ELOISE: Then I shall certainly stay a little longer—he is such a gay fellow.

ESTEBAN (*glancing at her swiftly*): The soul of jocularity.

RAOUL: I think we will not discuss him.

ESTEBAN: You seem rather strange this morning, Raoul.

ELOISE: Monsieur le Compte had a headache. He tells me he is a martyr to them.

ESTEBAN: A headache in your presence, Madame, must surely denote a deficiency of gallantry.

RAOUL (*crossly*): Laboured, Esteban—very laboured.

ELOISE: On the contrary—a delightful compliment.

RAOUL: I will leave you, Esteban, to deliver some more.

ESTEBAN: I must admit I am puzzled.

RAOUL: Why?

ESTEBAN: Your manner is so very odd.

RAOUL: My manner is the same as usual

ELOISE (*brightly*): Then you must change it, Monsieur le Compte.

ESTEBAN (*looking from one to the other*): I don't understand.

ELOISE: It is my fault entirely. I have been very rude this morning—I have insulted Monsieur de Vriaac's hospitality—I have made complaints—the house is very badly managed. I am far too outspoken—it has always been my failing in life. I apologise humbly.

RAOUL (*icily*): It is of no consequence.

ESTEBAN: It's absurd, Raoul, to take offence so easily—you should be ashamed.

ELOISE: There were several mice in my bedroom last night.

RAOUL: There were not.

ELOISE: Please don't be so definite—it might be misconstrued.

ESTEBAN: *My* château is in a dreadful state of disrepair, Madame. I should be so grateful if you would visit it some time and give me the value of your advice.

ELOISE: I should be charmed.

ESTEBAN: You will be here alone this evening?

ELOISE: Quite possibly—except for the support of the Church.

ESTEBAN: Perhaps you would do me the honour of supping with me?

ELOISE: How kind you are.

ESTEBAN: The kindness would be yours. I am a lonely man.

ELOISE: I accept with pleasure.

ESTEBAN: A thousand thanks. My coach shall fetch you at eight o'clock.

ELOISE: Eight o'clock.

ESTEBAN: I shall leave you now, Raoul. I am not wholly unconscious of a certain strain in the atmosphere —perhaps my departure will alleviate it. Madame! (*He bows over her hand, smiles almost knowingly, and goes out.*)

ELOISE: What an enchanting man!

RAOUL: I'm glad you find him so congenial.

ELOISE: Such chivalrous manners—such gallantry.

RAOUL: You must see more of one another.

ELOISE: Doubtless we shall.

RAOUL: Your designs may be more effective with him than with me.

ELOISE: Don't be crude, Raoul.

RAOUL: I hope you will excuse me now—I must prepare for the journey.

ELOISE: I haven't thanked you yet for allowing me to stay here. It will be so peaceful—the country is entrancing at this time of the year.

RAOUL: I hope you will be very comfortable.

ELOISE: I doubt that—but I'll try.

RAOUL (*with a triumphant smile*): Good-bye.

ELOISE (*altering her tone*): Just a moment, Raoul. I wish to ask you a service.

RAOUL: Indeed.

ELOISE: Yes. Will you please allow Adrienne to marry Jacques Rijar as soon as possible?

RAOUL: What!

ELOISE: He is obviously a good and nice young man. I can guarantee him an excellent position in Paris. I still have influence in some quarters.

RAOUL: Have you taken leave of your senses?

ELOISE: Now keep calm, Raoul.

RAOUL: Your impertinence is beyond belief.

ELOISE: They are deeply in love.

RAOUL: Rubbish.

ELOISE: I ask you quite seriously—in the name of many past memories—just grant me this.

RAOUL: I refuse to discuss the matter.

ELOISE: If you agree—I'll torment you no further.

RAOUL: I've already taken steps to prevent that.

ELOISE: I might almost go out of your life for ever. Please, Raoul. They adore one another—why shouldn't they be happy?

RAOUL: Adrienne is betrothed to Miguel de Santaguano—and it is he that she shall marry or no one.

ELOISE: She shall not!

RAOUL: How can you prevent it?

ELOISE: Easily. By telling her who I am and taking her away with me.

RAOUL: You wouldn't dare.

ELOISE: I'd dare anything.

RAOUL: It would ruin her life.

ELOISE: I don't want to tell her—yet, anyhow—but if either of us is going to ruin her life it shall be me—I can ruin it more happily for her in the long run.

RAOUL: I defy you—do you understand?—I defy you.

ELOISE: Raoul!

RAOUL: I have no more to say.

ELOISE: We shall see!

He walks off into the library. ELOISE, *left to herself,*

strides about the room, obviously perplexed. Suddenly a thought strikes her. She ponders for a moment, and a smile spreads over her face. She runs to the stairs.

(*Calling*) Alice—Alice——

After a moment ALICE *comes down the stairs.*

ALICE: Madame.

ELOISE: Ask Mademoiselle Adrienne and Monsieur Rijar to come here immediately.

ALICE: Yes, Madame.

ELOISE: And bring me my leather travelling case.

ALICE (*surprised*): Madame!

ELOISE: My *leather* travelling case—you understand—quickly.

ALICE: Yes, Madame. (*She goes off upstairs.*)

ELOISE *goes swiftly over to the library door, listens carefully for a moment, and then very quietly turns the key in the lock.* ADRIENNE *and* JACQUES *come downstairs, followed by* ALICE *with an oblong leather case, which she hands to* ELOISE.

ELOISE: Thank you, Alice. Find Father Clement as quickly as you can. Say I wish to speak to him urgently.

ALICE: Yes, Madame. (*She curtseys and goes out into the hall.*)

ADRIENNE: What's the matter? What's happening?

ELOISE: Wait. (*She pulls the bell by the fireplace.*) You're going on a journey—both of you.

JACQUES: Madame—please explain.

ELOISE: Promise me—promise me you'll do as I tell you.

JACQUES: But I——

ADRIENNE: I promise—oh, *I* promise.

ELOISE *goes up to* JACQUES *and looks at him carefully.*

ELOISE: Just a moment—before we go any further. Are your father and mother both living?

JACQUES (*surprised*): Yes.

ELOISE: You're sure?

JACQUES: Of course—quite sure.

ELOISE: I'm *so* glad—I get so muddled.

HUBERT *enters.*

ELOISE: Hubert.

HUBERT: Yes, Madame.

ELOISE: Is Monsieur le Compte's coach ready to leave for Paris?

HUBERT: Yes, Madame. He gave orders for it some time ago.

ELOISE: Good—that is all for the moment.

HUBERT: Yes, Madame. (*He bows and goes out.*)

ELOISE: Listen, my dears—you're going to be married.

JACQUES: Married!

ELOISE: Yes—by force if necessary.

ADRIENNE: How—when—where?

ELOISE: Here and now.

JACQUES: No—no——

ELOISE: No more ridiculous scruples, please—I will arrange everything. If Monsieur le Compte refuses to settle any money on you I will use my influence to get you a secretaryship in Paris, and I can assure you of one thing—it will be a far better paid job than this one.

JACQUES: But, Madame——

ADRIENNE: Be quiet, Jacques!—It's wonderful. Oh, Madame—I trust you absolutely—you're an angel from heaven.

ELOISE: Now whatever happens keep calm—don't be surprised at anything, and do what I tell you.

FATHER CLEMENT *enters from the terrace·—he looks faintly surprised.*

FATHER CLEMENT: You sent for me, Madaıne?

ELOISE: Yes, Father Clement. I want you to do a small service for me.

FATHER CLEMENT: Service?

ELOISE: Yes—a marriage service.

FATHER CLEMENT: What right have you to ask me that, Madame?

ELOISE: That is beside the point. Will you marry these two young people at once?

FATHER CLEMENT (*to* ADRIENNE): Mademoiselle—do my ears deceive me?

ELOISE (*impatiently*): Will you or will you not?

FATHER CLEMENT: Monsieur Rijar——

JACQUES: We both wish it, Father Clement.

FATHER CLEMENT: Does Monsieur le Compte know of this?

ELOISE: No—and I don't intend him to until it's all over.

FATHER CLEMENT (*making a movement*): I see.

ELOISE: Where are you going?

FATHER CLEMENT: To tell him of this disgraceful plot.

ELOISE: Oh, no you're not. (*She stands in front of the library door.*)

FATHER CLEMENT: Let me pass, Madame.

ELOISE: Will you marry these two people?

FATHER CLEMENT: Certainly not.

ELOISE: I think you will. (*She takes two pistols from the leather travelling case and levels them at him.*)

FATHER CLEMENT (*iumping back*): You're mad—you're mad——

ELOISE: Go on, start.

FATHER CLEMENT (*shouting*): Help! help!—Monsieur le Compte—help! help!

ELOISE: Unless you start the marriage service immediately I shall shoot—I shall just aim at both legs—it will be very, very painful but not mortal.

FATHER CLEMENT: Help!—it's infamous—help!

ELOISE: Unless you have started by the time I count three I shall shoot. Now then——

RAOUL *begins to batter at the library door.*

ELOISE: Don't worry—the door's locked. Go on.

FATHER CLEMENT, *with a trembling hand, grasps his prayer book. He is staring at* ELOISE *as though hypnotised.*

One—two——

FATHER CLEMENT, *in a quavering voice, begins to intone in Latin.* RAOUL'S *efforts to get in wax louder.* JACQUES *and* ADRIENNE *kneel down as the curtain falls.*

CURTAIN

ACT III

SCENE: *It is about eight o'cloak in the evening.*

RAOUL *is seated at supper by himself. His expression is extremely morose. The curtains are drawn.* RAOUL, *with an exclamation of annoyance, rises and tugs the bell rope viciously and returns to the table.* HUBERT *enters.*

RAOUL: Hubert.

HUBERT: Yes, Monsieur le Compte.

RAOUL: This pie is disgusting.

HUBERT: In what way, Monsieur le Compte?

RAOUL: In every way—the pastry is heavy—the apples are undercooked—and there are cloves in it.

HUBERT: There are always cloves in apple pie, Monsieur le Compte.

RAOUL: The meat was disgusting, too.

HUBERT: I'm very sorry, Monsieur le Compte.

RAOUL: Bring me some cognac—I wish to get drunk.

HUBERT: Yes, Monsieur le Compte. (*He goes out.*)

RAOUL *rises irritably, pulls aside the curtains, gazes out on to the terrace, and then returns to the table.* HUBERT *re-enters with a bottle of cognac.*

RAOUL: Sit down.

HUBERT (*obediently sitting*): Yes, Monsieur le Compte.

RAOUL: You shall drink with me.

HUBERT: Yes, Monsieur le Compte.

RAOUL: Go on, pour it out. (HUBERT *fills two glasses.*) I'll give you a toast. (*He raises his glass.*) To hell with everything!

HUBERT (*also raising his glass*): To hell with everything!

They both drain them.

RAOUL (*taking the bottle*): Another toast.

HUBERT (*apprehensively*): Do you think it's wise, sir?—you haven't drunk seriously for a long time.

RAOUL (*refilling glass*): I don't care.

HUBERT: Very well, Monsieur le Compte.

RAOUL: Debauchery—that's the thing—unbridled debauchery! (*He drinks.*)

HUBERT: Yes, Monsieur le Compte.

RAOUL: Are there any women in the village?

HUBERT: Several, Monsieur le Compte—I believe.

RAOUL: I have the worst possible motives for wishing to see crowds of women.

HUBERT: I am glad Father Clement has gone, Monsieur le Compte.

RAOUL: What has that to do with it?

HUBERT: He would not have approved.

RAOUL: That's why he has gone.

HUBERT: I understand, Monsieur le Compte.

RAOUL: *You* propose a toast now, Hubert.

HUBERT: I, Monsieur le Compte?

RAOUL: Yes—go on——

HUBERT (*rising*): Madame la Marquise de Kestournel.

RAOUL (*banging his glass on to the table*): Stop!

HUBERT: I'm sorry, Monsieur le Compte.

RAOUL: Why do you do that?

HUBERT: Her name sprang to my lips—I apologise.

RAOUL (*bitterly*): Sentimentalist!

HUBERT: Madame la Marquise is such a romantic figure——

RAOUL: No—hard as iron—hard and unrelenting. (*He drinks.*)

HUBERT: Forgive me, Monsieur le Compte, if I venture to disagree with you.

RAOUL: No one has any right to be romantic, after a certain age. (*He pours himself out another glass of cognac.*)

HUBERT: Madame la Marquise will never be old.

RAOUL (*rising angrily*): Why should you torment me too?

HUBERT: I torment you, Monsieur le Compte? Nothing could be further from my thoughts!

RAOUL (*pacing the room*): Everyone torments me—everyone defies me—I am made a laughing-stock—— (*He drinks.*)

HUBERT: Please don't upset yourself, Monsieur le Compte.

RAOUL: You have courage—I will say that for you.

HUBERT: That is another thing you have lost with your youth, Monsieur le Compte. Courage!

RAOUL: What do you mean?

HUBERT: You are afraid of yourself.

RAOUL: Get out of my sight.

HUBERT (*rising*): Very well, Monsieur le Compte. (*He goes towards the door.*)

RAOUL: Stop a moment. (HUBERT *pauses.*) Why did you never tell me all this before?

HUBERT: You wouldn't have listened, Monsieur le Compte.

RAOUL: Am I such a fool?

HUBERT: Please—I—I——

RAOUL: You've known me longer than anyone else—answer me.

HUBERT: May I have a little more cognac?

RAOUL: Yes—take it.

HUBERT (*taking it*): Thank you.

RAOUL: Now then—am I a fool?

HUBERT (*after drinking hurriedly*): Yes, Monsieur, le Compte.

RAOUL (*sitting down again*): What remedy do you suggest?

HUBERT (*grasping the bottle and leaning forward*): Allow me, Monsieur le Compte.

RAOUL: That is no remedy—a few moments back you were advising me against it.

HUBERT: A little warms the heart, Monsieur le Compte.

RAOUL: That's it, is it—I'm cold-hearted? (*He drinks.*)

HUBERT: Yes, Monsieur le Compte.

ROAUL: And stubborn, I suppose, and disagreeable?

HUBERT: Yes, Monsieur le Compte.

RAOUL: Splendid—magnificent—what else?

HUBERT (*encouraged*): Middle-aged.

RAOUL: How dare you!

HUBERT (*firmly*): You are at the cross-roads—you must either grow older or younger.

There comes a loud peal of the bell in the hall.

RAOUL: See who it is, Hubert.

HUBERT: Yes, Monsieur le Compte.

He goes off. RAOUL, *left alone at the table, buries his head in his arms.* ESTEBAN *enters.*

ESTEBAN: Good evening, Raoul.

RAOUL (*looking up*): Cross-roads.

ESTEBAN: I beg your pardon.

RAOUL: You're middle-aged, too.

ESTEBAN: What's the matter?

RAOUL (*pulling himself together*): Nothing is the matter.

ESTEBAN: What are you talking about?

RAOUL: A choice of evils, my friend, that's all.

ESTEBAN: I thought you were going to Paris?

RAOUL: I am—the city of sin—I long for it!

ESTEBAN (*astonished*): My dear Raoul!

RAOUL (*excitedly*): Vivid scarlet sin—it warms one up, you know.

ESTEBAN: You seem to grow more and more peculiar each time I enter the house.

RAOUL (*rising and embracing him*): Esteban—— (*He waves a glass of cognac.*) Sevigla iyiz! Hurrah! (*He drains it.*)

ESTEBAN (*amiably*): Hurrah!

RAOUL: Have some? (*He brandishes the bottle.*)

ESTEBAN (*regarding him quizzically*): Not just now—I want to know what's happened.

RAOUL: Nothing—everything!

ESTEBAN: Thank you. I understand perfectly.

RAOUL: I'm a fool—a middle-aged—stubborn—disagreeable fool!

ESTEBAN: Excellent—also hysterical and apparently drunk.

RAOUL: No—not yet.

ESTEBAN: Where is everybody?

RAOUL: Scattered—leaves on the wind.

ESTEBAN (*gently*): Wouldn't you like to sit down?

RAOUL: Yes, very much.

ESTEBAN: Well, do so.

RAOUL (*sitting down*): There—are you satisfied?

ESTEBAN: No. Why are you drunk?

RAOUL: I'm not—very.

ESTEBAN: You are.

RAOUL: Don't bully me.

ESTEBAN: What has happened?

RAOUL: Someone opened a window and everything blew away! (*He giggles.*)

ESTEBAN (*impatiently*): Where is Madame la Marquise?

RAOUL (*with an effort*): St. Cloud. A charming house overlooking the river. Do you like the river?

ESTEBAN: No, I do not.

RAOUL: Neither do I—it's enervating, I fear—sadly enervating.

ESTEBAN: For heaven's sake pull yourself together.

RAOUL: Never again—I've been together too long.

ESTEBAN (*sitting down opposite him*): Now listen to me, Raoul—you must try quite quietly to explain.

RAOUL (*leaning forward confidentially*): Certainly. (*He sits back again.*)

ESTEBAN: Go on then—I'm waiting.

RAOUL: How old are you?

ESTEBAN: Forty-six.

RAOUL: Allow me to congratulate you—you don't look a day over thirty-five.

ESTEBAN: Never mind about that—go on.

RAOUL: The whole affair is very unfortunate.

ESTEBAN: *What* affair?

RAOUL: Being middle-aged.

ESTEBAN (*rising angrily*): Will you or will you not explain?

RAOUL (*aggrieved*): Don't be so restless, Esteban—it worries me.

ESTEBAN: What exactly has taken place in this house since I left this morning?

RAOUL: Catastrophe—regeneration—disaster—fulfilment.

ESTEBAN *walks over and pulls the bell rope.* RAOUL *subsides in his chair.*

RAOUL: What are you doing?

ESTEBAN: My poor, poor Raoul.

HUBERT *enters.*

Hubert, some strong black coffee.

HUBERT: It is already brewing, Monsieur le Duc.

ESTEBAN: Good. Where is Madame la Marquise?

HUBERT: She has left, Monsieur le Duc.

ESTEBAN: Left?

HUBERT: Yes—this afternoon.

ESTEBAN: Where is Father Clement?

HUBERT: He has left, too, Monsieur le Duc.

ESTEBAN: And Mademoiselle Adrienne?

HUBERT: She went to Paris with Monsieur Rijar.

ESTEBAN: With Monsieur Rijar?

HUBERT: Yes—they were married at one o'clock.

ESTEBAN (*astounded*): Married! Are you mad!

HUBERT: No, Monsieur le Duc.

ESTEBAN: That will do, Hubert. Bring the coffee as soon as possible.

HUBERT: Yes, Monsieur le Duc. (*He goes out.*)

RAOUL: Hubert is my only friend in the world.

ESTEBAN: What does all this mean?

RAOUL: Faithful and true—true as steel—Toledo! Esteban, do you remember Toledo?

ESTEBAN: Perfectly.

RAOUL: So do I. (*He reaches out for the cognac.*)

ESTEBAN (*preventing him*): No more.

RAOUL: Bigoted—that's what you are—bigoted!

ESTEBAN: You've had enough.

RAOUL (*affably*): Too much, Esteban—far, far too much.

ESTEBAN: The coffee will pull you round.

RAOUL: You must never leave me, Esteban—I am devoted to you.

ESTEBAN: Good.

RAOUL: You are so gay—and care-free—it's very stimulating.

ESTEBAN: I'm glad.

RAOUL (*portentiously*): Life, Esteban, is nothing but a game of see-saw.

ESTEBAN (*absently*): What?

RAOUL: I said life is a game of see-saw.

ESTEBAN (*thinking*): Oh yes—yes, certainly.

RAOUL: One is either up or down. I have been down for years.

ESTEBAN: And now you are up?

RAOUL: Yes, high, high up—I am sitting on a cloud—I know all there is to know and I forgive everybody.

ESTEBAN: That is exceedingly magnanimous of you.

RAOUL: I forgive my wife—— (*He rises and stands in front of the picture.*) Do you hear, Hélène—I forgive you freely—you traded on my loneliness and my weakness, and you married me relentlessly, but I forgive you—having achieved the protection of my name and the uninspired but solid comfort of my home. You forsook me utterly and rushed with almost wanton enthusiasm to the arms of your true love, the Church! Your theories were above reproach, but your practices were unfriendly. You were virtuous and noble according to your lights, but, alas, those lights were completely obscured by the dreariness of your conversation. In fact, my dear, dear Hélène, you were a determined and unmitigated bore! But I forgive you—there! Esteban, help me! (*He drags a chair to the fireplace and mounts it a trifle unsteadily.*)

ESTEBAN: Raoul—what are you doing?

RAOUL: Help me—help me.

ESTEBAN, *laughing, drags up another chair, and together with some effort they dislodge the picture from the wall and convey it to the ground.* RAOUL *lays it gently down with its face to the floor and then subsides on to the couch with a sigh of relief.*

RAOUL: At last—at last I have the courage!

HUBERT *enters with coffee on a tray. He places it upon the table.*

ESTEBAN: Thank you, Hubert.

HUBERT: Have you supped, Monsieur le Duc?

ESTEBAN: No, not yet.

HUBERT: Can I bring you anything?

ESTEBAN: Thank you, no—not at the moment—later perhaps.

HUBERT: Very good, Monsieur le Duc.

He goes out. ESTEBAN *pours out some coffee and takes it over to* RAOUL *on the couch.*

ESTEBAN (*peremptorily*): Here—drink this.

RAOUL (*grandly*): Your personality is so dominant that I have no choice but to obey, but please understand it is with the very greatest reluctance.

ESTEBAN: Go on, drink it.

RAOUL (*waving the cup*): Good-bye, Paradise. (*He drinks.*)

ESTEBAN: Fool's Paradise.

RAOUL: It's very hot.

ESTEBAN: Good.

RAOUL: I suppose I had better have some more?

ESTEBAN: By all means.

He takes the cup over to the table and refills it.

RAOUL: Just like old times.

ESTEBAN (*returning with the cup*): Extremely.

RAOUL: That thought rejuvenates me more than the coffee.

ESTEBAN: Well, for God's sake dwell on it.

RAOUL: You mustn't be cross with me—I have been sorely tried.

ESTEBAN: Drink it up now—we'll have a little fresh air, I think. (*He goes across to the windows.*)

RAOUL: Be careful.

ESTEBAN: Why?

RAOUL: The moon——

ESTEBAN (*pulling back the curtains*): What about the moon?

RAOUL: It's very dangerous. (*He drinks off the second cup and grimaces.*) Ugh!

ESTEBAN (*opening the windows wide*): There!

RAOUL *rises and joins him and they both stand looking out over the valley.*

RAOUL: There are lights on the high road.

ESTEBAN: I don't see any.

RAOUL: There—through the trees.

ESTEBAN: Some coach, I expect—come in and sit down.

RAOUL: Fate never gives second chances.

ESTEBAN: What do you mean by that?

RAOUL: Nothing.

They both return into the room.

ESTEBAN: Now then. Is what Hubert said true?

RAOUL: Everything Hubert says is true—it's quite uncanny.

ESTEBAN: He says Adrienne is married to Jacques Rijar.

RAOUL: Correct.

ESTEBAN: Why did you allow it?

RAOUL: I didn't—they locked me in the library—she let me out when it was all over.

ESTEBAN: She?

RAOUL: Eloise.

ESTEBAN: Eloise?

RAOUL: Don't keep repeating everything I say—it's infuriating.

ESTEBAN: What do you mean by calling her Eloise?

RAOUL: It's her name, isn't it?

ESTEBAN: Well, considering that you met for the first time last night.

RAOUL: I've known her for years.

ESTEBAN: Well, why didn't you say so?

RAOUL: It's my life's secret.

ESTEBAN: Why should it be?

RAOUL: She is Adrienne's mother.

ESTEBAN (*astounded*): What!

RAOUL: She came back to torment me.

ESTEBAN (*slowly*): It's—it's not possible!

RAOUL: You don't know her?

ESTEBAN: Oh, yes, I do.

RAOUL: Not as well as I do.

ESTEBAN: Just as well.

RAOUL: What do you mean?

ESTEBAN: It's exceedingly fortunate that Adrienne married Jacques Rijar.

RAOUL: What has that to do with it?

ESTEBAN: Miguel would not have been quite suitable.

RAOUL: Why not?

ESTEBAN: He happens to be her brother.

RAOUL (*falling back*): Good God!

ESTEBAN: That's *my* life's secret.

RAOUL (*sitting down*): Forgive me—I feel very confused.

ESTEBAN: Where has she gone?

RAOUL: Eloise?

ESTEBAN: Yes, of course, Eloise.

RAOUL: I don't know.

ESTEBAN: Fool—blundering fool.

RAOUL: I wish I did. I'd tell her what I thought of her.

ESTEBAN: So should I.

RAOUL: She deceived me.

ESTEBAN: And me. When did you——?

RAOUL: Paris, 1716—when did you?

ESTEBAN: Madrid, 1713.

RAOUL: It's abominable—I loved her with all my heart.

ESTEBAN: Infamous. So did I.

RAOUL (*striding about the room*): Never will I forgive her—never—never——

ESTEBAN (*also striding*): Nor I——

RAOUL: Her memory is ashes in my mouth.

ESTEBAN: Splendid. From now onwards I cast her from my mind—absolutely.

RAOUL (*at table*): We'll drink to that.

ESTEBAN: Very well.

RAOUL *pours out two glasses of cognac.*

RAOUL (*raising his glass*): Eloise—to her destruction!

ESTEBAN (*raising his glass*): Eloise—to her damnation!

They both drain their glasses at one gulp. ELOISE *enters quietly from the terrace.*

ELOISE (*sweetly*): I do hope I'm not intruding?

They both turn and stare at her. RAOUL *drops his glass with a crash*—ESTEBAN *clutches the table for support.*

RAOUL (*recovering himself*): You!

ELOISE: Yes—I've been on the terrace for several minutes waiting for an opportune moment to appear—I seem to have found one.

RAOUL (*bitingly*): Very clever.

ELOISE: No, not really—a trifle theatrical, I fear—but there, as William Shakespeare said, "All the world is a stage."

ESTEBAN (*irritably*): Who was William Shakespeare?

ELOISE: A poet who was clever enough to persuade his own countrymen that he was only a playwright.

RAOUL: All of which does not excuse your effrontery in returning to this house.

ELOISE: Oh, Raoul, you're surely not going to begin all that again.

ESTEBAN: I think it would be advisable, Raoul, if you allowed me to handle this unpleasant situation.

RAOUL: On the contrary, I would prefer you to leave it to me.

ESTEBAN: You are in no condition to manage it with the requisite delicacy.

RAOUL: You are essentially a man of action, Esteban. Delicacy is beyond your—— Please leave us.

ELOISE (*lightly*): Well—while you are fighting it out I shall take a little coffee. It was cold on the terrace. (*She seats herself at the table and pours some coffee into* RAOUL'S *cup. She drinks it in silence.*)

RAOUL (*with bitterness*): I hope you are satisfied.

ELOISE: It's far too strong—I must speak to the chef.

ESTEBAN: Eloise, I think it only fair to tell you that we know all.

ELOISE: All what?

RAOUL: The full extent of your baseness.

ELOISE: Nonsense—I'm not in the least base.

ESTEBAN: You have betrayed us.

ELOISE: Nothing of the sort.

RAOUL: Lied to us.

ELOISE: I have not. You're behaving like idiots—both of you. Why don't you sit down and close the windows? There's a draught.

RAOUL: Close the windows, Esteban.

ESTEBAN: Close them yourself.

RAOUL (*icily*): Very well, I shall.

ELOISE: That's right. (RAOUL *goes over and closes the windows angrily.*) Now then we can talk.

ESTEBAN: Talk! What do you hope to achieve by talking?

ELOISE: A good deal. I'm glad that you both "know all", as Esteban so dramatically put it, because it saves a lot of wearisome explanation and leaves us free to arrive at a satisfactory conclusion.

RAOUL: It's too late.

ELOISE: "It's never too late to mend". Shakespeare again. You really must read him, it will improve your minds.

ESTEBAN (*with sarcasm*): What conclusion would you consider satisfactory?

ELOISE: I haven't quite decided yet—it's extremely difficult for me to choose. You see, your temperaments are so very opposite.

RAOUL: Choose!

ESTEBAN: What has that to do with it?

ELOISE (*surprised*): Well, one of you is going to marry me, I suppose?

RAOUL: Marry you!

ELOISE: Naturally.

ESTEBAN: You must be mad!

ELOISE: Really, Esteban, I expected more chivalry from *you*—Raoul is different. Hypocrisy seems to have blunted his sensibilities lately.

RAOUL: You seriously suggest that we should marry you!

ELOISE: I said one of you. Of course, our children complicate matters dreadfully.

ESTEBAN: It's shameful.

ELOISE: What is shameful?

ESTEBAN: For you to be so calm and—and callous.

ELOISE: What do you expect me to do? Hurl myself at your feet and scream?

RAOUL (*turning away*): This is insupportable!

ELOISE: I'm sorry—I'm rather enjoying it.

ESTEBAN: Your brazen attitude is appalling.

ELOISE: Come now, Esteban—you're not nearly as angry as you were when I came in.

ESTEBAN: Yes, I am.

ELOISE: And you, Raoul—haven't you succumbed to my charms in the least?

RAOUL: No.

ELOISE (*resignedly*): Well—well—I mustn't lose heart.

RAOUL: Please say what you have to say and begone.

ELOISE: With Esteban?

RAOUL: Certainly not—by yourself.

ESTEBAN: I will escort you, if you wish.

RAOUL (*quickly*): Where to?

ELOISE: At last—a gleam of gallantry.

RAOUL: You'll do nothing of the sort, Esteban.

ESTEBAN: Mind your own business, Raoul.

ELOISE (*gratefully*): Thank you, Esteban.

RAOUL (*bitterly*): Traitor.

ESTEBAN: Not at all—nothing can be gained by rudeness.

ELOISE: I entirely agree with you, Esteban.

ESTEBAN: Where do you wish to go?

ELOISE: I don't really know—I believe Switzerland is very attractive at this time of the year.

RAOUL (*confronting* ESTEBAN *furiously*): Take her to Timbuctoo and be damned!

ESTEBAN (*angrily*): Don't you speak to me like that!

RAOUL: False friend—double-faced false friend!

ESTEBAN: You must never drink again, Raoul—it's obviously very bad for you.

ELOISE: Drink! Has Raoul been drinking?

ESTEBAN: Violently.

ELOISE: For shame, Raoul. What would Father Clement say?

RAOUL (*to* ESTEBAN *wildly*): Traitor—dishonourable traitor.

ESTEBAN: Have a care—you go too far.

RAOUL (*beside himself*): Hypocrite! (*He slaps his face.*)

ELOISE: Oh, Raoul—that was *very* naughty of you!

There is a dead silence for a moment. The two men stand glaring at one another. ESTEBAN *steps back, clicks his heels together and bows haughtily.*

ESTEBAN: At your service. To-morrow morning perhaps?

RAOUL: No, now—here and now! (*He goes to the bell rope and tugs at it.*)

ELOISE (*conversationally*): Where shall I sit?

ESTEBAN (*without looking at her*): Please leave us.

ELOISE: Leave you—not for the world—I haven't been fought over for years.

RAOUL: *You* are not being fought over.

ELOISE: Nonsense, of course I am.

HUBERT *enters.*

RAOUL: Hubert, my rapier.

HUBERT: Yes, Monsieur le Compte. Have you finished with the coffee?

RAOUL: Quite.

HUBERT: Then I'll clear it away. (*He picks up the coffee tray and takes it out with him.*)

ELOISE (*rising*): We'd better move some of the furniture, hadn't we?

ESTEBAN: Eloise—please go.

ELOISE: Never—here, help me with the table.

She begins to drag the table up to the wall. ESTEBAN *perforce to help her.*

Raoul, dear, those chairs will be dreadfully in the way. Put them over by the window.

RAOUL, *without a word, moves the chairs.* ELOISE, *having placed the table satisfactorily, regards the room thoughtfully, stroking her face with her hand.*

That rug, Esteban. It would be so humiliating if you tripped over it.

ESTEBAN *silently takes up the rug.* RAOUL *is standing aloof with his back turned, looking out of the window.* ELOISE *fans herself with her hand.*

Gracious, the dust! If you are alive to-morrow, Raoul, you must really engage a housekeeper.

HUBERT *re-enters carrying a rapier.* RAOUL *turns.* ELOISE *takes it quickly.*

Here, Hubert—give it to me. (*She takes it from its sheath and tests the blade.*) Yes, that's all right—that will do, Hubert. (*She hands the rapier to* RAOUL.)

HUBERT: Yes, Madame. (*He bows and goes out.*)

ELOISE: I shall sit on the spinet. (*She climbs up on to the spinet and arranges herself comfortably.* ESTEBAN *draws his sword and he and* RAOUL *confront one another.*) Just a moment—Esteban, before you start will you be very kind and hand me an orange. I can *never* enjoy witnessing any spectacle unless I'm eating something.

ESTEBAN, without taking his eyes off RAOUL, takes an orange from the bowl on the table and hands it to her.

Thank you *so* much.

The duel begins. ELOISE bites her orange and begins to peel it rather carelessly. RAOUL and ESTEBAN give occasional grunts of rage. ELOISE punctuates their various thrusts and retreats with encouraging remarks.

Well done, Raoul. Splendid, Esteban. Be careful of that table. Oh! There, that's right. Look out, there's a piece of orange peel just there. I'm so sorry. Aha! That's better, Raoul. Really, considering your joint ages, you're doing magnificently. Ah, if only my dear husband were alive. He dearly loved a duel. (*Suddenly she snatches up a heavily embroidered cloth which is lying over the spinet beside her and flings it neatly across both their blades.*) Stop! That's enough now.

ESTEBAN and RAOUL, forced to desist, stand glaring at her and breathing rather heavily.

RAOUL: Stand aside, Eloise, immediately.

ELOISE (*firmly*): Put down your swords.

ESTEBAN: Eloise—get out of the way.

ELOISE: Raoul—give me your sword.

RAOUL: I'll do no such thing.

ELOISE (*with sudden fury*): Give it to me at once—I mean it—give it to me. (*She snatches his sword from his hand and flings it across the room.*)

RAOUL (*angrily*): Eloise!

ELOISE: That's enough, I tell you—you're far too old for this sort of thing. Duelling is for hot-tempered youth, not disgruntled middle-age, and it's a ridiculous habit anyhow.

ESTEBAN: Raoul insulted me. Honour must be satisfied.

ELOISE: Rubbish—he only slapped your face!

ESTEBAN: *Only* slapped my face!

ELOISE: Well, then, slap his if you're so annoyed about it.

ESTEBAN: I'll do no such thing.

ELOISE: Come along—I'll hold him. (*She grasps* RAOUL.)

RAOUL (*struggling*): Leave go of me.

ELOISE: Go on, Esteban.

ESTEBAN (*bursting out laughing*): Very well, I will! (*He lightly slaps* RAOUL'S *face.*)

RAOUL: My God—this is insufferable.

ELOISE: Now then embrace—both of you.

RAOUL: Never—stand aside.

ELOISE (*stamping her foot*): Embrace, I tell you!

ESTEBAN: I will if you will, Raoul.

RAOUL: I won't.

ELOISE: Yes, you will. Go on. (*She pushes him towards* ESTEBAN.)

RAOUL: This is ludicrous.

ELOISE: Extremely. Go on.

ESTEBAN *and* RAOUL *embrace.*

ESTEBAN: Disagreeable ass!

RAOUL: Damned fool!

ELOISE: That's right—now then, sit down quietly and listen. I have a confession to make.

ESTEBAN: Eloise, I——

ELOISE: Sit down, please—both of you.

ESTEBAN: Very well. (*He sits down.*)

ELOISE: Raoul.

RAOUL: I don't wish to hear any more.

ELOISE: Sit down.

RAOUL: I will *not* sit down.

ELOISE: Well, stand up then. (RAOUL *sits sulkily on the couch.*) You were both quite right when you accused me of lying to you. I did.

RAOUL: Aha!

ELOISE: Be quiet. I told you I had been married. I haven't.

ESTEBAN: What!

ELOISE: You have been the only men in my life ever —in this depraved age it's rather humiliating to admit it, but it's true. My career as a singer has been extremely successful and I have managed to amass a small but adequate fortune. When I was young and inexperienced I met you, Esteban, in Madrid. I loved you desperately, with all the misplaced heroism first love generally inspires. I gave birth to your child and left you because your marrying me would have meant disinheritance by your family and the ruin of your career. That may have been foolish of me, but I don't regret it. Two years later I met Raoul in Paris. He was attractive and sweet and loved me passionately. I came to live with him here, where Adrienne was born. The reason I left you, Raoul, was less romantic but equally understandable. Never once during the whole course of our relationship did you suggest marriage to me.

RAOUL (*shocked*): Eloise—I——

ELOISE: Shhh—don't protest. It was doubtless the fault of your upbringing. You were always faintly snobbish, even in your nicer moments. If I had been a designing woman I could have forced your hand. If I had possessed the soul of a courtesan I could have demanded a settlement—but instead, I chose to earn my living in a more self-respecting manner. Many men since then have made love to me, but none have won me. I preferred to preserve my integrity and wait, and now—now—I have come back, and God help you both.

ESTEBAN: What do you mean by that?

ELOISE: I mean that one of you is going to house, feed, protect and adore me until the day I die.

RAOUL: Eloise!

ELOISE: I mean it.

ESTEBAN: Is all this true?

ELOISE: Perfectly. I have been, technically speaking, a virtuous woman for sixteen years.

RAOUL: Why didn't you say so before?

ELOISE: Your manner to me has not been exactly conducive to intimate confidences.

RAOUL: I'm sorry.

ELOISE: Is that a genuine apology?

RAOUL (*turning away*): Quite.

ELOISE: Esteban, what have you to say?

ESTEBAN: I don't know. I feel bewildered.

ELOISE: Well—I'm quite content to wait—there's no hurry. Raoul, do you mind if I sleep in Adrienne's room to-night as she is not here?

RAOUL (*sulkily*): You can sleep where you like.

ELOISE: Thank you. That guest-room, as I said before, is most depressing, what with that loose shutter and the beetles——

RAOUL (*incensed*): If you searched the house from top to bottom you would not find *one* beetle.

ELOISE (*meekly*): You know best.

ESTEBAN: If, as you say, you have amassed a satisfactory fortune—why do you crave our protection?

ELOISE: What a mercenary question.

ESTEBAN: Quite a natural one.

ELOISE: I need companionship and domestic security. I have been battered by the world.

RAOUL: Nonsense.

ELOISE: You wouldn't be expected to understand—you were one of the batterers.

RAOUL: You'd better choose which of us you want, hadn't you?

ELOISE: Don't speak so ungraciously, Raoul, just because you happen to be ashamed of yourself.

ESTEBAN (*rising and taking her hand*): I shall be very honoured if you choose me, Eloise.

ELOISE (*smiling*): Always the soul of courtesy.

ESTEBAN: I mean it.

ELOISE: Thank you, Esteban—come along, Raoul.

RAOUL (*rising*): There's nothing for me to say.

ELOISE: Typical.

ESTEBAN: For shame, Raoul.

RAOUL: Do you love her?

ELOISE (*quickly*): That's not fair.

RAOUL: Do you?

ESTEBAN: Mind your own business.

ELOISE: There is one condition I wish to state—the one of you who is fortunate enough to win me must inform his child of the identity of his or her mother—the other shall go forever in ignorance. It will be better, I think.

RAOUL (*with determination*): Eloise—will you marry me?

ELOISE: Raoul—after sixteen years—this is so sudden!

ESTEBAN: Eloise—the choice is in your hands.

ELOISE: It's terribly difficult—couldn't you draw lots or something?

RAOUL: Please be serious.

ELOISE: Why?

RAOUL: Is it all such a tremendous joke?

ELOISE (*pensively*): It *is* funny.

RAOUL: I don't see it.

ELOISE: Never mind, dear.

ESTEBAN: I'd do all I could to make you happy.

ELOISE: I know you would, Esteban.

RAOUL (*suddenly*): I love you! (*He walks out on to the terrace.*)

ELOISE: There!

ESTEBAN: Is that true, do you think?

ELOISE: Yes.

ESTEBAN: How very, very odd.

ELOISE: Thank you.

ESTEBAN: You know I didn't mean that—I meant——

ELOISE: You should be used to Raoul's self-consciousness by this time.

ESTEBAN: Do you love him?

ELOISE: Of course.

ESTEBAN: Then—then——

ELOISE: I don't mind you looking relieved, Esteban.

ESTEBAN (*smiling*): You're a strange creature.

ELOISE: My dear. Good-night. (*She kisses him.*)

ESTEBAN: Good-night.

He goes out. ELOISE *walks over to the spinet and begins to play softly, then she sings a little song, at the end of which* Raoul *re-enters from the terrace.*

Raoul (*going towards her*): Eloise.

Eloise: Shhh—it's so peaceful here. We still have a lot of time for talking.

Raoul: I meant what I said. I do love you.

Eloise: That has been obvious since the first moment I came into the house.

Raoul: I didn't know.

Eloise: Dear Raoul—I did!

She continues to play. Raoul *goes to her slowly and rests his head on her shoulder as the curtain falls.*

CURTAIN

POST MORTEM

CHARACTERS

JOHN CAVAN
LADY CAVAN
SIR JAMES CAVAN
TILLEY
SHAW
BABE ROBINS
PERRY LOMAS
JENNER, a batman
CORPORAL MACEY
MONICA CHELLERTON
BERTIE CHELLERTON
KITTY HARRIS
EGGIE BRACE
DRAKE, a butler
ALFRED BORROW
MISS BEAVER
LADY STAGG-MORTIMER
THE BISHOP OF KETCHWORTH
SIR HENRY MERSTHAM
A BUTLER
SHAW (aged 39) TILLEY (aged 43)
BABE ROBINS (aged 32)

The action of this play should be continuous and the changes of scene managed as quickly as possible, during which the Auditorium should remain in darkness.

SCENE 1

The scene is a company headquarters in a quiet section of the Front Line in the Spring of 1917. *It is a roughly built shelter with a sloping corrugated tin roof. There is an entrance up* Right *centre which leads round into the front trench and a doorway left. At the back there is a sandbag wall reaching to within a few feet of the roof, through this opening can be seen the higher wall of the back trench topped with mud and grass and a few old tins, beyond this can be seen occasionally the flashes of guns far back. Every few moments during the whole scene there is the flare of a Verey light.*

It is about 8.30 *in the evening.*

(TILLEY, SHAW, BABE ROBINS *and* JOHN CAVAN *have just finished dinner and as the Curtain rises* JENNER, *the batman, is serving them with mugs of coffee.* ROBERT TILLEY *is a man of about thirty, pleasant looking, with certain authority as befits a Company Commander.* SHAW *is younger, about twenty-six, fattish and good-humoured, and inclined to be raucous in jollity.* BABE ROBINS *is nineteen, nice and clean looking, his face which is ordinarily cheerful, is now set ana strained.* JOHN CAVAN *is about twenty-seven or twenty-eight. He is tall, not remarkable looking in any way, his face is rather pale and his eyes look tired. He has had command of the Company for several months until a few weeks back, when* TILLEY *returned from leave after being wounded and took over from him.* SHAW *is seated on a bunk, left, with his legs stuck out in front of him, chuckling over a copy of the "Daily Mercury."* TILLEY *is sitting at the back of the table smoking.* JOHN *is sprawled on the bunk, right, and* BABE ROBINS *is at the end of the table, leaning against a post which supports the roof, and staring into space.* JENNER, *having given coffee to* TILLEY *and* JOHN, *offers some to* BABE.)

JENNER: Coffee, sir?

BABE (*focussing his attention*): Er—er—no thanks.

JENNER (*persuasively*): Nice and 'ot to-night, sir.

BABE: No thanks, Jenner. I don't want any.

JENNER *goes across to* SHAW.

JENNER: Coffee, sir?

SHAW (*taking a mug*): Thanks. Put in a couple of spoonfuls for me.

JENNER (*doing so*): Yes, sir.

JENNER *goes off left.*

SHAW (*laughing*): God! This paper's rich, so full of plums it's downright indigestible.

TILLEY: What is it? The *Mercury?*

SHAW: Of course. I wouldn't read anything else, not while I'm out here anyhow. A little honest English fun goes a long way out here. Have you read Lady Stagg-Mortimer's open letter to England? It's called "I gave my son."

TILLEY: And did she?

JOHN: Oh yes. I was in the O.T.C. with him for three months. Whenever she came to visit the camp he used to lock himself in the latrine. They hated one another.

TILLEY (*to* ROBINS): Want some port?

BABE: No thanks, Tilley.

SHAW (*reading delightedly*): "Every woman of England should be proud and glad to give and give and give, even the flesh of her flesh and the blood of her blood——"

TILLEY: And the tripe of her tripe. Sorry, John, I'd forgotten your father owns the bloody paper.

JOHN: Don't rub it in.

SHAW: One thing I will say about the *Mercury*, it's moral tone is sound and high, and it's very right-minded about the war. It thinks war is evil all right, but necessary. And it's absolutely beastly about the Germans. It criticises them most severely. Who is the *Mercury's* War Correspondent, Cavan?

JOHN: Damned if I know.

SHAW: He seems to be a fine upstanding lad and observant. He's actually noticed the way we all go over the top cheering and shouting "For God and Country."

JOHN: Oh, dry up! (*He laughs, and getting up, helps himself to port.*)

SHAW: You must have a nice talk to your father when you go home on leave. Tell him how we all kneel down and pray before an attack, you might take him a snapshot of it.

TILLEY: The light's not good enough.

SHAW: He could use a time exposure, surely you'd be willing to wait a few minutes for God and the *Mercury*!

BABE (*suddenly*): Has any word come from battalion headquarters, Tilley?

TILLEY: No.

BABE: They'd let us know at once, wouldn't they, if——

TILLEY: Perry will be back soon, he went to the M.O. to have his hand seen to. He'll know how Armitage is.

BABE: Perhaps they've taken him down!

TILLEY: Perhaps. Don't worry.

BABE (*rising*): I think I'll go and write a letter to his people, just to warn them. I don't go on duty till nine.

TILLEY: Right. Cheer up!

BABE: Thanks, Tilley.

BABE *goes out miserably.*

JOHN: Do you think they've taken him down?

TILLEY (*shaking his head*): No, he couldn't be moved. I doubt if he'll last more than a few hours.

SHAW: Bloody awful luck!

CORPORAL MACEY *enters and salutes.*

TILLEY: Yes, Corporal Macey?

CORPORAL: Mr. Shaw, sir, please.

SHAW (*looking up*): Yes?

CORPORAL: Carrying party just coming up with the R.E. material, sir.

SHAW (*rising and putting belt on*): All right. Fall in the working party. I'll come straight up.

CORPORAL: Yes, sir.

He salutes and exits.

TILLEY: Get things going as soon as you can, Shaw. I'll be round presently.

SHAW: Right.

He picks up his electric torch from the bunk, puts on his gas mask and tin hat and goes towards the doorway. PERRY LOMAS *enters. He is thin and looks nervy.*

His hand is bandaged.

SHAW: Hallo! How's the hand?

PERRY: Nothing much, thanks.

SHAW: Cheero!

SHAW *goes out.*

PERRY *takes off his helmet and mask and belt.*

TILLEY: Well, what did he say?

PERRY: It'll be all right in a day or so. He told me to rest it as much as possible, and gave me an anti-tetanus injection.

TILLEY: Good! You're on the new machine gun emplacement, aren't you?

PERRY: Yes. I'm going up at nine.

TILLEY: On your way you might take a look and see how number 8 platoon's getting on with their bit of parapet.

PERRY: All right. (*Calling*) Jenner—dinner please!

JENNER (*off*): Coming, sir.

PERRY *sits down at the table.* TILLEY *continues to write in his note-book.* JENNER *brings in a plate of soup, puts it down in front of* PERRY *and exits.*

PERRY (*starting his soup*): Armitage is dead.

TILLEY (*looking up*): When?

PERRY: Just before I left the Aid Post.

TILLEY: I thought as much. It looked pretty hopeless.

JOHN: Poor kid!

PERRY: He's well out of it.

TILLEY (*quietly*): Shut up, Perry.

JOHN: Somebody's got to tell him.

TILLEY: Tell who—Robins?

PERRY: I think he knows.

JOHN: No. He's waiting for news, he's in his

dug-out, I'll tell him presently.

There is a pause.

TILLEY (*rising*): Well, if the Adjutant calls up, give me a shout. I've got to go through these bloody returns with the Company Sergeant Major.

JOHN: All right, Bob.

TILLEY *goes out.*

JENNER *re-enters with a plate of meat and potatoes and exits with the empty soup plate.* JOHN *goes on reading his magazine.* PERRY *rises, takes* SHAW'S *"Mercury" from his bunk and props it up in front of him on the table. There is silence.* PERRY *reads a little and then throws the paper on the floor.*

PERRY (*angrily*): Oh, Christ!

JOHN: What's up?

PERRY: That muck makes me sick!

JOHN (*wearily*): What does it matter?

PERRY (*bitterly*): "I gave my son." "Women of England!" "God and Country." Your father owns the blasted rag. Why don't you do something about it?

JOHN (*smiling*): What could I do?

PERRY: Tell him the truth for f change!

JOHN: He knows—he's not a aool!

PERRY: You mean he's an ambitious hypocrite?

JOHN: Of course.

PERRY: Do you like him at all?

JOHN: No. I admire him rather.

PERRY What for?

JOHN:: For getting what he wants. He's a good climber.

PERRY: What does your mother think about him?

JOHN: I do wish you'd shut up, Perry. There's no sense in working yourself up into rages.

PERRY: I'm sorry. It gets in my mind and I can't get it out—all that mealy mouthed cant being shoved down the people's throats!

JOHN: The demand creates the supply, I think. The civilian public must enjoy its war; and it also has to reconcile it with a strong sense of patriotism and a nice Christian God. It couldn't do that if it had the remotest suspicion of what really happens.

PERRY: Do you think it will ever know?

JOHN: I hope so, later on, much later, when it's all over.

PERRY (*violently*): Never, never, never! They'll never know whichever way it goes, victory or defeat. They'll smarm it all over with memorials and Rolls of Honour and Angels of Mons and it'll look so noble and glorious in retrospect that they'll all start itching for another war, egged on by dear old gentlemen in clubs who wish they were twenty years younger, and newspaper owners and oily financiers, and the splendid women of England happy and proud to give their sons and husbands and lovers, and even their photographs. You see, there'll be an outbreak of war literature in so many years, everyone will write war books and war plays and everyone will read them and see them and be vicariously thrilled by them, until one day someone will go too far and say something that's really true and be flung into prison for blasphemy, immorality, lese majesty, unnatural vice, contempt of court, and atheism, then there'll be a glorious religious revival and we'll all be rushed across the Atlantic to conquer America, comfortably upheld by Jesus and the Right!

JOHN (*laughing*): Wonderful, Perry—simply wonderful!

PERRY: Don't laugh, I mean it. Stop laughing!

JOHN (*continuing*): I can't help it.

PERRY: You're not really laughing anyhow—you're as sick as I am inside.

JOHN: Not quite. I don't think poor old England is as bad as all that.

PERRY: It isn't poor old England particularly; it's poor old Human Nature. There isn't a hope for it anywhere, all this proves it.

JOHN: You're wrong. There are a few moments among these war years of higher value than any others, just a few every now and then.

PERRY (*sarcastically*): Christian value, I suppose you mean? Christian forbearance, nobility of spirit, Lady Stagg-Mortimer.

JOHN: You know I don't mean that!

PERRY: What do you mean then?

JOHN: You should see it quicker than I. You're a poet, aren't you?

PERRY: I was.

JOHN: Cheer up, Perry!

PERRY: I envy you, anyway. You've got a damned philosophic outlook, that's what you've got.

JOHN: Somebody must be learning something from all this.

PERRY: Nobody's learning anything. It's too big, too utterly futile.

JOHN: You can't be sure. Years and years and years ahead we may know.

PERRY: *We* may know.

JOHN: I didn't mean "we" personally. I'm taking a God's-eye view.

PERRY: Are you happy on your cloud, watching kids

like Armitage torn to pieces, screaming in bloody pain—will it gratify your omnipotence as God to see his mother's face when she opens the telegram. He's an only son, I believe. He had his twenty-first birthday last week when we were out of the line—we had a grand evening—you remember, you were there——

JOHN: Yes, I was there.

PERRY: He wasn't even killed in an attack or a raid, no glory, just stupid chance.

JOHN (*quietly*): Look here, Perry, I've been here longer than you and I'm going to give you some advice whether you like it or not. You're heading for a smash. Perhaps because you've got more temperament than I, or more imagination, or less control, but whatever it is, shut it off, keep it down, crush it! We can none of us afford a personal view out here, we're not strong enough—no one is strong enough. There's just a limited number of things we can bear to think about, sleep, warmth, food, drink, self preservation, no more—no more than that.

PERRY: Voluntary reversion to animalism.

JOHN: Not voluntary, compulsory.

PERRY: Aren't you touched by it any more? Not now, I don't mean now when everything's comparatively quiet, but when we're in the thick of it, floundering through mud in an attack, treading on men's faces, some of them not dead, with the bloody din of the barrage in our ears, and thin human screams cutting through it—quite clearly like penny whistles in a thunderstorm——

JOHN: I'm all right then—too much to do, no time.

PERRY: What about when it's over and we fall back sometimes, back over that idiotic ground, having to go quickly, not hearing people groaning or crying for water—when we flop down in a dug-out, safe, for the moment, time to think then, isn't there—can you help thinking then ?

He rises during this and stands over JOHN'S *bunk.*

JOHN : I believe something will come out of it—something must, when those who do get through go back home, they'll be strong enough to count somehow.

PERRY : Not they. They'll slip back into their smug illusions, England will make it hot for them if they don't. Remember we're a Christian country.

JOHN : I'm waiting, treading water, waiting to see.

PERRY : You'll probably be blown to pieces if you wait long enough. Then you'll never see.

JOHN : I'm not so sure. I have a feeling that one might see the whole business just for a second before one dies. Like going under an anæsthetic, everything becomes blurred and enormous and then suddenly clears, just for the fraction of a fraction of a moment. Perhaps that infinitesimal moment is what we're all waiting for really.

PERRY (*irritably*) : Well, in that case the war is highly to be commended, it's providing thousands of your infinitesimal moments per day per person. Very comforting !

JOHN : Just as comforting as anything else. Time is very interesting. Nobody has found out much about it, perhaps there isn't any, perhaps it's just a circle and Past and Future are the same. Funny if the current got switched and we all started remembering twenty years hence and looking forward to last Tuesday.

PERRY : God forbid that I should ever look forward to any of the last Tuesdays I've lived through.

JOHN : What's your particular Devil?

PERRY : God, I think.

BABE ROBINS *comes in. He looks at* PERRY *anxiously.*

BABE : Perry!

PERRY : Yes?

BABE : What's happened about Armitage? Have they taken him down yet?

PERRY (*after a slight pause*) : No, Babe—it wouldn't be any use—he's dead.

BABE : Oh, I see.

There is a silence. BABE *stands quite still.*

PERRY (*awkwardly*) : Don't worry about him, kid, he didn't have much pain, he was unconscious. (*He shoots a bitter look at* JOHN *and says more loudly*) Unconscious!

PERRY *goes out abruptly.*

BABE *sits down by the table.*

BABE (*breaking the silence, dully*) : I'd just written to his mother saying he'd been pretty badly hit. She's—she's awfully nice, they live in Somerset.

JOHN (*rising*) : If I were you I'd have a spot of whisky. (*He goes to the table and pours some whisky into a mug and gives it to him.*)

BABE (*taking it*) : Thanks awfully. (*He gulps it down.*)

JENNER *comes in and piles all the dinner things on to a tray*)

JENNER (*to* BABE) : Shall I have a cup of tea ready for you, sir, when you come off duty?

BABE *doesn't answer.* JOHN *speaks quickly.*

JOHN : Very good idea! I'd like a cup now, can you hurry it along, Jenner?

JENNER : Yes, sir.

He goes off with the tray.

JOHN *instinctively puts his arm round* BABE'S *shoulders.* BABE *sits still for a moment, then gently disengages himself and walks over to the bunk, left.*

BABE (*unsteadily*) : Don't say anything to me, will you ? I don't want to blub and make a fool of myself. You see we were at Sandhurst together and school, we've been together all along, for years really. I shall miss him—very much—(*His voice breaks so he stops talking.*)

JOHN (*practically*) : Look here, old chap, you'd better stay here quietly for a little. I don't go on until midnight, we'll just swap duties. I'll take over your covering party now, and you can do my tour for me at twelve. That'll give you time to steady yourself a bit.

BABE : Thanks ever so much, it's awfully decent of you.

He fumbles in his pocket for a cigarette. JOHN *hastily hands him a tin from the table.* BABE *lights one and puffs at it.* JOHN *puts on his belt and gas mask and hat.*

JOHN : Lend me your torch, will you ? I think Shaw's pinched mine.

BABE (*giving it to him with a slight smile*) : Here.

JOHN : Thanks. Cheero.

As he is about to go out he meets TILLEY *coming in. He speaks quietly.*

Look here, Bob—(*he points to* BABE)—he's a bit knocked out over Armitage, if you've no objection I'll do his covering party. He'll go on for me later.

TILLEY : That's all right.

JOHN : Thanks.

TILLEY *sits at the table, and bringing a pile of loose papers out of his pocket, proceeds to check them through with a pencil. He glances over at* BABE *once or twice.*

TILLEY: There's some port left in the bottle, Babe, d'you want a drop?

BABE: No thanks, Tilley.

PERRY *re-enters and begins to put on his belt, gas mask, etc. He looks at his watch.*

PERRY: I make it five to nine—is that right?

TILLEY (*looking at him*): Yes. Try and get that emplacement done to-night. I want to avoid any work on it in the daylight.

PERRY: If it only stays quiet the way it has the last three nights, and that machine-gun from the sunken road doesn't start pooping at us—we'll get through it in a few hours.

TILLEY: Right. I'll be along later.

There is a sudden outbreak of machine-gun fire, several bullets whistle over the top of the shelter.

(*Jumping to his feet*) Blast! They've spotted the wiring party.

*There is another burst of fire—*TILLEY *and* PERRY *stand listening.*

PERRY: They must have got them in that flare.

TILLEY: I'll go and have a look.

They both move towards the entrance. CORPORAL MACEY *dashes in.*

CORPORAL: Mr. Cavan been 'it, sir, got him just as 'e was getting out of the trench.

TILLEY: Anyone else hit?

CORPORAL: No, sir.

TILLEY: Bring Mr. Cavan in here, quick!

CORPORAL: Yes, sir.

He goes off.

JENNER *enters with a cup of tea.*

TILLEY: Jenner!

JENNER: Yes, sir?

TILLEY: Get the stretcher-bearers!

JENNER: Yes, sir.

He puts the cup of tea on the table and rushes off.

PERRY *flings several papers and magazines off the bunk downstage and makes a pillow from a pack that is lying nearby.* *Two* MEN *carry in* JOHN *and lay him on the bunk.* BABE *jumps to his feet.*

BABE (*shrilly*): What's happened? What's happened?

TILLEY: Quiet—get some water—quickly!

He stands looking at JOHN *carefully.* BABE *hurries over with a mug of water.* TILLEY *takes it from him, and kneeling down, hoists* JOHN'S *head up a little and forces some water between his lips.* PERRY *stands a little way off watching, his hands are twitching nervously.*

BABE (*bursting into sobs*): It's my fault! It's my fault! He was doing my duty for me, it ought to have been me. Oh Christ! It ought to have been me! (*He crumples up against the table.*)

TILLEY: Shut up—for God's sake be quiet!

JOHN (*opens his eyes and smiles, speaking painfully*): I'll know now, Perry—I'm right, I bet you I'm right—I'll know—I'll know——

Two STRETCHER-BEARERS *come in as the* LIGHT *fades out and there is complete darkness and silence except for the distant rumbling of guns.*

END OF SCENE I

SCENE II

SIR JAMES CAVAN'S *house in Kent. It is a spring evening, about nine o'clock in the year* 1930. *The scene is* LADY CAVAN'S *bedroom. It is a comfortable and charmingly furnished room, and the view from the window is magnificent. First, low wooded hills, then the Romney Marshes, and beyond them, the sea.*

LADY CAVAN *is seated by the window at a bridge table playing Canfield Patience. She is a graceful-looking old lady. The twilight is fading rapidly, and every now and then she pauses in her game to look out at the distant lights coming to life along the coast. When the curtain has been up for a few moments* JOHN *walks quietly into the room. He is in uniform and looks exactly as he did in the preceding scene. As he comes in, there seems to be a distant rumble of guns a long way off, and the suggestion of a Verey flare shining briefly and dying away. He stands by the table opposite to* LADY CAVAN. *She sees him and puts down the pack of cards slowly.*

LADY C. (*in a whisper*): Johnnie!

JOHN: Hullo, mother!

LADY C.: I daren't speak loudly or move, you might disappear.

JOHN: I won't disappear. I've only just come.

LADY CAVAN holds out her arms. JOHN comes round the table and kneels on the floor by her chair. She holds him tightly and very still.

LADY C.: It can't be a dream, I'm wide awake.

JOHN: I don't believe I've quite got away yet really. I can still hear the guns. (*He suddenly bends and clutches his stomach.*) Oh God!

LADY C. (*whispering*): Does it hurt terribly, my darling?

JOHN: Just a bit—it'll pass off.

LADY C.: Keep very still for a minute.

JOHN: Darling Mum!

LADY C.: Will it matter if I turn on the reading lamp? It's so dark and I do want to see you.

JOHN *makes a movement.*

Don't move. I can do it with my left hand.

She switches on a small lamp on the table.

There! That's better!

JOHN (*smiling*): Much better. (*He fidgets a little.*)

LADY C.: Are you uncomfortable?

JOHN: A little bit.

LADY C.: I'll leave go of you if you promise not to go away again, without warning me.

JOHN: I promise. (*He kisses her.*)

JOHN *gets up and sits opposite to her at the table.*

Good old Canfield! (*He puts his hand across the table and takes hers.*)

LADY C.: I got it out yesterday.

JOHN: Without cheating?

LADY C. (*shaking her head*): No.

JOHN (*looking out of the window*): How lovely and quiet it is!

LADY C. (*in a strained voice*): Oh darling! You weren't in very great pain were you, when——

JOHN: No—hardly any at all.

LADY C.: They said you couldn't have been because

it was all over so quickly, but I wasn't sure.

JOHN : Don't let's think about that.

LADY C. : A little of course, like just now, that can't be helped. (*She suddenly crumples on to the table with her head in her arms.*)

JOHN (*stroking her hair*) : Mum—don't—please, don't !

LADY C. (*brokenly*) : I'm a silly old fool, wasting precious time——

JOHN : It doesn't matter about time, really it doesn't —don't cry !

LADY C. : I'm not crying, it's something inside twisting horribly like it did years ago when—when—I couldn't cry then, I tried to because I thought it would be a relief, but it was no use, I couldn't, not for ages, and then only over stupid trivial things. (*She raises her head and sits back in her chair.*) Oh Johnnie—how dreadfully tired you look !

JOHN : We all look tired I'm afraid.

LADY C. : Why didn't you come sooner ?

JOHN (*surprised*) : Sooner ? I wasn't hit until a few minutes ago.

LADY C. : Thirteen years ago.

JOHN (*wondering*) : Oh !

LADY C. : Didn't you know ?

JOHN : I thought you looked a little older, I wondered why.

LADY C. : I nearly died last year. I'm glad I didn't now, although I was sorry then. I should have missed you.

JOHN (*stricken*) : Oh Mum, that would have been unbearable. (*He clutches her hand again.*)

LADY C. : We'd have found each other somehow.

JOHN : Thirteen years—then—it's—it's——

LADY C.: 1930.

JOHN: How funny that sounds! I wonder where I've been!

LADY C.: Can't you remember?

JOHN: No—not a thing—I just swapped duties with Babe because he was so upset over Armitage, I hopped over the parapet with the covering party. It was all pretty quiet, then there was a flare and a lot of row suddenly, and I fell down and couldn't get up—I remember Perry looking at me though, just for a second, that was later, I was in the shelter again—he's there now—I can see him now—Perry——

LADY C. (*gripping both his hands*): No, no, darling—not yet—stay a little longer—not yet—please, please, please—(*His voice breaks.*)

JOHN (*quite naturally*): All right, darling—don't fuss.

LADY C.: I won't ask any questions—don't try to remember anything—ask me things and I'll answer, ordinary things; there have been tremendous changes everywhere, London looks quite different, you should see Regent Street, and Park Lane, and you can telephone to America quite easily, your father does it from his office every day—just as though he were speaking to the next room——

JOHN: Father—where is he?

LADY C.: In London. He comes down for week-ends.

JOHN: Still the *Mercury*?

LADY C.: Yes.

JOHN: Oh God!

LADY C.: A million copies a day, I believe.

JOHN: Is he just the same?

LADY C.: He's fatter.

JOHN: And is he still—I mean—still going on like he used to?

LADY C.: Yes. It's Viola Blake at the moment.

JOHN: Who's she?

LADY C.: A film actress, very pretty and quite civil, she pronounces it Vi*o*la.

JOHN: Sounds like a shaving stick!

LADY C.: They all came down here one day, a huge party of them with cameras and things and she acted all over the garden with a bright yellow face.

They both laugh a little.

JOHN: Did you mind?

LADY C.: No, I rather enjoyed it.

There is a pause for a moment.

JOHN (*quietly*): What's happened to Monica?

LADY C. (*swiftly*): Monica's married, Harriet's married, too, quite a nice little man called Stokes; he's a writer. Of course he's completely under her thumb, she was always domineering, even when you were children, wasn't she?

JOHN (*thoughtfully*): Yes.

LADY C.: And she's become a Christian Scientist, it's made her a trifle hard I think, but she seems very pleased with it. They have a child, poor little thing!

JOHN: How old is Harriet?

LADY C.: Forty-two.

JOHN: Then I must be forty?

LADY C.: No, darling, no, you're not. Don't think about that.

JOHN (*patting her hand*): Don't be frightened—go on talking! You said Monica was married.

LADY C.: Yes, she married very well.

JOHN: Who?

LADY C.: Bertie Chellerton.

John: Oh!

There is a pause.

Is she happy?

LADY C.: I believe so. I haven't seen her for years, except in the illustrated papers.

JOHN (*putting his head down*): I hope she's happy!

LADY C.: Please don't worry your head about her, darling. She seems to lead a lovely life, full of excitements and fun.

JOHN: I can't help worrying a bit. You see I'm still in love with her, I haven't had time not to be.

LADY C. (*sadly*): I see.

JOHN: You never cared for her much, did you?

LADY C.: I tried to like her, Johnnie, for your sake.

JOHN: Yes, I knew that.

LADY C.: I never thought she, was worthy of you.

JOHN: All mothers think that don't they?

LADY C.: Perhaps they do.

JOHN: It's inevitable, I expect. A sort of jealousy without meaning to be.

LADY C.: I expect it is.

JOHN: So she married Bertie Chellerton. I don't think I've ever seen him. Is he nice?

LADY C.: He looks quite pleasant.

JOHN: Was she upset when—thirteen years ago?

LADY C.: She wrote me a very sweet letter.

JOHN: I'm glad. When did she marry?

LADY C.: 1920.

JOHN: Ten years ago?

LADY C.: Yes.

JOHN: It's nice to think she waited a bit. I want to see her awfully.

LADY C.: Oh no—no.

JOHN: Yes, mum, I must really, some time. Are they in love still?

LADY C.: I suppose so. They go to the Opera together, in the *Tatler*. (*She turns away.*)

JOHN (*impulsively*): I'm sorry, dearest. We won't talk about her any more.

LADY C.: You're right. I am jealous, really. You see, you're all I've got, all I've ever had. Harriet never counted as much as you did, and now, in this strange moment between life and death I want you all to myself, if I can't have you quite all, don't let me know, there's a dear boy! (*She tries to smile but doesn't succeed very well.*)

JOHN: I didn't mean to hurt you.

LADY C.: Don't be silly. Of course you didn't.

JOHN: I love you with all that's best in me—always.

He gets up and wanders about the room. LADY CAVAN *watches him—he stops in front of a picture.*

I remembered that picture the other day, quite suddenly, just before an attack, wasn't it funny? I saw it as clearly as though someone had held it in front of my nose.

LADY C.: You always liked it, even when you were tiny.

JOHN: It isn't very good really, is it?

LADY C.: Your Aunt Lilian painted it when she was a girl. I was brought up to think it very beautiful indeed. I suppose it is dreadfully amateurish.

JOHN: The sheep look a bit lop-sided. Apart from that, it's all right.

LADY C.: Sheep are very difficult.

JOHN *picks up a book from the table by the bed.*

JOHN (*looking at it wonderingly*): "*Post-Mortem*" by Perry Lomas—Perry Lomas!

LADY C. (*rising*): Put it down, darling—don't open it—please put it down. (*She comes over and takes it from him.*)

JOHN: Is it new?

LADY C.: Yes—it's only just published.

JOHN: Perry! So he came through all right.

LADY C.: He sent it to me, he said he thought you would have liked him to, I've got the letter somewhere, it's a bitter book and terribly sad.

JOHN: War?

LADY C.: Mostly. It's caused a great sensation. There's a rumour that it's going to be burnt publicly or something——

JOHN: Good God, why?

LADY C.: They say because it's blasphemous and seditious and immoral and lots of other things.

JOHN: They?

LADY C.: The Press.

JOHN: The *Mercury*?

LADY C.: Yes. I'm afraid the *Mercury* started all the trouble. Alfred Borrow wrote a violent attack on the front page. He's City Editor now and very important.

JOHN: That slimy little man who used to be father's secretary?

LADY C.: Yes.

JOHN: What did you think of it, mother?

LADY C.: I could hardly bear it, but I think that was because of you. There are hundreds of war books now, they're the fashion, perhaps it's a good thing for those who forget too easily.

JOHN: But they can't burn Perry's book just because

a rag like the *Mercury* makes a stunt of attacking it!

LADY C.: The *Mercury's* very powerful.

JOHN: So he's done it. He said somebody would. Give it to me, mother. I want to read it.

LADY C.: No, no, don't! What's the use?

JOHN: I must see father.

LADY C.: That wouldn't do any good. He doesn't care whether it's good or bad. It's just a scoop for the paper——

JOHN: Please give it to me.

LADY C.: Very well.

JOHN *takes it and opens it at random.*

JOHN: I think I know it somehow. Where is Perry—in London?

LADY C.: Yes. (*She smiles wistfully.*) You're going to see him, too, I suppose?

JOHN: I must. I must see them all, I've got to know what's happening.

LADY C. (*pleading*): I can tell you everything that's happening if you'll only stay here quietly with me. I can tell you better than they can——

JOHN: That's why I came back—to find out something.

LADY C.: There's nothing, nothing worth finding out——

JOHN: I must see for myself.

LADY C. (*holding him imploringly*): Listen to me, John, Johnnie, my darling, look at me! There's only one thing in the world worth finding, worth catching hold of, if only for a moment, and that's here in this room between you and me. Don't you understand, I don't want you to be hurt any more. Stay, ask me anything, I'll be able to answer, I know now, I'll tear the truth out of infinity for you, even if I break my heart in doing it, only stay, don't leave me !

JOHN: You don't understand. There's a fraction of a fraction of a second when you have a chance of seeing everything for yourself if only you're strong enough. I must be strong enough. That's why it all happened; that's why I'm here, I must try, even if I fail, I must try. Let me go, darling, please!

LADY C.: No, no, no!

JOHN: I won't go back finally without seeing you again. I promise, I swear it.

LADY C.: It isn't that. Go back now finally, say good-bye my own dearest and go, but don't open your eyes——

JOHN (*looking at her strangely*). How much have you ost?

LADY C.: Everything, but you.

JOHN: Everything—everything you've ever believed?

LADY C.: Yes. I'm too old to find new creeds and the old ones are all gone, swept away!

JOHN: God?

LADY C.: Whose God? There are so many, and they're all so foolish.

JOHN: Life Force, Force for Good, something?

LADY C.: Death Force, Force for Evil, Nothing, equal in futility!

JOHN: You're denying what you said just now. What of this that is here, between us?

LADY C.: A poor little spark, flickering for an instant in Eternity. What can that matter?

JOHN: It does matter, it does, it must——

LADY C.: Then stay, stay! There's such a little

time left, and I'm so lonely.

JOHN: I'll come back, but I must go now——

LADY C. (*brokenly*): Please, please!

JOHN (*taking her in his arms and holding her close, her face is hidden in his coat—he speaks very gently*): Listen, Mum, you understand really. It's just because you're tired that you're finding it hard to be brave. I felt like that often enough in the Line, the effort to be made seems too big for one's strength, immense and frightening, but it isn't too big actually once you start. You must steel your heart, darling, and let me go. I know about War—a bitter and cruel knowledge, horror upon horror, stretched far beyond breaking point, the few moments of gallant beauty there, are not enough measured against the hideous ages of suffering! Now, I must know about Peace, I must know whether by losing so much we have gained anything at all, or whether it was just blind futility like Perry said it was, I must know whether the ones who came home have slipped back into the old illusions and are rotting there, smug in false security, blotting out memory with the flimsy mysticism of their threadbare Christian legend, or whether they've had the courage to remember clearly and strike out for something new—something different! I must know for myself, it's the urge inside me that's carved this brief moment out of Time. You do understand, don't you?

LADY C.: Yes, dear. I understand. Come back once more, you promised!

JOHN: I'll come back. I swear it.

They cling together and for a moment it seems as though they are illumined by the vivid unnatural light of a Verey flare. There is a faint rumbling of guns in the distance. As the flare fades away LADY CAVAN *speaks:*

LADY C.: Take care of yourself, my dearest dear!

In the gathering darkness, JOHN'S *figure moves away from her and disappears into the shadows. There is complete darkness for a moment, then twilight returns to the garden and then the room.* LADY CAVAN *is seated at the table by the window. She holds a pack of cards in her hand, and thoughtfully places one on those lying on the table as the* LIGHTS FADE *and——*

THE CURTAIN FALLS

SCENE III

The Chellerton's house in Mount Street. The scene is Monica's sitting-room. It is furnished in quite good ultra modern taste, although tending slightly to exaggeration.

When the curtain rises MONICA *is lying on the sofa attired in rather bizarre pyjamas, which, in her epoch, have taken the place of tea-gowns and negligees. She is reading "Vogue," smoking and listening to a panatrope; one of the new kind which has been set with twelve records and seems to show no signs of flagging.* MONICA *is not exactly handsome, nor pretty, but somehow brilliant looking. She has the reputation of being witty and her parties are always successful.* JOHN *is standing at the head of the sofa just behind her, she hasn't seen him yet and goes on reading. He comes slowly down to the foot of the sofa.*

JOHN: Hallo, Monica!

MONICA (*looking up*): My God!

JOHN: Don't be frightened, please!

MONICA (*wide-eyed, staring at him*): John?

JOHN: Yes, I've come back for a little.

MONICA (*opening and shutting her eyes rapidly*): I'm stark staring mad!

JOHN (*wonderingly*): You have changed—tremendously!

MONICA: I suppose this is a dream?

JOHN: Not exactly, at least, I don't know, perhaps for you it is!

MONICA: What else could it be?

JOHN: Some sort of magic.

MONICA (*rallying*): I don't know what to say quite.

JOHN: Are you pleased to see me?

MONICA: I don't know, it's such a shock—(*her voice softens.*) Yes, of course I'm pleased to see you—dear John.

She puts out her hand with a slight effort, JOHN *takes it and she jerks it away again instinctively.*

JOHN: I wish you wouldn't be frightened!

MONICA: I'm not. Not exactly frightened, but you must admit it's a little shattering for me.

JOHN: I suppose it must be.

MONICA: I expect it's the effect of all those damned war books, getting on my nerves; I'll take some aspirin when I wake up. I wish I could remember when I went to sleep—it is after dinner, isn't it?

JOHN: Yes. (*He looks at his watch.*) It's just nine

MONICA: Have you dined?

JOHN: Yes, a little while ago.

MONICA: You look awfully tired. Would you like a drink or something! (*She laughs.*) Oh—it seems funny offering a ghost a drink!

JOHN: I'm not quite a ghost yet, and I should like some brandy.

She rises and moves over to the bell, never taking her eyes off him.

MONICA (*pressing the bell*): Do sit down, John dear—you can sit down, can't you?

JOHN: Could we stop the gramophone first?

MONICA: I'd forgotten it was going. (*She stops it.*)

JOHN : Does it go on playing for ever ?

MONICA : Practically !

He comes over to it.

You see that sinister little arm keeps on slapping them on and snatching them off all by itself, horrid, isn't it ?

JOHN : Good idea really, saves all that business of winding.

MONICA : It's certainly convenient, but rather scare making, don't you think ? Everything's absolutely terrifying nowadays. I'm seriously thinking of going into a monastery.

She said this at dinner a few nights ago and everybody laughed. JOHN *smiles, rather absently.*

JOHN : Oh, Monica ! (*He sits down.*)

MONICA (*sensing disapproval*) : What's the matter ?

JOHN : Nothing.

MONICA : Cigarette ? (*She offers him a box.*)

JOHN (*looking at her as he takes one*) : Yes—thanks.

She lights it for him as DRAKE, *the butler, enters.*

DRAKE : You rang, my lady ?

MONICA : Yes, bring some brandy, please. (*To* JOHN.) Would you like some coffee ?

JOHN : No, thank you.

MONICA (*to* DRAKE) : Just brandy then.

DRAKE : Very good, my lady.

He goes out.

MONICA (*conversationally*) : He's called Drake. Isn't he sweet ?

JOHN (*smiling*) : Frightfully sweet.

MONICA : Once when we were dining out we saw him in a very grand car in Eaton Square, and Eggie said 'Drake is going West, lad.' You'll like Eggie, he's terribly funny.

JOHN: Who's Eggie?

MONICA: Eggie Brace. He's Lord Verilow's son, you know, our old friend impoverished nobility, very enjoyable. Eggie's one of your father's toadies, he writes snappy gossip for the *Mercury*. You must have seen him, he's always with your father.

JOHN: I haven't seen father yet.

MONICA: Darling Jumbo! We all worship him, particularly when he comes over Napoleonic—he's too lovely.

JOHN: I remember now. Maisie Lorrimer used to call father "Jumbo."

MONICA (*surprised*): Maisie Lorrimer! Why she's been dead for years, she fell out of something or other.

JOHN: Lots of things happen in thirteen years!

MONICA (*hurriedly*): You'll see Eggie soon. He and Kitty Harris are coming to fetch me, we're going to a gloomy party at the Friedlanders. (*She pauses.*) Will Kitty and Eggie be able to see you as well, I mean, if they come before I wake up?

JOHN: Yes, I expect so. Drake saw me all right, didn't he?

MONICA: You can never tell with Drake. He has such perfect manners. If he came in and found John the Baptist playing the gramophone without his head, he wouldn't flicker an eyelash! We'll see how many glasses he brings.

> JOHN *laughs.* DRAKE *re-enters with a tray on which there are two big glasses and a decanter. He pours some brandy into one and hands it to* MONICA. *Then he pours some into the other glass and hands it to* JOHN.

JOHN: Thank you.

DRAKE *goes out.*

MONICA: There now! He probably thinks you're going to a fancy dress ball or something.

JOHN: Monica!

MONICA: Yes, John?

JOHN: Come off it.

MONICA: What do you mean?

JOHN: There's so much to say—we haven't said anything yet.

MONICA (*turning away*): I don't understand.

JOHN: Yes, you do. You must, inside, you can't have changed as much as all that.

MONICA: You're not approving of me, are you? (*She laughs.*)

JOHN: I haven't seen you yet.

MONICA: You mustn't be pompous, dear.

JOHN: Isn't it any use?

MONICA (*irritably*): Isn't what any use?

JOHN: How old are you?

MONICA: Thirty-three, and doing nicely thank you.

JOHN: I keep on seeing you as you were and then trying to fit it in with you as you are.

MONICA: This isn't a very comfortable dream!

JOHN: Don't shut me out, it's awfully important. I've only got a little while.

MONICA: I'm not shutting you out. I'm delighted to see you again. I've just told you.

JOHN: Have you any children?

MONICA: No.

JOHN: What a shame!

MONICA: Why? Do you think I ought to have?

JOHN: Not if you don't want to.

MONICA: I'm not very good at children, you know.

Not that I don't like them, I do really, when they're funny and nice.

JOHN (*smiling*): And other people's?

MONICA: Exactly. Violet Furleigh's children for instance. They adore me, and I play with them for hours. They always look forward to the week-ends that I'm going to be down there. But I'm afraid I can only be maternal in small doses.

JOHN: I see.

MONICA: You don't. You've got a Victorian look in your eye.

JOHN: Should we have had children if we'd married, I wonder?

MONICA (*in a softer voice*): You were terribly in love with me, weren't you?

JOHN: Yes.

MONICA: Poor old John!

JOHN: Weren't you, with me?

MONICA: Of course. You knew I was, but it's a long time ago, isn't it? (*Her voice rises slightly.*) Isn't it?

JOHN: For you.

MONICA: You mean—you're still—still there?

JOHN: I'm afraid so.

MONICA: I see.

There is silence for a moment.

JOHN: I was a fool to come.

MONICA: I feel awfully stupid, as if I were going to cry.

She rises abruptly and goes to the window.

JOHN: Nothing to cry about.

MONICA: I'm not so sure.

JOHN: Monica!

She doesn't answer.

Monica!

MONICA (*turning*): Don't speak, please. I want to wake up, I want to wake up!

JOHN: I'll go. (*He gets up.*) I don't want to upset you.

MONICA: John—don't go—please!

The door opens and KITTY HARRIS *and* EGGIE BRACE *enter.* KITTY *is young and pretty and consistently silly.* EGGIE *is moon-faced and has a slight stammer which never interferes with his good remarks and enhances some of his bad ones.*

KITTY: Darling, you're not dressed or anything! (*She sees* JOHN.) Oh!

MONICA (*mechanically*): Kitty, this is John Cavan—Lady Catherine Harris, Lord Brace——

KITTY (*shaking hands vaguely*): How do you do——

EGGIE: How do you do! (*Then to* MONICA.) Jumbo's in great form to-night. He's gone trumpeting off to one of his conferences surrounded by bishops and deans. We've got the Home Secretary to stop all sales of this Lomas book. That's what they're all up to to-night. They want to get it publicly burnt like J-J-Joan of Arc. The *Mercury* Printing Presses are fairly bouncing up and down like V-v-virgin B-brides, waiting to be ravished by the story. Poor Lomas is for it all right, I haven't read the damned thing myself, but it's full of bits from all accounts——

KITTY: I've read it, it's marvellous! I found a copy tucked away in Hatchard's just before the fuss started—it's probably worth millions now!

EGGIE: Can't we have a drink or something?

MONICA: Of course.

She goes towards the bell but DRAKE *has anticipated her and enters with a large tray of drinks which he places on a side table and exits.*

KITTY *switches on the panatrope so the ensuing conversation is naturally pitched rather more loudly.*

EGGIE (*waving a whisky bottle at* JOHN) : Drink ?

JOHN : No thanks.

EGGIE : Kitty ?

KITTY (*using her lip-stick*) : Yes, please. Small one !

EGGIE : You'll have to hurry, Monica. You know what Millie is over her musical parties.

KITTY : Poor Millie ! Her house is much too small——

EGGIE : Even for c-c-chamber music.

Everybody laughs except JOHN

(*To* MONICA) Drink ?

MONICA : No, I've got some brandy somewhere.

EGGIE (*continuing the conversation*) : And her head's much too big.

MONICA : I'm not coming to the Friedlanders !

KITTY : Monica !

MONICA : I want to talk to John.

KITTY : Bring him, too.

EGGIE (*to* JOHN) : Yes, it wouldn't take you long to change, would it ?

JOHN : These are the only clothes I have.

KITTY : Do come, it's sure to be agony.

JOHN : No thanks, really—I think I'd feel out of it.

KITTY : How absurd ! You could talk about the War. Nobody who can talk about the War's out of it now, are they, Eggie ?

EGGIE : I think the War's a bore, a b-b-bore war.

KITTY: Not very funny, my sweet, that will do for your column.

MONICA: I quite agree. It is a great bore, but John and I are not going to talk about the War, are we, John?

JOHN: I think I must be getting along, Monica. I've got to see Perry.

MONICA: Who on earth's Perry?

JOHN: Just an old friend of mine, nobody you know.

EGGIE (*to* MONICA): What's happened to Freddy?

MONICA: He's in Paris with Laura.

EGGIE: Somebody told me that, but I couldn't b-b-bring myself to believe it—you're beautifully composed about it.

MONICA: I don't see any reason to be anything else.

KITTY: Monica's always composed, aren't you, dear?

EGGIE: Hard as nails, utterly ruthless, when l-l-love is o-o-over how little lovers thingummy bob——

MONICA (*sharply*): Shut up, Eggie!

KITTY: Freddy's a fool anyhow! I always thought so.

MONICA: You didn't always show it!

KITTY: And Laura's a half-wit, they're admirably suited.

EGGIE: Go carefully, Kitty. There may be t-t-tendrils of affection still twining round Monica's stony heart! I shall write a dear little bit about Freddy and Laura being in Paris. Where are they—at the Ritz?

MONICA: You're too late, it's already in the *Standard*.

EGGIE: Did Burford ring you up?

MONICA: Don't be ridiculous, Eggie! As if I'd

talk about my private affairs to the Press.

EGGIE: The Press seems to have a pretty good rough idea of them!

KITTY: Don't quarrel, you two!

EGGIE (*injured*): Nobody ever gives me any news, I always have to scavenge round for it, it's a great mistake writing about people you know.

MONICA (*sharply*): If it was really *writing* it wouldn't matter so much!

KITTY (*taking* EGGIE's *arm*): Give up, Eggie, Monica's remarkably snappy to-night.

They both move away slightly towards the panatrope.

JOHN (*quietly to* MONICA): Good-bye!

MONICA (*with sudden intensity, unheard by the others*): Please stay—you owe it to me—you haven't given me a chance yet!

JOHN: Get rid of them—for God's sake!

KITTY (*coming down*): Darling—do hurry!

MONICA: I told you, I'm not coming.

KITTY: Just for a few minutes?

MONICA: No—(*Almost wildly*)—No!

KITTY: Well, you needn't snap my head off just because you've got a bit of private nonsense on. (*She looks at* JOHN *and laughs.*) I do hope he'll be a comfort, darling, he looks a bit gloomy to me—Eggie!

EGGIE: What?

KITTY: Put on the "Blue Danube" dear and come away!

EGGIE: What for? (*He stops the panatrope.*)

KITTY: Monica wants us to go!

EGGIE: How inhospitable! Is this true, Monica?

MONICA: Yes. I may join you later, I don't know, I'll see.

KITTY (*catching* EGGIE's *arm*): Come on!

EGGIE (*gulping down his drink*): All right!—"Impoverished Peer asked to leave Lady Chellerton's House in Mount Street." "Full story on Page 8." (*He waves genially to* JOHN.) See you later!

KITTY (*to* MONICA): Good-bye, darling—have fun! (*To* JOHN.) Good-bye!

JOHN: Good-bye!

MONICA: Good-bye!

EGGIE *and* KITTY *go out*.

MONICA: I'm sorry, John.

JOHN: What for?

MONICA: All that.

JOHN: Why—it's part of your life, isn't it?

MONICA: They don't matter a bit.

JOHN: Don't apologise for them, that makes it worse.

MONICA: I hate them, particularly Eggie, he's got a mind like a third-rate housemaid.

JOHN: You said he was a darling a little while ago, and terribly funny!

MONICA: He can be sometimes, but he wasn't to-night.

JOHN: That was my fault. I was the wrong note.

MONICA: Yes, that's probably true. (*She flings herself down on the sofa.*) Anyhow you've managed to make me utterly miserable if that's any comfort to you.

JOHN: I'm sorry!

MONICA: Why did you come? You might have known it would be a failure.

JOHN: How could I know? I've been too far away to know anything but the more concrete horrors.

MONICA: You're not going to begin about the War,

are you ? I couldn't bear it.

JOHN : Why couldn't you bear it ?

MONICA : Because it's over and done with and boring to the last degree.

JOHN : It isn't over and done with for me !

MONICA : You're dead, don't be silly, you're dead !

JOHN : I couldn't die until I was free.

MONICA : What do you mean ?

JOHN : You've made it just a little easier for me, only a few more minutes left, I must go——

He goes towards the door. MONICA *rises swiftly and intercepts him.*

MONICA : No, no, forgive me, I didn't mean it. I wouldn't have talked like that if I hadn't been puzzled and bewildered and scared ! Give me a chance to explain, I can't change back all in a minute, but I'll try. I swear I will, if you want me to, enough !

JOHN (*gently*) : It doesn't matter, Monica. It's only my personal view ! You go your own way and don't be upset. You've got a life to live, I haven't. Don't worry about me !

MONICA : I loved you ! I swear I did. (*She is crying now.*)

JOHN (*leading her down to the sofa*) : There, there ! That's all right—I know you did——

MONICA (*suddenly clinging to him*) : I could love you again, if you wanted me——

JOHN (*drawing away*) : No, Monica, don't say that !

MONICA (*wildly*) : It's true.

JOHN (*remotely*) : Our love wouldn't meet now, there's a gap of too many years !

MONICA (*whispering*) : John, don't be so dreadfully stern and sure. Kiss me, just once, won't you ? Even if it's only to say good-bye—won't you, please?

JOHN: Of course.

He kisses her, she twines her arms round his neck and relaxes in his embrace. BERTIE CHELLERTON *enters. He is amiable-looking, about forty, a trifle puffy from good living, but possessing a certain charm. He is obviously embarrassed but covers it more or less successfully after the first start.* MONICA *and* JOHN *break away.*

BERTIE: I'm so sorry to come bursting in like that. I'd no idea you were at home!

MONICA (*with an effort*): It doesn't matter, dear. John, this is my husband—John Cavan!

BERTIE (*shaking hands*): Of course. Monica's often spoken of you. How are you?

JOHN (*suddenly*): I'd like to apologise—you see Monica and I were engaged once, years ago, and—and —we hadn't seen each other since. That's why——

BERTIE: I know—I know—don't say any more, please. It was my fault for blundering in. Monica and I understand one another perfectly, we've been married too long to be anything but just good friends. You were killed in 1916, weren't you?

JOHN: 1917.

BERTIE: Yes, of course. There was a great pal of mine in your show—Teddy Filson. Do you remember him?

JOHN: Yes. Quite well.

BERTIE: I must be getting along now. I'm supposed to be at the Pavilion with Mary and Jack. They've got a box or something. I was bringing this telegram to put on your desk, Monica, it's from the Burdon's asking us down on the 20th. D'you want to go?

MONICA: I'll think about it and let you know later.

BERTIE: Right. (*He smiles at* JOHN.) Cheero! (*Then under his breath to* MONICA.) For God's sake, lock the door next time. That was damned awkward!

He goes out.

There is a silence for a moment. JOHN *starts laughing—a strained laugh.*

MONICA: Don't, John, please!

JOHN: I can't help it. It's funny.

MONICA: You'll never forgive me now, will you?

JOHN: Forgive you?

MONICA: You know what I mean.

JOHN: There's nothing to forgive, honestly there isn't. It hasn't anything to do with it.

MONICA: I'm sorry I've let you down.

JOHN: I don't matter. It's you that matters.

MONICA (*smiling*): Mattered—past tense, please—mattered once, a long while ago, not any more, not now.

JOHN (*suddenly sitting down and burying his face in his hands*): Oh God! It's all so silly!

MONICA: Don't be miserable, please—if you'd come back all right years ago and we'd married as we'd planned, it might all have been different.

JOHN (*looking up*): I wonder!

MONICA: This won't last, will it—this feeling that I've got now? It'll pass away when I wake up, won't it?

JOHN: I expect so.

MONICA: I couldn't bear it if it didn't. I just couldn't bear it—I wish you wouldn't look at me like that.

JOHN: Good-bye, Monica dear. I'm really going this time, and I won't worry you again ever, even in dreams, I promise! Never think I regret having loved you, I'm grateful to you for a lot of happiness. It was jolly planning a future, it passed the time.

MONICA: Yes, it passed the time all right—and that's all I've done ever since, though I don't know what right you have to accuse me. Oh, I know you didn't actually in so many words, but your eyes did—you died young, who are you to judge, you hadn't yet found out about everything being a bore.

JOHN *quietly goes away, but she goes on talking without seeing him—the* LIGHTS *begin to fade.*

I don't see why I shouldn't try to justify myself really. I'm quite nice and kind to people. I don't cheat or lie, or steal, I like being popular and having people in love with me; why shouldn't I? There's no harm in that, really, all the fuss that's made about having affairs, it's silly! I might have had an affair with you just now if Bertie hadn't come in. Funny having an affair with a ghost—funny having an affair with a ghost——

She speaks the last few lines in the pitch dark, the panatrope blares out, but the LIGHTS *don't go up.*

CURTAIN

SCENE IV

The scene is PERRY LOMAS' *sitting-room. It is poorly furnished, there is a bed on one side of the stage, and a few books about. One or two cane armchairs and a table in the centre.*

When the curtain rises PERRY *is seated at the table writing. There is a tray of half-eaten food which he has pushed on one side. Lying on the table just beyond the paper upon which he is writing, is a revolver.* PERRY *is still thin and nervy looking. His hair is scantier than in Scene I and grey.* JOHN *appears in the pool of light shed over the table from a hanging lamp.*

JOHN: Perry?

PERRY (*not looking up*): Yes?

JOHN: It's me—John!

PERRY (*peering at him*): Oh, sit down.

JOHN: Don't you recognise me?

PERRY: Wait a minute till I've finished this.

JOHN: But, Perry!

PERRY: Wait, wait a minute, please!

JOHN *sits down.* PERRY *goes on writing. He finally reads through the letter he has finished, and putting it into an envelope, seals it down. He sits back and looks at* JOHN, *then he smiles.*

I thought you'd have vanished by the time I looked up again.

JOHN: I'm awfully glad to see you, Perry.

PERRY: Well, you're only just in time.

JOHN: What do you mean?

PERRY (*taking up the revolver*): Good-bye!

He is about to place it to his head when JOHN *leans over and grabs his arm.*

JOHN: Stop—no—not yet—Perry.

PERRY: So you're tangible, that's surprising!

JOHN: Give me that gun.

PERRY: If this is my brain beginning to snap I'm damned if I'm going to wait and watch it happen. (*He tries to lift his arm again.*) I'm going to anticipate it!

JOHN (*struggling with him*): Not yet, please not yet, Perry.

PERRY: Let me go, damn you!

JOHN: Don't be a fool!

PERRY: That's not being a fool, there are thousands of ways of being a fool in life, but not in death. You must know all about that.

JOHN: I don't, I don't know anything, but I'm beginning to. It isn't as swift as you think.

PERRY: Don't put me off, there's a good chap. It's all I've got to look forward to.

JOHN: Just a few minutes can't make any difference.

PERRY: Why should I listen to you? My mind's made up. I'm all ready.

JOHN: I want to know why you're doing it.

PERRY: That's easy.

JOHN: Tell me. Put that revolver down, and tell me.

PERRY: Heart to heart talk with spook, very difficult.

JOHN: Please!

PERRY: You always got your own way when you were alive, it's clever of you to keep it up when you're dead. (*He puts the revolver down.*) There! Would you like a drink, I believe there's still some left?

JOHN: No thanks.

PERRY (*looking at him curiously*): I remember you so clearly, in those last few moments lying on the bunk. I hated it, seeing you brought in like that. It came so unexpectedly. After all there hadn't been any heavy shelling, everything was quiet and you were so very very alive always, even when you were tired. What have you been up to all this time?

JOHN: I don't know, waiting, I suppose.

PERRY: Where?

JOHN: I don't know that either.

PERRY: Haven't you met any spirits yet, socially?

JOHN: Not one.

PERRY: Haven't you even been in touch with Sir Oliver Lodge?

JOHN: No.

PERRY: Well you ought to be ashamed of yourself, a fine upstanding ghost of your age, shilly shallying about and getting nowhere. I don't know what the spirit world's coming to, and that's a fact!

JOHN: It's what I was talking to you about, the infinitesimal moment, don't you remember? You see it's "now" for me and "then" for you.

PERRY (*flippantly*): And "two for tea and tea for two!"

JOHN: Don't evade me by being flippant, Perry, it's not kind.

PERRY: You're so earnest, so very earnest.

JOHN: You can't talk, you're earnest enough to commit suicide.

PERRY: True—true!

JOHN: And you won't even tell me why!

PERRY: It's difficult to tabulate it in words.

JOHN: Try. I do want to know.

PERRY: Curioser nor a cat!

JOHN: Why, Perry, why?

PERRY: A sort of hopelessness which isn't quite despair, not localised enough for that. A formless, deserted boredom, everything eliminated, whittled right down to essentials, essentials which aren't there.

JOHN: Are you sure?

PERRY: Yes, quite sure, for me, anyway.

JOHN: Personal view again.

PERRY: There's nothing else, that's all there is for any of us.

JOHN: No, you're wrong. There must be something more.

PERRY: Still floundering about after ultimate truths? Really, Master John, you're dead enough to know better.

JOHN: I'm beginning to wish I were.

PERRY: Why?

JOHN: I'm getting scared. I wasn't when I started.

PERRY: What's upset you?

JOHN: Change and decay. (*He laughs suddenly.*)

PERRY: Oh good! Splendid! You're coming along nicely.

JOHN: I thought that would please you.

PERRY: It doesn't please me exactly, but it's interesting.

JOHN: I suppose it is.

PERRY: Where did you start?

JOHN: Mother!

PERRY: How did that go? How did you find her?

JOHN: Strong and clear as always.

PERRY: That's the only form of sex that really holds.

JOHN (*with sudden fury*) : Go to hell! You'll never find peace, not in a million deaths.

PERRY : Don't get rattled!

JOHN : Your bitterness is too bitter, deep down in your heart, nullifying any chance you might have.

PERRY : You mustn't be superior just because you've got a mother. I haven't. Never have had since I was two. No compromise for me.

JOHN (*looking down*) : I'm sorry.

PERRY : So you bloody well ought to be. Coming it over me with your mother love, and Christmas decorations and frosted robins!

JOHN : Shut up—do shut up! (*He buries his face in his hands.*)

PERRY : Well, who else? Who else have you seen?

JOHN : Why should I tell you? You won't understand, I don't like you enough really!

PERRY : You used to.

JOHN : That was different.

PERRY : And you've remembered to come and see me in your brief moment.

JOHN : I had to come.

PERRY : Why? It couldn't have been admiration of my point of view, reverence for my brain, you always thought me unbalanced.

JOHN : I feel sort of sorry for you.

PERRY : Very kind I'm sure. Lady Bountiful bringing me a basket of goodies from the grave.

JOHN : Don't misunderstand me. Not that sort of sorry.

PERRY : You're gibbering, old dear, just gibbering. Not being quite honest trying to fit half truths together, but they're too jagged and unmanageable. Better stop trying and come off your perch.

JOHN: What do you mean?

PERRY: I know why you're here, even if you don't.

JOHN: Tell me then!

PERRY: A gesture to memory, rather a gallant gesture, particularly from you, a farewell salute to things that have lain unsaid between us.

JOHN (*embarrassed*): Oh, Perry! Don't be such an ass.

PERRY: It's true! Nothing to be ashamed of. Look at me, through the me that's here, back to the me that you knew, and remember a little and be nice, because—because I'm feeling pretty low really. (*He looks fixedly at* JOHN *smiling, but his eyes are filled with tears.*)

JOHN (*wonderingly*): Vulnerable, over me?

PERRY: I never said I wasn't vulnerable.

JOHN: So that's why I came.

PERRY: I think so.

JOHN: Youth is a long way away, isn't it?

PERRY: Yes, it doesn't matter any more.

JOHN: Oh God! What a muddle!

PERRY (*gently*): You haven't answered my question. Who else have you seen?

JOHN: Nobody.

PERRY (*smiling*): Liar!

JOHN: Nobody I expected to see anyhow.

PERRY: Monica Chellerton, I suppose!

JOHN: Do you know her?

PERRY: No, I know of her. I remembered that you were engaged to her when I saw of her marriage years ago—I've watched her progress since then. Did she let you down very hard?

JOHN: I don't think, perhaps, it was altogether her fault.

PERRY: What did you expect?

JOHN: I don't know.

PERRY: Why wasn't it her fault?

JOHN: Circumstances, environment, money, all those silly people hemming her in.

PERRY: She could get out if she wanted to.

JOHN: Not as easily as all that.

PERRY: Why are you making excuses for her? It isn't her that you love, you'd stored up a pretty little sentimental memory, separated from reality by war, then you came back and took her by surprise before she had time to play up. Damned unfair I call it!

JOHN: Do you mean she was always playing up, even before?

PERRY: I expect so, it's her job.

JOHN: She loved me once.

PERRY: I'm sure she did, as much as she could. Don't worry about her, there are deeper sorrows than that. Hang around a bit longer and you'll see.

JOHN: I know about your book.

PERRY: Do you?

JOHN: Is it true that they're going to burn it?

PERRY: I expect so.

JOHN: Damn their eyes!

PERRY: They haven't got any to damn! They can't see, they can only grope with their instincts and the principal one, as usual, is fear. They're afraid my book might start something, that if they let it get by, it might encourage someone else to write a better one, clearer, more concise in simpler phrases. I tried to be as simple as possible, but I didn't succeed, that's what's wrong with the book. You have to talk to dogs in bone language and it's difficult, particularly if you don't care for dogs.

JOHN: Is it because of the book that you're going to—to——

PERRY: Kill myself?

JOHN: Yes. Have they got you down? Is that why?

PERRY: Lord no! I'm not killing myself because of the book, that's trivial compared with the rest. It was true you see, as true as I could make it, and that's that. I've got it out of me. It was received as I expected it to be received—outraged squeaks and yells. But none of that matters, even to me, now.

JOHN: What is it then?

PERRY: Deeper than that, far, far deeper. One little ego in the Universe, mine, humiliated and shamed into the dust by being alive. You're all right, you're safe. You're naturally idealistic, I never was. You're young. I never was. You're mercifully dead. This coming back to see is all very well, a good trick but no more. It's really as futile as everything else because as usual there's been a blunder. You're not the right sort to come back, you'll never see, your eyes are too kind. You can try, that's all, but you won't get far.

JOHN: It's nerves, this hatred in you. Nerves, you're ill! You've been working yourself to death over writing this book and now it's done, you're suffering from a reaction. You should go away quietly into the country somewhere and rest.

PERRY: Oh, John, good old John, how typical of you! Do you remember that night when somebody or other died and I was a bit upset and you told me to control my mind? You gave me a list of things to think about, a jolly little list, sleep, warmth, drink, food, self-preservation. You gave me that list, without a trace of irony, do you remember?

JOHN: I was right. This is the smash I was warning you about, but it's come later than I thought.

PERRY: You said that you believed something would come out of the war, that there was a reason for all that ignorant carnage, all that vitality and youth dying as bravely as it could not knowing why, years and years hence, you said, we shall see, something will rise out of the ashes, didn't you, didn't you?

JOHN: I still believe that.

PERRY: Hurry then, don't waste time with me.

JOHN: It may be that I've come back too soon.

PERRY (*rising irritably*): Come back again then. If your curiosity is tenacious enough, it can hold you indefinitely suspended between the grave and the stars; you can keep on coming back, but don't stay now, you've picked a bad moment.

JOHN: Why so bad? What is it? What's happening?

PERRY: Nothing's happening, really. There are strides being made forward in science and equal sized strides being made backwards in hypocrisy. People are just the same, individually pleasant and collectively idiotic. Machinery is growing magnificently, people paint pictures of it and compose ballets about it, the artists are cottoning on to that very quickly because they're scared that soon there won't be any other sort of beauty left, and they'll be stranded with nothing to paint, and nothing to write. Religion is doing very well. The Catholic Church still tops the bill as far as finance and general efficiency goes. The Church of England is still staggering along without much conviction. The Evangelists are screeching as usual and sending out missionaries. All the other sects are flourishing about equally. Christian Science is coming up smiling, a slightly superior smile, but always a smile. God is Love, there is no pain. Pain is error. Everything that isn't Love is error, like Hell it is. Politically all is confusion, but that's nothing new. There's still poverty, unemployment, pain, greed, cruelty, passion and crime. There's still meanness, jealousy, money and disease. The competitive sporting spirit is being admirably fostered, particularly as regards the Olympic games. A superb preparation for the next War, fully realised by everyone but the public that will be involved. The newspapers still lie over anything of importance, and the majority still believes them implicitly. The only real difference in Post War conditions is that there are so many men maimed for life and still existing, and so many women whose heartache will never heal. The rest is the same only faster, and more metricious. The War is fashionable now, like a pleasantly harrowing film. Even men who fought in it, some of them see in it a sort of vague glamour, they've slipped back as I knew they would. Come and see if you must, John. You can stand up under a few blows in the guts, you're strong in courage and true as far as you know, but what are you doing it for? Why not be content with the suffering you've had already out there. All the rest is unnecessary and doesn't help. Go back to your mother for the time that's left, say good-bye to her, be sweet to her as you're sweet to everybody and just a little sweeter, that may be worth something although it passes in a flash. A kid like you isn't going to do any good in all this muck. Hold close to your own love wherever it lies, don't leave it lonely while you wander about aimlessly in chaos searching for some half formulated ideal. An ideal of what? Fundamental good in human nature! Bunk! Spiritual understanding? Bunk. God in some compassionate dream waiting to open your eyes to truth? Bunk! Bunk! Bunk! It's all a joke with nobody to laugh at it. Go back to your mother while you can.

JOHN: Cheer up, Perry.

PERRY: You'll see, I'm right. You'll see.

JOHN: You've given yourself away a bit.

PERRY: How do you mean?

JOHN: You laugh at me for being an idealist, but you're a greater one than I, far greater——

PERRY: Magnificent sophistry, you'll be saying everything's God's Will in a minute.

JOHN: I'm only idealistic about individuals really, that's why I came back. I can only see causes and effects through a few people, the people I love. But you're different, capable of deeper depths and further heights, because your ideals catch at life itself, away beyond me Perry, far beyond, you've been clutching at a star beyond my vision, looking to a future that's too dim for me even to imagine. It must be heartbreaking to be a poet!

PERRY: Cheering my last moments, that's what you're doing, aren't you? (*He smiles rather wearily.*)

JOHN (*picking up the revolver and handing it to him*): Here!

PERRY (*taking it*): Thanks. What's a little death among friends?

JOHN: Better than life among enemies. Poor old Perry! I see that much.

PERRY: An epigram and from you, oh John, how glorious!

JOHN (*rising*): Good-bye, Perry!

PERRY (*rising also and standing above the table*): Thanks for coming. You've made a strange difference. I'm deeply deeply grateful!

JOHN suddenly puts his arms round PERRY tightly, then turns away and disappears into the shadows.

JOHN (*as he goes*): Good-bye, old dear!

PERRY (*huskily*): Cheero!

As the LIGHTS FADE, PERRY lifts the revolver to his head. He is smiling. The shot rings out in the dark.

CURTAIN

In the pitch darkness the voices of BABE ROBINS, TILLEY, SHAW, and PERRY are heard.

TILLEY: He's still breathing.

BABE (*hysterically*): Will he die—will he die?

SHAW: Shut up, Babe.

PERRY: He's not quite unconscious, look at his eyes. I believe he opened his eyes.

SCENE V

Scene :—The private office of SIR JAMES CAVAN *in the "Daily Mercury" Building, London. The room is large and luxuriously furnished. The three windows look out over roof tops, and as it is evening, electric light signs can be seen flashing in the distance. The big table in the centre is placed in readiness for a conference. Note-books and pencils at each place and chairs drawn up. On the sideboard there is an elaborate cold supper laid out. There is a sofa downstage left, and Sir James' desk downstage right. There are two or three telephones on it and neat piles of letters and papers. Far away, down below somehow can be heard the faint rumble of printing presses.*

When the curtain rises SIR JAMES *and* ALFRED BORROW *are seated on the sofa,* MISS BEAVER *is standing primly just above it with her note-book.* SIR JAMES *is fattish and pink and shrewd.* ALFRED BORROW *is also shrewd but in a different way. He is a measly looking man. They are both in dinner jackets.* MISS BEAVER *is watery and pale, but obviously efficient, otherwise she would not be there.* JOHN *comes quietly in from the door downstage left.* SIR JAMES *stops talking abruptly and rises to his feet.*

SIR JAMES : John ! My son, my boy ! (*He very beautifully takes* JOHN *in his arms.*)

JOHN (*wriggling away*) : Hallo, father !

SIR JAMES : I can't speak in this great, great moment

I can't speak, my heart is too full!

JOHN: Is it?

SIR JAMES (*with one eye on* BORROW *and* MISS BEAVER): You have passed from life into death, and back again from death into life to see your old father——

BORROW whispers something to MISS BEAVER and she makes a few shorthand notes.

Borrow, this is my son, John, you remember him? John, you remember Borrow, don't you?

JOHN: Yes.

SIR JAMES: Borrow is now the live wire of the *Mercury*.

BORROW: This is very moving. I can only say welcome!

JOHN: How do you do! Thank you so much. How do you do!

BORROW (*shaking hands*): We need you. Men like you—England needs you, you must tell England everything.

SIR JAMES: Your mother will be so happy. So, so happy! We must telephone her. Miss Beaver, get through immediately to her ladyship. How happy she will be!

JOHN: I've seen mother.

SIR JAMES: Good, splendid! How happy it must have made her.

BORROW: Return of Sir James Cavan's only son after thirteen years! His mother, a white-haired Patrician lady smiled at our special representative with shining eyes. "My son," she said simply. Just that, but in those two words the meed of mother-love was welling over.

JOHN (*impersonally*): Worm, stinking little worm!

BORROW: A full page, nothing less than a full page. Have you any photographs of yourself aged two, then aged eight, then aged thirteen? Hurray for school-days! Then seventeen, just enlisted, clear-eyed and clean-limbed, answering your country's call. "We're out to win," said Sir James Cavan's son, smilingly. Just that, but in those simple words what a wealth of feeling, what brave brimming enthusiasm.

JOHN (*dreamily*): Filth—scavenging little rat!

BORROW: "Death of Sir James Cavan's only son." "Thank God!" said Sir James Cavan huskily to our Special Representative, "he died fighting." Lady Cavan when interviewed was reserved and dry-eyed, her mother-grief was too deep for tears. "He was my only son," she said clearly. "Now he is gone, but he would like to think we are carrying on, so we will, we will carry on!" Just those few words, so simple, but oh, what a wealth of heroic suffering lay behind them!

JOHN: I can't touch you with words or blows, the nightmare is too strong.

BORROW: What do you think of the modern girl? What do you think of the longer skirts? Do you think bicycling women make the best wives? Do you think the Talkies will kill the Theatre? What do you think of the dear little Princess Elizabeth? Do you think this vogue of war literature will last?

He walks up and down followed closely and in step by MISS BEAVER, *taking notes mechanically.*

We will off our hats to Sir Lawrence Weevil for saying "Thank God, we've got a Navy." We take off our hat to Lady Millicent Beauchamp for giving birth to a baby daughter. We take off our hat to Cedric Bowleigh for making coloured paper toys and being photographed in the nude. We take off our hat to the Duchess of Lyme for appearing at the " Down with Cancer " matinee as the infant Samuel. We take ofl our hat to Lieutenant John Cavan for returning from Death; returning from the grave; returning from the other side; returning from the spirit world; returning from the hinterland; returning from the Beyond. (*He turns to* SIR JAMES) What do you think best?

SIR JAMES: Hinterland.

BORROW: Miss Beaver.

MISS BEAVER: Beyond.

BORROW: Returning from beyond the hinterland.

SIR JAMES: Sunday. Save it all for Sunday.

The telephone rings. MISS BEAVER *goes to it.*

MISS BEAVER (*at phone*): Yes. Just a moment. (*To* SIR JAMES) It's that painted strumpet, Viola Blake, Sir James.

SIR JAMES: Thank you, Miss Beaver. (*He goes to telephone.*)

MISS BEAVER (*relinquishing telephone*): I think she's drunk again.

SIR JAMES (*at phone*): Hallo! Yes, Viola; no, Viola; yes, Viola; no, Viola; yes, a conference. Very busy. Yes, darling; no, darling, later darling. Good-bye, darling.

SIR JAMES *hangs up the receiver and comes over to* JOHN.

Long exciting legs, my boy, but no brain.

BORROW: Miss Viola Blake in a private interview admitted that she only used plain cold cream and a loofah. " Exercise," she said, " is absolutely essential, every morning I ride and skip and play tennis and hunt in season. In the evenings I read and write and listen to good music. If I marry it must be a strong good man who will understand me. I'm really very old-fashioned in spite of the parts I play. I never use hot or cold water, or soap or cosmetics or massage. Just plain cold cream and a loofah—cold cream and a loofah—away with blackheads—cold cream and a loofah!"

MISS BEAVER: Silly drunken harlot! Any more notes, Sir James?

SIR JAMES: Not at the moment, Miss Beaver, but I'd like you to wait. Have a glass of champagne? We'll all have a glass of wine. The others will be here in a moment.

MISS BEAVER: No champagne for me, thank you. Just plain cold cream and a loofah!

She laughs wildly and sits down in a corner. BORROW *pours out three glasses of champagne and hands one to* JOHN, *one to* SIR JAMES *and keeps the other himself.*

SIR JAMES (*lifting his glass*): A Toast to the War, and the heroic part played in it by my son!

BORROW (*lifting his glass*): To the War!

JOHN: To the War! (*He drains his glass*) More, please!

BORROW *takes* JOHN'S *glass and refills it.*

SIR JAMES: John, my boy, this is a great moment.

JOHN (*lifting his glass*): Here's to you, father. Liar, hypocrite, conscientious money grubber, political cheat, licentious sentimentalist—my father.

JOHN *drinks.*

SIR JAMES (*jovially*): Thank you, my boy, thank you—a great moment.

BORROW: Lieutenant John Cavan drinks to his father. "Father and I have always been good pals," he said to our representative. "Even when I was so high he was my ideal of what a man should be." Then this serious war-scarred young soldier gave one of his rare smiles. "I see no reason to change that early impression," he said. Such a simple unemotional sentence and yet what a wealth of pride and adoration lay behind it.

SIR JAMES: The Bishop should be here. Why is he so late?

MISS BEAVER: It will be lovely to see a Bishop close to—what a lucky lucky girl I am!

BORROW: I can't think what's detaining the old fool!

SIR JAMES: And Lady Stagg-Mortimer!

MISS BEAVER: And Sir Henry!

JOHN: Lady Stagg-Mortimer. I remember her name—she gave her son!

SIR JAMES: A truly remarkable woman, deeply religious and a wonderful mother!

JOHN: We were talking about her a minute ago, reading that tripe. I'm glad she's coming. I want to see her.

SIR JAMES: The best type of womanhood in the world.

MISS BEAVER: Faded.

BORROW: Embittered.

SIR JAMES: Sexually repressed.

MISS BEAVER: Snobbish.

BORROW: Plain.

SIR JAMES: A truly remarkable woman!

The BUTLER *enters.*

BUTLER: Lady Stagg-Mortimer!

LADY STAGG-MORTIMER *comes slyly into the room. She is tall and thin like a scraggy Burne Jones. Her manner is alternatively ingratiating and authoritative.*

She is in a russet evening gown—her voice is shrill and high. She shakes hands with SIR JAMES.

LADY S.-M.: How do you do? I should like a tongue sandwich, but no sherry. Sherry is the beginning of the end. (*To* BORROW) How do you do? (*She shakes hands—to* JOHN) How do you do? (*She shakes hands.*)

SIR JAMES: My son—from beyond the hinterland!

LADY S.-M.: How interesting! If you're going to stay I'm afraid we must erase your name from the Roll of Honour. (*She looks at* MISS BEAVER) That woman is showing too much neck!

BORROW: Too much neck, Miss Beaver—make a note.

LADY S.-M.: It's indecent! Merely intended to arouse the beast in men, that's all she does it for. I know that kind, sly and quiet and utterly unreliable. Where's the Bishop?

SIR JAMES: Where's the Bishop, Borrow?

BORROW: Miss Beaver, where's the Bishop?

MISS BEAVER (*going to telephone*): I'll find out.

LADY S.-M.: All that efficiency is all very well, but it's false. Look at the way she moves her hips when she walks!

MISS BEAVER (*at telephone*): Where's the Bishop? Very well. (*She hangs up*) He's downstairs washing his hands.

LADY S.-M.: Pert, too. They're all alike, look at her hair.

JOHN: I want to go back now. This is no use! I want to go back.

SIR JAMES: You can't. You must stay and help us, you're one of our most valuable allies, you shall speak at the conference—you're fresh from the Great War——

BORROW: The Great War for Civilisation!

MISS BEAVER: The Great War for Freedom!

LADY S.-M.: The Great War for God!

SIR JAMES: You will be able to prove that this book by Perry Lomas is a living lie to be stamped out—defaming the memory of the Great War for humanity.

JOHN: What do you know of war? How did you see it, sitting at home here? Could any of the truth of it possibly have filtered through to your minds? How? By what channels? The newspapers, perhaps, the edited drama of cautious war correspondents, photographs of devastated areas, casualty lists, the things you were told by men on leave, men who spared you out of courtesy to your ignorance, who parried your idiotic questions because they were tired and wanted to rest a little. They said it was "All right, not so bad," that it would soon be over, and that you weren't to worry. And they went back, some of them almost gladly, because they loved you and were relieved to find how little you knew, others, less sentimental, were glad for different reasons. There's a quality in war that doesn't quite fit in with your gaudy labels, "God and Country!" "Martyred Belgium!" "The Great Sacrifice!" And all the rest of the cant you manufactured. There's a quality that you could never know, never remotely imagine, beyond your easy patriotism and your prayers. Beyond even what love you have, something intangible and desolately beautiful because it's based upon the deepest tragedy of all, disillusion beyond hope. Strangely enough your whole religion is founded on that same tragedy, though in comparison with the war, the crucifixion becomes microscopic in importance. Christ was one man, the War was millions.

LADY S.-M.: You're a very interesting young man. You must come to lunch. Can you manage next Tuesday, or if not you might dine on the 25th. Quite a small party. Don't forget.

JOHN: You're nothing but a silly hypocrite, so confused you don't even know yourself. You did well in the War, didn't you? You ran a hospital, and organised gratifying charity matinees and screeched out patriotic speeches at the top of your lungs. You even sang to the wounded. God help them! You achieved notable glory by writing an open letter to the Women of England when your son was killed. "I Gave My Son," it was called. In that very heading you stole from him his voluntary heroism, you used his memory to exalt yourself in the eyes of sheep. You implored other mothers to "give" their sons as you did, proudly and gladly. You'd better pray quickly to your tin-pot God, pray that your son never knows, he'll hate you even more than he did when he died.

LADY S.-M. (*affably*): It always comforts me to think that there is a little bit of England out there in France that is me! Part of *me!*

JOHN: I knew him, d'you hear me, I knew your son.

LADY S.-M.: No one will ever know how we women of England suffered, suffered, suffered! We gave our loved ones, but proudly! We'd give them again—again——

JOHN: He hated you, your loved one.

LADY S.-M. (*looking at* MISS BEAVER): Is it necessary

for that woman to be present during the conference, Sir James ?

SIR JAMES : I'm afraid so, she must take notes.

LADY S.-M. : Tell her to remain in the corner then, and not to look at the Bishop. At all costs she mustn't look at the Bishop.

The BUTLER *enters.*

BUTLER (*announcing*) : The Bishop of Ketchworth, Sir Henry Merstham.

The BISHOP *enters, followed by* SIR HENRY. *The* BISHOP *is genial and smiling.* SIR HENRY *is tall and austere. He wears a monocle and carries his head a trifle on one side.*

BISHOP : Forgive me, Sir James, I was detained. How do you do ! Ah, Lady Stagg-Mortimer, what a pleasure to be sure. (*He shakes hands with* SIR JAMES *and* LADY STAGG-MORTIMER.

SIR HENRY (*sepulchrally*) : I was also detained, in the House, a very stormy meeting. (*He shakes hands*) Ah, Lady Stagg-Mortimer.

LADY S.-M. : Don't forget you're lunching with me on Tuesday, and dining on the twenty-fifth. Quite a small party.

SIR JAMES : You both know my Right Hand, don't you, Mr. Borrow ?

BISHOP : Certainly. How do you do ! (*He shakes hands with* BORROW.)

SIR HENRY (*doing the same*) : How do you do !

SIR JAMES : This is my son from the Spirit World.

BISHOP (*shaking hands with* JOHN) : Very interesting. How do you do !

SIR JAMES (*to* SIR HENRY) : My son, from Out There.

SIR HENRY : Out where ?

BISHOP: The War, my dear Henry, the War.

SIR HENRY: Oh, the War. (*He shakes hands absently with* JOHN) I was in Paris quite a lot during the war, very depressing, but still I took up a philosophical attitude over the whole thing. It was a time when we all had to pull our weight in the boat. No use grumbling, no use grumbling at all.

BISHOP: Let us get on with the Conference. I must get to bed early, I have a Confirmation to-morrow at Egham. Very tedious.

SIR JAMES: A glass of champagne?

BISHOP: No thank you, I never take it, except at weddings, as a special gesture.

SIR JAMES: Sir Henry?

SIR HENRY: Afterwards, I should like some afterwards.

SIR JAMES: Very well. Lady Stagg-Mortimer!

He motions her to a seat at the table. He also indicates chairs for the BISHOP *and* SIR HENRY. BORROW *sits on his left, with* MISS BEAVER *behind his chair.*

My son on my right.

JOHN *sits down.*

LADY S.-M. (*confidentially to* SIR HENRY): Such a nice looking boy. He knew Alan you know, my Alan. They were the closest friends. We used to have such happy times when they were home on leave, just the three of us. They treated me just as though I were one of them, not an old woman at all. Oh, dear—— (*She sniffles, and fumbles for her handkerchief.*)

SIR HENRY: Dear Lady Stagg-Mortimer, memory is a cruel thing, is it not? There—there—— (*He pats her hand.*)

SIR JAMES (*rising to his feet at the head of the table*): We have met together to-night in order to discuss a very serious matter, to wit, the rising tide of Sedition, Blasphemy and Immoral Thought which, under the guise of "War Literature," is threatening to undermine the youth of our generation.

SIR HENRY: Hear, hear!

LADY S.-M.: Excellently put.

BISHOP: Delightful, quite delightful!

SIR JAMES: In order to decide upon a course of action which will uproot this—this—er—canker in our midst once and for all, I have called together in secret conclave three of the most brilliant and most powerful people of our time. My old friend the Bishop of Ketchworth, whose finger is ever upon the religious pulse of the nation——

LADY S.-M. (*skittishly blowing him a kiss*): Dear Bishop!

SIR JAMES (*continuing*): Sir Henry Merstham, whose sane and uncompromising decisions in his capacity as adviser on the committee of censorship, have gone so far towards ridding our theatres and libraries of much that is base and unwholesome——

LADY S.-M.: All the same, Sir Henry, you should never have allowed them to produce that play about the Monk and the Chilian Ambassadress.

SIR JAMES: I never read the play, I was having a few weeks' holiday in Taormina.

LADY S.-M.: Very reprehensible!

BISHOP (*brightening up*): Taormina—what an enchanting spot. Dear, dear, how time flies!

SIR JAMES (*continuing*): Lady Stagg-Mortimer, whose indefatigable zeal in charity organizations, whose unswerving loyalty to her country, and whose passionate upholding of Englishwomen's rights, have made her name a byword, and her opinion a force to be reckoned with——

LADY S.-M.: Don't listen to him, Bishop, he's flattering me.

SIR JAMES: And last, but by no means least—my son! My own flesh and blood, returned by a miracle from the valley of the shadow, to give us the value of his personal war experience, the benefit of that splendid spirit of patriotism which caused him to lay down his life for God and Country. And, if necessary, the strength of his youthful right arm, in defence of those heroes who died for us, and whose memory is being defamed daily by these writers of so-called War books, who treat England's victory as ignoble, and the glory of her sacrifices as futile.

JOHN (*quietly*): Death in War is above being defamed, even by you.

BORROW (*dictating to* MISS BEAVER): At the termination of Sir James Cavan's emphatic speech, John Cavan, his only son——

MISS BEAVER: Returned from B. the H.?

BORROW: Yes, returned from B. the H.—looked up at his father with a proud smile. "Dad's right," he said. Just two simple words, but somehow, somehow, one understood.

BISHOP: We're here to discuss a book, I understand, a very unpleasant book. Let's get on with it. (*He smiles, and shuts his eyes.*)

SIR JAMES: You have all read this outrage?

BISHOP: Outrage? Another outrage! Some poor little girl I suppose, set upon in a country lane by some great hairy man! What happened—what happened?

He is quite excited, so SIR HENRY *calms him.*

SIR JAMES: I was referring to this book "Post-Mortem" by a man called Perry Lomas.

JOHN: A Poet.

LADY S.-M.: I've read it. I felt humiliated and ashamed.

JOHN: Good for you.

SIR HENRY: The book is a disgrace.

SIR JAMES: Bishop, I want your opinion on this book.

BISHOP: Which book?

SIR JAMES: "Post-Mortem" by Perry Lomas. I sent it to you.

BISHOP: Very kind of you, I'm sure. I appreciate it very much.

SIR JAMES: Have you read it?

BISHOP: Alas, no. You see I have been so very occupied, what with one thing and another, and now there's this Confirmation at Egham to-morrow——

SIR JAMES: Borrow. The Bishop of Ketchworth's opinion of "Post-Mortem."

BORROW: Miss Beaver. The Bishop of Ketchworth's opinion of "Post-Mortem."

MISS BEAVER (*producing a typewritten paper*): Here it is.

SIR JAMES (*taking it and handing it to the* BISHOP): Will you sign here, please?

BISHOP: Where are my glasses?

SIR HENRY (*picking them up from the table*): Here.

BISHOP: Thank you.

He puts them on and signs the paper, breathing rather heavily. When he has done so he sits back with a sigh and closes his eyes again. SIR HENRY *removes the glasses from his nose, and replaces them on the table.* SIR JAMES *takes the paper, and coughs, preparatory to reading it aloud.*

SIR JAMES (*reading*): Letter from the Bishop of Ketchworth to the Editor of the *Daily Mercury.* " Sir, with regard to the sentiments expressed in your editorial of May 14th concerning the book ' Post-Mortem,' I should like to say that I am in complete agreement with you on every point. Writing such as this, I will not dignify it by the name of Literature——

BORROW *smiles and exchanges a glance with* SIR JAMES.

—should not only be forbidden publication in a Christian country, but ignominiously burnt.

SIR JAMES (*continuing*): It is a vile book and an ungodly book. Its content is blasphemous in the extreme——

JOHN: Etc., etc., etc., etc., etc., etc., etc.—signed The Bishop of Katchbush."

SIR JAMES (*smiling*): My son! (*He pats his head.*)

JOHN (*jerking away*): Don't touch me.

SIR HENRY: Have you written to the Home Office?

SIR JAMES: That is what I want you to do. I also want you to write a detailed letter to me for my next Sunday Edition.

SIR HENRY: I gather that pressure has already been brought to bear upon the publisher to suspend the book pending a decision from the Home Office?

SIR JAMES: Certainly, certainly.

BORROW: I myself have bought twenty copies, first editions, you understand. Possibly very valuable one day. (*He smiles.*)

BISHOP (*waking up*): I have a first edition of "Alice in Wonderland."

LADY S.-M. (*rising*): Let me speak, I must speak now.

SIR JAMES: Borrow. Lady Stagg-Mortimer's speech.

BORROW: Miss Beaver. Lady Stagg-Mortimer's speech.

MISS BEAVER (*producing another typewritten sheet*): Here it is.

BORROW *reads the speech, while* LADY STAGG-MORTIMER *gesticulates and opens and shuts her mouth silently.*

BORROW (*reading*): Open letter to the Women of England. "Women of England. Mothers, sweethearts and wives——

JOHN: Sisters, and cousins, and aunts, and prostitutes, and murderesses.

SIR JAMES (*fondly, petting his head*): My son! Proceed, Lady Stagg-Mortimer.

BORROW (*continuing*): —I have a message for you from my heart, the heart of a mother, who, like many of you, made the great sacrifice of her own flesh and blood in the great War for Humanity. Twelve years have passed since Britain's glorious victory was consummated in the signing of the Armistice. During those twelve years we have gone our ways, working and living, gallantly crushing down our sorrows, and, as a tribute to our glorious dead—carrying on!

JOHN: What else could you have done?

BORROW (*continuing*): —Now, at a critical period in the progress of our nation towards world supremacy, we are faced with a contingency so sinister in its potential evil, so imminently and insidiously perilous, that the very contemplation of it appals me. I refer to——

(*Stops abruptly*) Miss Beaver, what's that?

MISS BEAVER (*scrutinising the paper*): I can't think, I must have left some lines out. I apologise.

SIR JAMES: Let me see.

BORROW *hands him the paper, he stares at it.*

Can't make head or tail of it. (*He hands it back*) Be more careful in future, please, Miss Beaver.

MISS BEAVER (*bursting into tears*): It's the first time I've ever made a mistake. Oh dear, oh dear——

LADY S.-M. (*frantically*): Never mind, never mind, go on with the speech—I must continue my speech.

BORROW (*continuing*): —Etc., etc.—the Union Jack.

LADY S.-M.: Go on from there, quickly, quickly!

BORROW (*continuing*): These puling men who write war books, blackening the name of our heroes, putting blasphemous words into the mouths of our soldiers, picturing them as drinking whisky and rum in the trenches, and making obscene jokes, and behaving like brutes. These men. These slandering scoundrels, should be taken out and shot!

JOHN (*losing control*): Shut up, shut up! Stop!

He hammers the table with his fist. The BISHOP *wakes up with a start.*

BISHOP: An air raid, an air raid, quickly, the coal cellar!

JOHN: The nightmare is wearing thin. I can't stay much longer.

SIR JAMES: Have some champagne.

JOHN: I see you clearly, even though a web of time separates us. You are representative. You are powerful. You always were and you always will be. This is delirium, the delirium of dying, but the truth is here, mixed up with my dream, and infinitely horrible. The

War was glorious, do you hear me? Supremely glorious, because it set men free. Not the ones who lived, poor devils, but the ones who died. It released them from the sad obligation of life in a Christian world which has not even proved itself worthy of Death.

LADY S.-M.: Charming, quite charming.

JOHN: War is no evil compared with this sort of living. War at least provides more opportunities for actions, decent instinctive clear actions, without time for thought or wariness, beyond the betrayal of fear and common-sense, and all those other traitors to humanity which have been exalted into virtues. It is considered eminently wise to look before you leap. But that is thin and over protective wisdom. Your only chance of seeing at all is after you have leapt. War makes you leap, and leap again into bloody chaos, but there are redeeming moments of vision which might, in smug content, be obscured for ever.

SIR JAMES: England is proud of you, my son.

JOHN: England doesn't know me, or any like me. England now can only recognise false glory. Real England died in defeat without pretending it was Victory.

There is the faint sound of guns far away.

Listen—listen—can't you hear the guns?

SIR JAMES: He sacrificed his life for God and Country.

BORROW: God and Country.

They all chant "God and Country" in a monotone, quite softly, an accompaniment to JOHN's *voice as it rises. The guns sound nearer.*

JOHN: Listen—listen—you can hear them more clearly now—blasting your Christianity to pieces. You didn't know, did you? You didn't realise that all the sons you gave, and the husbands you gave, and the lovers you gave in your silly pride were being set free. Free from your hates and loves and small pitiful prayers, for Eternity. You wouldn't have let them go so easily if you'd known that, would you? They've escaped—escaped. You'll never find them again either in your pantomime hell or your tinsel heaven. Long live War. Long live Death, and Destruction and Despair! Through all that there may be a hope, a million to one chance for us somewhere, a promise of something clearer and sweeter than anything your bloody gods have ever offered. Long live War—Long live War——

JOHN *is laughing hysterically.* SIR JAMES *and the others continue to chant "God and Country." The guns grow louder and louder as the lights fade.*

In the pitch dark there is suddenly dead silence. Then, PERRY'S *voice is heard, speaking quietly.)*

PERRY'S VOICE: I think he opened his eyes.

There is a far off splutter of machine-gun fire.

SCENE VI

SCENE :—TILLEY, SHAW, BABE ROBINS *and* JOHN *are seated round a dinner table. Dinner is over, and they are drinking coffee and brandy. There is no light anywhere but immediately over the table, beyond its radius is blackness.* TILLEY *is forty-three, iron grey, and wearing pince-nez.* SHAW, *at thirty-nine, is extremely corpulent, and pink.* BABE ROBINS, *aged thirty-two, has the appearance of any average young man in the motor business. All three of them look fairly prosperous. They are wearing dinner jackets, and smoking cigars, and there is somehow less life in them than there was when they were together in War.* JOHN *is the same as he has been all through the play.*

JOHN (*raising his glass*) : I give you a Toast. "To Contentment."

TILLEY : Contentment ?

JOHN : Yes, and Peace and Plenty.

SHAW : This really is the damnedest dream I've ever had.

BABE : Good old John. Contentment, Peace and Plenty. (*He drinks.*)

TILLEY : Why not ? (*He drinks.*)

SHAW : Excellent brandy. (*He drinks.*)

BABE : Pity old Perry isn't here.

TILLEY : I think it's just as well.

JOHN : Why ?

TILLEY : He wouldn't fit.

SHAW: He is a bit impossible, I'm afraid. I saw him the other day, changed beyond recognition, and now all this business about his book.

JOHN: You never liked him, did you, Tilley?

TILLEY: Oh, he was all right, then. He had to conform more or less, we all had to.

BABE (*laughing loudly*): You bet we did!

JOHN: You were always a stickler for discipline, Tilley.

TILLEY: Certainly. Sheer common-sense.

JOHN: Are you still?

TILLEY: How do you mean?

JOHN: In civil life, do you still insist on immortal souls forming fours?

SHAW (*laughing, and reaching for some more brandy*): Immortal souls! I say——!

JOHN: Only a phrase—meaning nothing—I apologise.

TILLEY: I must be getting home soon.

JOHN: Where is home?

TILLEY: Hampstead.

JOHN: It's nice, Hampstead.

TILLEY: The air's good, anyhow.

JOHN: Wife and children?

TILLEY: Yes.

JOHN: How many?

TILLEY: Two. Both boys.

JOHN: You're married too, aren't you, Shaw?

SHAW: Yes.

JOHN: Children?

SHAW (*suddenly resentful*): Mind your own business.

JOHN: Sorry.

SHAW: What is all this, anyhow?

JOHN (*raising his glass*) : " Family life. Home Notes. Christians Awake ! "

TILLEY : Irony seems out of place in you, John, alive or dead.

JOHN : Do you remember Armitage, Babe ?

BABE : What ?

JOHN : I said, do you remember Armitage ?

BABE : Of course I do. Why ?

JOHN : How has his memory stayed with you ? Is he still clear in your mind ? Important ?

BABE (*sullenly*) : I don't know what you mean.

JOHN : You loved him then.

BABE (*jumping to his feet*) : Look here, don't you talk such bloody rot.

JOHN : Don't misunderstand me. There is no slur in that. It was one of the nicest things about you, wholehearted, and tremendously decent. It must be a weak moral code that makes you wish to repudiate it. Love among men in war is gallant and worth remembering. Don't let the safe years stifle that remembrance.

TILLEY : Sentimentalist.

JOHN : You're my last chance, you three. Don't resent me. There is so much I want to know. This is only a dream to you, so you can be honest. It's easier to be honest in a dream. I know barriers are necessary in waking life, barriers, and smoke screens, and camouflage. But here, in unreality, we're together again for a little. Let me see where you are and what you're doing. Is there no contact possible between you and me just because I'm dead ? Is it as final as all that ? Are you happy with your wives, and children, and prosperity, and peace ? Or is it makeshift ?

SHAW : I wish I knew what you were getting at.

JOHN: I'm trying to find a reason for survival.

TILLEY: Life is reason enough, isn't it?

JOHN: No, I don't believe it is.

TILLEY: Nonsense. Morbid nonsense.

JOHN: Have you completely forgotten that strange feeling we had in the war? Have you found anything in your lives since to equal it in strength? A sort of splendid carelessness it was, holding us together. Cut off from everything we were used to, but somehow not lonely, except when we were on leave, or when letters came. Depending only upon the immediate moment. No past, no future, and no conviction of God. God died early in the war, for most of us. Can you remember our small delights? How exciting they were? Sleep, warmth, food, drink, unexpected comforts snatched out of turmoil, so simple in enjoyment, and so incredibly satisfying.

TILLEY (*bitterly*): What about the chaps one knew being blown to pieces? Lying out in the mud for hours, dying in slow agony. What about being maimed, and gassed, and blinded? Blinded for life?

JOHN: There was something there worth even that. Not to the individual perhaps, but to the whole. Beyond life and beyond death. Just a moment or two.

TILLEY: To Hell with your blasted moment or two. I'm going home.

JOHN: To Hampstead?

BABE: What's the matter with Hampstead? That's what I want to know. What's the matter with Hampstead?

JOHN: The air's good, anyhow.

SHAW: You make me sick, trying to be so damned clever.

JOHN: When your boys grow up, Tilley, and there's another war, will you be proud when they enlist?

BABE: There won't be another war.

JOHN: There'll always be another war. Will you let them go? Will you?

TILLEY: I don't flatter myself that it would be in my power to stop them.

JOHN: You could shoot them.

SHAW (*belligerently*): If I had sons, and there were a war, I'd shoot them if they didn't go.

JOHN: Excellent sentiments, but why? From what motives?

SHAW: Because I don't believe in shirking one's responsibilities.

JOHN: To what would your sons be responsible?

SHAW: To the decent standards I'd taught them. To the things I'd brought them up to believe.

JOHN: What would you bring them up to believe?

SHAW: I'll tell you, and you can sneer as much as you like. I'd bring them up to believe in God, and the necessity of standing by their country in time of need, and to play the game according to the rules.

JOHN: And if they made their own rules, and didn't accept God, and didn't consider their country important enough. You'd shoot them?

SHAW: Yes, I would. And that's that.

JOHN: Well, you'd better pray for another war for your sons that are not yet born, because it will all be just as you want. They'll grow up and go off to fight gallantly for their God and country according to the rules, and you'll be proud, quite rightly proud, because they'll be nice, decent boys. I'm quite sure of that. What happens to them out there will be entirely beyond your comprehension, *then*. Even now, after only thirteen years, you've forgotten the essential quality. Then, you'll be more forgetful still because you'll be old. You say truculently that you'd shoot them if they didn't go. Try with all your might to be brave enough to shoot them when they come back.

BABE (*hysterically*): Stop talking like that! Leave us alone! Let us wake up!

JOHN: Hard luck, Babe. You might have died instead of me. Do you remember?

BABE: I didn't ask you to take over the covering party, you offered to, it was your own fault——

JOHN (*gently*): Don't worry about that.

BABE: Let me go. Let me wake up.

JOHN: It will be over very soon now.

BABE: Oh God! Oh God! (*He buries his head in his arms, and sobs.*)

From out of the shadows comes BABE, *as he was in Scene I, in uniform, aged nineteen. He stands still behind the chair. Guns sound faintly, far away.*

JOHN: You see? Life hasn't compensated him enough for not dying.

SHAW (*to* BABE): Shut up. Pull yourself together, for God's sake!

JOHN: Interesting that. "For God's sake."

SHAW: Go away. Damn your eyes! Get out—get out!

JOHN: Your mind is solemn now, and you're scared. You never used to be scared.

SHAW: Get out! Go away!

JOHN (*calling sharply*): Shaw—Shaw—come here a minute. Make us laugh. You were always clowning. Come out, you lazy old bastard.

SHAW *comes out of the shadows, and stands behind his older self. He winks at* JOHN *and grins broadly. The sound of guns accompanies him.*

JOHN: That's better. More comfortable. Tilley?

TILLEY (*quietly*): I hate you. You won't get me.

JOHN: Why do you hate me?

TILLEY: Stirring up trouble. Bloody Ghost!

JOHN: You were always more intelligent than the others; is that why you're so set against remembering?

TILLEY: You're not as I remember you anyhow. You're a complete stranger. Whatever you've learnt in death hasn't improved you. I intend to forget this dream even before my eyes open.

JOHN: Why—why?

TILLEY: I prefer to remember you as a damn good soldier, a nice uncomplicated boy without overtones. Tuck yourself up on your abstract plane, your fourteenth dimension, wherever you are, and keep your inquisitive hands off my soul. I'm all right. I accept life and peace, as I accepted death and war. They're equal as jobs, and I'm a worker.

JOHN: To what end?

TILLEY: I don't know, any more than you, and I care less. I'm passing the time, do you see? Just passing the time. (*He points contemptuously to* SHAW *and* BABE) They're malleable, those two, and there are millions like them, easily swayed through their sentimental emotions. You were clever enough to get them on their weaknesses. "Hard luck, Babe, you might have died instead of me." Excellent psychology. You got him on the raw. Hero-worship. "Greater love hath no man, etc., etc." Heart interest. Sex confusion. He'll be like that until he dies. Then Shaw, with his Public School belligerence, shooting his mythical sons in a fine fury of right-minded patriotism. Look how you got him. "Come here a minute, make us laugh, come out, you lazy old bastard!" Chaps! Good old camaraderie! "Damn good times we had together." Of course he'd respond to that treatment. Look at him, fashioned for conviviality, round and pink and jolly, and sentimental as a housemaid. You can't catch me out so easily.

JOHN: All the same, you were sorrier than any of them when they carried me in—dying.

TILLEY: You were a very good second in command. I always hated losing reliable men.

JOHN: Was that all?

TILLEY: Absolutely.

JOHN: I don't believe it.

TILLEY: Funny, personal vanity hanging on so long.

JOHN: It wasn't all. It wasn't all. There was more warmth than that, I felt it.

TILLEY: You were delirious. What you felt doesn't count.

JOHN (*wildly*): I'm not dead yet. There are still a few more seconds——

TILLEY: Get on with it and don't waste my time.

The lights begin to fade, and the guns sound louder.

JOHN: I can't yet. I've got to see mother—I promised——

TILLEY: Hurry, hurry, I'm tired—don't keep us all hanging about.

The lights go out. In the dark TILLEY'S *voice is heard speaking authoritatively. He says: "Hoist him up a little higher—gently—give me the water."* BABE'S *voice says: "Is he—done for?"*

SCENE VII

SCENE :—*The lights come up slowly on the Left-hand side of the stage.* LADY CAVAN *is playing Patience by the window.* JOHN *is standing by the table.*

JOHN (*urgently*) : Mother.

LADY C. (*rising*) : So soon?

JOHN : Yes.

LADY C. : It's all right. I won't cry or make a fuss.

JOHN (*holding her in his arms*) : Dearest.

LADY C. : It's for ever, isn't it—this time?

JOHN (*whispering*) : Yes.

LADY C. : Tell me something. Could you—could you stay if things had been worth it?

JOHN : Perhaps. I don't know. I think so.

LADY C. : You're going—willingly?

JOHN : Yes.

LADY C. : What of me—what of me? (*Brokenly*) Wouldn't I be enough?

JOHN : Only for a little, then you'd die and leave me—terribly alone. I never wanted to be born.

LADY C. : I see.

JOHN : Only a few more years, Mum, be brave.

LADY C. : Do you think there's any chance anywhere in that great void for us to be together again?

JOHN : Maybe. One in a million.

LADY C. : I'm still alive enough to mind. I know it's foolish.

JOHN: I'm on the border line and should be near to knowing; perhaps in eternity the mists will clear, but I doubt it.

LADY C. (*very quietly*): I love you, my darling—with all the love that has ever been. It doesn't matter about eternity, wherever you are, in however deep oblivion your spirit rests this love will be with you. I know it so very strongly—far beyond the limits of my understanding. I love you, my dear, dear one—I love you.

JOHN: Dearest Mum—good-bye.

LADY C. (*kissing him very tenderly*): Good-bye Johnnie.

The lights fade and go out.

SCENE VIII

The lights come up slowly revealing the dug-out, exactly as it was at the close of Scene I, except that the STRETCHER-BEARERS *have advanced as far as the bunk upon which* JOHN *is lying. They make a movement preparatory to lifting him on to the stretcher.* JOHN *moves and opens his eyes.*

JOHN: You were right, Perry—a poor joke!

He falls back. TILLEY *motions the* STRETCHER-BEARERS *away, and then with infinite tenderness lifts* JOHN *on to the stretcher as the Curtain falls.*

CURTAIN.

Methuen World Classics

Aeschylus (two volumes)
Jean Anouilh
John Arden
Arden & D'Arcy
Aristophanes (two volumes)
Peter Barnes
Brendan Behan
Aphra Behn
Edward Bond (four volumes)
Bertolt Brecht (three volumes)
Howard Brenton (two volumes)
Büchner
Bulgakov
Calderón
Anton Chekhov
Caryl Churchill (two volumes)
Noël Coward (five volumes)
Sarah Daniels
Eduardo De Filippo
David Edgar (three volumes)
Euripides (three volumes)
Dario Fo
Michael Frayn (two volumes)
Max Frisch
Gorky
Harley Granville Barker
Henrik Ibsen (six volumes)
Lorca (three volumes)
Marivaux
Mustapha Matura
David Mercer
Arthur Miller (three volumes)
Anthony Minghella
Molière
Tom Murphy (two volumes)
Peter Nichols (two volumes)
Clifford Odets
Joe Orton
Louise Page
A. W. Pinero
Luigi Pirandello
Stephen Poliakoff
Terence Rattigan (two volumes)
Ntozake Shange
Sophocles (two volumes)
Wole Soyinka
David Storey
August Strindberg (three volumes)
J. M. Synge
Ramón del Valle-Inclán
Frank Wedekind
Oscar Wilde